A
SEMANTIC STRUCTURE ANALYSIS
OF
2 PETER

by
Edna Johnson

Edited by
John Callow

Summer Institute of Linguistics, Inc.
7500 W. Camp Wisdom Rd.
Dallas, TX 75236

The Greek text is used by permision
of the United Bible Societies.

Copies may be obtained from
Academic Book Center
Summer Institute of Linguistics, Inc.
7500 West Camp Wisdom Road
Dallas, Texas 75236

PREFACE

It has been a privilege and a challenge to work on this Semantic Structure Analysis of 2 Peter. To have been able to spend so much time studying the Epistle and getting to know its teaching more thoroughly has been a privilege, and to grapple with some of the exegetical difficulties it presents has been a challenge.

My sincere thanks go to Elaine Beekman, Faith Blight, Karelin Seitz, and all those others at the International Linguistics Centre, Dallas, who have put so much time and effort into preparing the manuscript for publication.

My particular thanks are also due to John Callow for his expert advice, which shed light on problem areas; for his criticism, which was always constructive; and for his encouragement throughout. I am also indebted to Michael Martens for help received from his unpublished manuscript on the discourse structure of 2 Peter.

I am very aware of the inadequacies and shortcomings of this analysis, but I trust that, until more light is thrown on those exegetical problems which as yet are unsolved, it will be of some use to those involved in the translation of this Epistle.

Edna Johnson
January 1988

Table of Contents

ABBREVIATIONS

DBL	doublet
EUP	euphemism
HYP	hyperbole
ICC	*The International Critical Commentary*
JER	*The Jerusalem Bible*
KJV	*The Holy Bible* (King James Version)
LIT	litotes
MET	metonymy
METR	metaphor
NEB	*The New English Bible*
NOT	*Notes on Translation*
NIV	*The New International Version of the Bible*
PERS	personification
PHIL	*The New Testament in Modern English* (J. B. Phillip
RL	receptor language
RSV	*The Revised Standard Version of the Bible*
SIM	simile
TEV	*Today's English Version of the Bible*
UBS	United Bible Societies

ampli.	amplification
circ.	circumstance
comp.	comparison
conces.	concession
contraexpect.	contraexpectation
desc.	description
evid.	evidential
(exc)	exclusive
grds.	grounds
ident.	identification
illus.	illustration
(inc)	inclusive
neg.	negative

0. GENERAL INTRODUCTION

0.1 The Theory On Which A Semantic Structure Analysis Is Based

This volume is an analytical commentary on 2 Peter. It is based on a theory of semantic structure that is set forth in "The Semantic Structure of Written Communication" (Beekman, Callow, and Kopesec 1981). It has been prepared with the needs of the Bible translator particularly in view. Like other commentaries, it aims to arrive at the meaning that the original writer intended to communicate to the original recipients. It differs from most other commentaries, however, in that it is consciously based on a theory of the structure of meaning. Consequently, a consistent and comprehensive approach to the analysis of the meaning is applied to the total document, whether that meaning is conveyed by the smallest segments of the written communication (i.e., morphemes or words) or by the largest segments (i.e., the major constitutents of the document or the whole document itself).

A detailed section on the theory and presentation of semantic structure analyses is not included here, since the reader may refer to previous SSA's (Col. and 2 Thess.) for this information. A chart of the relations is included, and it would be well to notice the following also:

1. Parentheses are used in the display text to enclose implicit material that has been made explicit. However, in some cases it is difficult to decide what is implicit material and what is actually a component of meaning of the Greek word being translated.
2. An asterisk following a word indicates that the word is not being used in its primary meaning in contemporary English.

0.2 The Use Of A Semantic Structure Analysis

The SSA represents a step beyond the standard exegetical or critical commentary in that the needs of the translator have been uppermost in the minds of those preparing it. How should a technical commentary of this nature be used? How does it relate to other available aids?

It can be seen that the SSA consists of a series of "displays" of the semantic units followed by a number of discussions. These discussions are presented under three main headings:

BOUNDARIES AND COHERENCE: this section discusses evidence for the identification of the unit.

PROMINENCE AND THEME: this section sets forth evidence for the theme (and purpose) of the unit.

NOTES: these are concerned with decisions made about
1. the relational structure of the unit. Often there are points that need explanation, justification, and/or the presentation of alternative possibilities.

2. the information content of the unit. Often commentators differ quite markedly concerning the intended meaning of the text. In the propositional display, an attempt has been made to decide between the options on objective linguistic grounds. The bases for many such decisions are presented in the notes. At times no conclusive evidence has been found for resolving one of these exegetical ambiguities. In such cases the option that appears to the analyst to be the most likely is included in the display of the unit, and the alternative interpretations are discussed in the notes.

The display of a unit and the notes which follow it should be used along with other commentaries or versions. Where there is obvious agreement, the translator can move ahead with confidence. Where the display appears to depart from the versions or commentaries, or where a number of alternatives occur, then the discussion that accompanies the displays should be studied carefully to see what factors led to the decision represented in the display. The user should then be in a good position to form his own factually-based judgement as to the best interpretation.

It is important to understand that the SSA display text is not a translation in the commonly accepted sense. It is a presentation of the meaning of the Greek text, in propositional English surface structure form, and with various restrictions. For instance, abstract nouns are avoided as much as possible and the finite form of the verb is normally used. Words are used only in their primary senses. For **live** metaphors, the point of comparison (i.e., the full meaning of the figure intended to be communicated by the original author) is given in the display text. As a result, the display text does not always sound like the natural, flowing English which should mark any good translation. The making explicit of implicit material may make it seem too overloaded with information and too interpretative for a translation. However, its primary purpose is to be a source of information, not a model for word-by-word translation into another language. Any natural translation into another language will follow the patterns of that language.

The bibliography attached to the SSA indicates the source materials consulted by the analyst(s). By referring to such material, the analyst kept himself aware of the different exegetical choices at a given point, and often of factors to be weighed in reaching an exegetical decision. However, in many cases, the information derived from the source materials had to be reworked and reworded by the analyst(s) to conform to the general linguistic orientation of the SSA. Hence, detailed acknowledgement of individual sources for every piece of information involved in each exegetical decision is generally not practicable, but tends to be done where a minority or unusual decision is being discussed.

0.3 Chart Of Relations Involving Communication Units

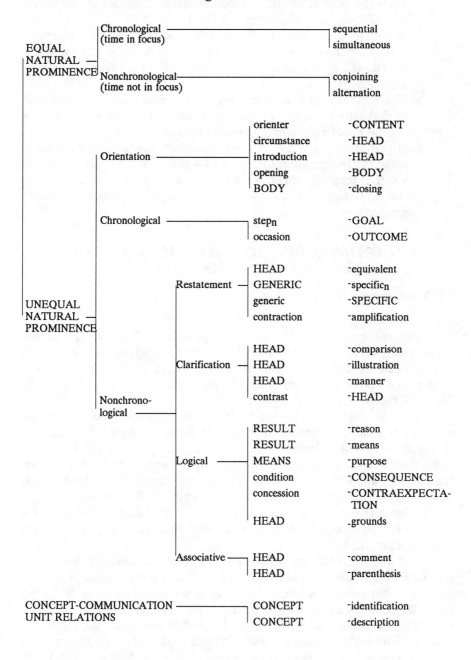

NOTES:

1. Since the Second Epistle of Peter is nonnarrative, not all the narrative relations are included in this chart.
2. The relations are given in the order in which they are most commonly found in the Greek of the New Testament; thus, a RESULT is usually followed by the reason for it, as signalled by *hoti, gar, dia* + accusative, etc.
3. The naturally prominent member of a paired relation is shown in capital letters. In one or two cases, there does not seem to be a natural head, e.g., contraction-amplification.
4. It should be noted that marked prominence devices can be used to make the less prominent member of a pair as prominenet as the one which is naturally prominent. Also, thematic prominence can reverse the natural prominence, so that, for example, a purpose will be of greater prominence than its means.

1. THE INTRODUCTION TO THE SEMANTIC STRUCTURE ANALYSIS OF 2 PETER

1.1 The Communication Situation

1.1.1 The Identification And Status Of The Participants

The writer of the epistle professes himself to be *Sumeōn Petros doulos kai apostolos Iēsou Christou* 'Simon Peter, servant and apostle of Jesus Christ' (1:1), and, although there has been much debate as to whether the epistle was written by Peter, or by someone else, the preponderance of opinion seems in favour of the view that he was the author.

There is nothing stated in the letter as to where it was written from, and there seems to be little known on the matter. Some commentators think that it was probably written from Rome, as was his first epistle, shortly before his martyrdom. However, there is no real evidence to suggest that it was written from Rome, although clearly Peter is very conscious that his death is imminent, as we see from 1:14, where he tells his readers that he will "soon put off" his mortal body. He is eager to write the letter to them so that after his death it will serve to remind them of the important matters he puts before them in it (1:15).

The recipients of the letter are described as *tois isotimon hēmin lachousin pistin* 'those who have received a faith of equal standing with our own' (1:1), but no specific church or group is mentioned by name. In 3:1 we are told that they had received an earlier letter from Peter, and, if that letter is 1 Peter, then the recipients of both letters are the same, i.e., Christians "scattered throughout Pontus, Galatia, Cappadocia, Asia, and Bithynia" (1 Pet 1:1). However, if 3:1 refers to some other letter now lost, it is difficult to say with any certainty to whom this present letter is addressed.

All that can be said then, of the recipients of this letter, is that they were believers who had received a previous letter from Peter; they were firmly established in the truth (1:12); they knew the teachings of the prophets and the apostles (3:3), including the writings of Paul (3:15-16); their spiritual stability was threatened by false teaching, which advocated an immoral way of life and discredited belief in the return of the Lord Jesus Christ in judgement (chapters 2 and 3).

1.1.2 The Occasion And Purpose Of The Letter

Peter wrote this letter as a reminder to its recipients of truths which they knew already (1:12-15 and 3:1-2). His purpose in doing so is to warn and to exhort. He warns them of false teachers who will try to undermine their Christian beliefs (2:1--3:4), and of the need to withstand this by growing in the grace and knowledge of the Lord Jesus Christ (3:17-18). He exhorts them to live holy lives, in response to all that the Lord has done for them (1:3-21), and in expectation of his return in judgement (3:11-13).

Peter wants his readers to realise the importance of true knowledge in their endeavours to live in a godly manner (1:2,3,5,6,8; 3:18), and he also wants them to realise that the grounds for this is the testimony of the Old Testament prophets and the teachings of the apostles (1:16-21; 3:2; 3:15-16).

A sense of urgency motivates Peter to write as he does. He knows that his death will be sudden and unexpected (1:14), and he wants to make sure that his readers will have a permanent reminder of his warning and exhortation when he is no longer there to remind them personally (1:13 and 15).

1.2 The Overview

1.2.1 The Constituent Organization of 2 Peter

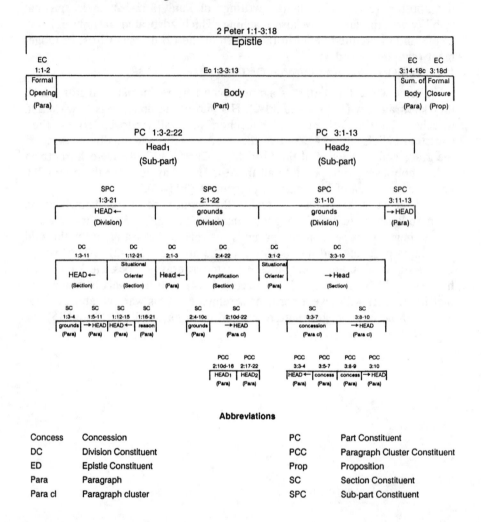

Abbreviations

Concess	Concession	PC	Part Constituent
DC	Division Constituent	PCC	Paragraph Cluster Constituent
ED	Epistle Constituent	Prop	Proposition
Para	Paragraph	SC	Section Constituent
Para cl	Paragraph cluster	SPC	Sub-part Constituent

1.2.2 The Thematic Outline of 2 Peter

2 PETER 1:1--3:18 (Epistle) THEME: Exert yourselves to the utmost to develop a stable Christian character, since false teachers will entice you to behave wickedly, and since the Lord Jesus Christ will certainly come back to judge people; at that time God will destroy this present world and there will be new heavens and a new earth where only righteous people will live.

EPISTLE CONSTITUENT 1:1-2 (Paragraph) (Role: Formal opening of the Epistle) THEME: I, Simon Peter, am writing this letter to you, whom God has caused to believe in Christ just as we(exc) believe in Christ. I pray that God will bless you greatly.

EPISTLE CONSTITUENT 1:3--3:13 (Part) (Role: Body of the Epistle) THEME: Exert yourselves to the utmost to develop a stable Christian character, since false teachers will entice you to behave wickedly, and since the Lord Jesus Christ will certainly come back to judge people; at that time God will destroy this present world and there will be new heavens and a new earth where only righteous people will live.

    PART CONSTITUENT 1:3--2:22 (Sub-part) (Role: Head₁ of 1:3–3:13) THEME: Exert yourselves to the utmost to develop a stable Christian character, since false teachers will entice you to behave wickedly; God will certainly destroy them.

        SUB-PART CONSTITUENT 1:3-21 (Division) (Role: Head of 1:3--2:22) THEME: Exert yourselves to the utmost to develop a stable Christian character.

            DIVISION CONSTITUENT 1:3-11 (Section) (Role: Head of 1:3-21) THEME: Exert yourselves to the utmost to develop a stable Christian character.

                SECTION CONSTITUENT 1:3-4 (Paragraph) (Role: Grounds for 1:5-11) THEME: God has given us(inc) everything that we need in order that we(inc) might live eternally and in order that we(inc) might be godly.

                SECTION CONSTITUENT 1:5-11 (Paragraph) (Role: Head of 1:3-11) THEME: Exert yourselves to the utmost to develop a stable Christian character.

            DIVISION CONSTITUENT 1:12-21 (Section) (Role: Situational Orienter for 1:3-11) THEME: I intend to remind you very frequently about these matters (1:3-11) because they are true.

                SECTION CONSTITUENT 1:12-15 (Paragraph) (Role: Head of 1:12-21) THEME: I intend to remind you very frequently about these matters (1:3-11).

                SECTION CONSTITUENT 1:16-21 (Paragraph) (Role: Reason for 1:12-15) THEME: You can be sure that these matters are true, because we ourselves(exc) witnessed that our(inc) Lord Jesus Christ is supremely great, and because what the prophets say about him is completely reliable also.

SUB-PART CONSTITUENT 2:1-22 (Division) (Role: Grounds for 1:3-21) THEME: There will be false teachers among you, who will behave wickedly and will entice you to behave in the same way as they do; God will certainly destroy them.

DIVISION CONSTITUENT 2:1-3 (Paragraph) (Role: Head of 2:1-22) THEME: There will be false teachers among you, who will behave wickedly and will entice you to behave in the same way as they do; God will certainly destroy them.

DIVISION CONSTITUENT 2:4-22 (Section) (Role: Amplification of 2:1-3) THEME: Because these false teachers will behave wickedly and will entice people to behave in the same way as they do, God will destroy them.

SECTION CONSTITUENT 2:4-10c (Paragraph) (Role: Grounds for 2:10d-22) THEME: It is certain that God knows how to rescue those who are godly, and that he knows how to keep those who are unrighteous until the time when he will punish them.

SECTION CONSTITUENT 2:10d-22 (Paragraph cluster) (Role: Conjoined Heads of 2:4-22) THEME: Because these false teachers will behave wickedly and will entice people to behave in the same way as they do, God will destroy them.

PARAGRAPH CLUSTER CONSTITUENT 2:10d-16 (Paragraph) (Role: Head$_1$ of 2:10d-22) THEME: Because these false teachers will behave wickedly God will destroy them.

PARAGRAPH CLUSTER CONSTITUENT 2:17-22 (Paragraph) (Role: Head$_2$ of 2:10d-22) THEME: Because these false teachers will entice people to behave wickedly God has reserved darkest hell for them.

PART CONSTITUENT 3:1-13 (Sub-part) (Role: Head$_2$ of 1:3–3:13) THEME: You ought to behave in a godly manner, since the Lord Jesus Christ will certainly come back to judge people, and at that time God will destroy this present world and there will be new heavens and a new earth where only righteous people will live.

SUB-PART CONSTITUENT 3:1-10 (Division) (Role: Grounds for 3:11-13) THEME: Although certain people will ridicule the fact that you believe that the Lord Jesus Christ will come back, nevertheless he will certainly come back to judge people, and at that time God will destroy this present world.

DIVISION CONSTITUENT 3:1-2 (Paragraph) (Role: Situational Orienter for 3:3-10) THEME: I am writing this letter to you in order to stimulate you to remember what the holy prophets said and what our(inc) Lord and Saviour commanded.

DIVISION CONSTITUENT 3:3-10 (Section) (Role: Head of 3:1-10) THEME: Although certain people will ridicule the fact that you believe that the Lord Jesus Christ will come back, nevertheless he will certainly come back to judge people, and at that time God will destroy this present world.

SECTION CONSTITUENT 3:3-7 (Paragraph cluster) (Role: Concession to 3:8-10) THEME: There will be certain people who will ridicule the fact that you believe that the Lord Jesus Christ will come back to judge people.

PARAGRAPH CLUSTER CONSTITUENT 3:3-4 (Paragraph) (Role: Head of 3:3-7) THEME: There will be certain people who will ridicule the fact that you believe that the Lord Jesus Christ will come back.

PARAGRAPH CLUSTER CONSTITUENT 3:5-7 (Paragraph) (Role: Concession to 3:3-4) THEME: Those people (3:3c) know that what they say (3:4b-f) is not true.

SECTION CONSTITUENT 3:8-10 (Paragraph cluster) (Role: Head of 3:3-10) THEME: The Lord Jesus Christ will certainly come back to judge people, and at that time God will destroy this present world.

PARAGRAPH CLUSTER CONSTITUENT 3:8-9 (Paragraph) (Role: Concession to 3:10) THEME: The Lord Jesus Christ has not yet come back to judge people because God is forbearing towards you.

PARAGRAPH CLUSTER CONSTITUENT 3:10 (Paragraph) (Role: Head of 3:8-10) THEME: The Lord Jesus Christ will certainly come back to judge people, and at that time God will destroy this present world.

SUB-PART CONSTITUENT 3:11-13 (Paragraph) (Role: Head of 3:1-13) THEME: You ought to behave in a godly manner, since God will destroy everything like this (3:10) and since only righteous people will inhabit the new heavens and the new earth which will then come into being.

EPISTLE CONSTITUENT 3:14-18c (Paragraph) (Role: Summary of 1:3–3:13) THEME: Do all you can to behave in a godly manner, and guard against those who will entice you to doubt what now you firmly believe.

EPISTLE CONSTITUENT 3:18d (Proposition) (Role: Formal closure of the Epistle) THEME: I pray that our(inc) Lord and Saviour Jesus Christ may be glorified forever.

2. THE PRESENTATION AND DISCUSSION OF THE SEMANTIC UNITS OF 2 PETER

2 PETER 1:1–3:18
(Epistle)

THEME: *Exert yourselves to the utmost to develop a stable Christian character, since false teachers will entice you to behave wickedly, and since the Lord Jesus Christ will certainly come back to judge people; at that time, God will destroy this present world and there will be new heavens and a new earth where only righteous people will live.*

RELATIONAL STRUCTURE	CONTENTS
opening	(1:1-2) I, Simon Peter, am writing this letter to you, whom God has caused to believe in Christ just as we(exc) believe in Christ. I pray that God will bless you greatly.
BODY	(1:3–3:13) Exert yourselves to the utmost to develop a stable Christian character, since false teachers will entice you to behave wickedly, and since the Lord Jesus Christ will certainly come back to judge people; at that time, God will destroy this present world and there will be new heavens and a new earth where only righteous people will live.
summary	(3:14-18c) Do all you can to behave in a godly manner and guard against those who will entice you to doubt what you now firmly believe.
closing	(3:18) I pray that our(inc) Lord and Saviour Jesus Christ may be glorified now and forever.

COHERENCE OF THE EPISTLE

The situational coherence of this epistle is significant. Peter is writing the letter to a group of believers to remind them of certain truths which are known to them already. His purpose in doing so is to stir them up, so that they will behave according to their Christian principles and not be deceived by false teachers who will entice them to behave wickedly. This unity is shown by the situational orienters, 1:12-21 and 3:1-2. and also by the first person forms referring to Peter and the apostles, and the second person forms referring to the recipients of the letter, in chapters 1 and 3.

The Epistle begins with reference to the Lord Jesus Christ, in 1:1-2, and ends with reference to him, in 3:18d, whilst there are frequent references to the members of the Godhead throughout the letter. This referential coherence will be discussed in more detail in connection with the unity of the Body.

With regard to structural coherence, the Epistle consists of the opening (1:1-2), the body (1:3–3:13), the summary (3:14-18c), and the closing (3:18d). Unlike his first Epistle, in which Peter ends with personal remarks and greetings, he draws this Epistle to a close with a summary or recapitulation in 3:14-18c. In this he reiterates his exhortations to live godly lives, and also his warnings about those who will entice them to abandon their Christian beliefs. He then returns to his prayer of 1:2, that those to whom he is writing should grow in grace and in the knowledge of the Lord Jesus Christ. Finally, in 3:18d, there is a brief doxology consisting of a single sentence. this ending is consistent with the way the Epistle opens, and the sense of urgency which is apparent throughout. Peter clearly feels the necessity to communicate his message directly and forcefully, without any other matters which might distract attention from its importance.

An alternative analysis might be to regard 3:14-18c as being a constituent of the body, in a contraction-amplification relationship with 1:3–3:13. This would mean that the Epistle would follow the normal pattern for letters of that day, i.e., the opening, the body, and the closing. However, I have chosen to regard 3:14-18c as a unit which is distinct from the body, although related to it. This view is supported by the fact that the chiastic structure of the body is clearly reflected in the structure of 3:14-18c. For a detailed discussion of this see the discussion of coherence for 1:3–3:13 and 3:14-18c.

PROMINENCE AND THEME

The body is clearly the most prominent of the four constituent parts of the Epistle, so that the theme of the Epistle will be based on the most prominent information of the body. The theme for the whole discourse, therefore, will be discussed in connection with the prominence and theme of the body itself.

EPISTLE CONSTITUENT 1:1-2
(Paragraph) (Role: Formal opening of the Epistle)

THEME: *I, Simon Peter, am writing this letter to you, whom God has caused to believe in Christ just as we(exc) believe in Christ. I pray that God will bless you greatly.*

BOUNDARIES AND COHERENCE

The initial boundary of this unit coincides with the opening of the Epistle.

There is some discussion amongst commentators as to whether there

RELATIONAL STRUCTURE				CONTENT
	HEAD₁	HEAD		(1:1a) (I), Simon Peter, (am writing/sending this letter to you),
		desc. of "I"		(1:1b) (I) who serve Jesus Christ and who am an apostle appointed by Jesus Christ/who represents Jesus Christ.
HEAD₁	HEAD₂	HEAD		(1:1c) (I am writing/sending this letter to you) whom (God has) caused to believe (in Christ) just as (he caused) us(exc) to believe (in Christ).
		comment	HEAD	(1:1d) We(inc) are equally privileged in believing in Christ,
			reason	(1:1e) because Jesus Christ (who is) God (whom) we(inc) (worship/serve) and (who is) the one who saves us(inc) is righteous.
	HEAD₁			(1:2a) (I pray that God) may act very graciously towards you,
HEAD₂	HEAD₂			(1:2b) and (I pray that God may cause) you to be very much at peace,
	grounds			(1:2c) since you (truly/personally) know God and Jesus (who is) our(inc) Lord.

should be a break between verses 2 and 3, or whether the paragraph should continue, since the punctuation is difficult to decide. The possibilities are:

1. There may be a comma after verse 2, which would make verses 3 and 4 an explanation of the greeting, i.e., grace and peace are multiplied in knowing him, because God has given us all we need etc.
2. There may be a full stop after verse 2, which would mean that there is no main verb in the sentence (3-4), thus making it an anacoluthon. Verses 3 and 4 introduce the body of the Epistle, and provide a grounds for the exhortation which follows in 1:5-11.

Although either of these alternatives makes reasonable sense, the latter has been followed, since verse 2 provides a typical formal greeting to bring to a close the opening of the letter. The same formula fulfils that function in 1 Peter 1:2.

The unity of this paragraph lies primarily in the established pattern for the beginning of a letter of this period, which is as follows:

1. The sender identifies himself, using the nominative case. Here it is *Sumeōn Petros doulos kai apostolos Iēsou Christou* 'Simon Peter a servant and apostle of Jesus Christ'.
2. Those to whom the letter is written are identified, using the dative case. Here, *tois isotimon hēmin lachousin pistin* 'those who have received a faith as precious as ours'.
3. The sender greets the recipients, the greeting normally taking the form of a prayer that the Lord will bless the recipients. In the letters of Paul, this is usually expressed without a verb, but, in both of his letters, Peter uses the verb *plēthuntheiē* 'may it abound, increase'.

The unity of the paragraph is strengthened by references to the first two persons of the Godhead:

Iēsou Christou 'Jesus Christ' (1:1)

tou theou hēmōn kai sōtēros Iēsou Christou 'God and our Saviour Jesus Christ' (1:1)

tou theou kai Iēsou tou kuriou hēmōn 'God and Jesus our Lord' (1:2)

The use of other lexical items relating to the Christian faith further strengthens the unity of the paragraph:

pistin 'faith' (1:1)

dikaiosunē 'righteousness' (1:1)

charis 'grace' (1:2)

eirēnē 'peace' (1:2)

As we have seen above, there are three parts to this constituent of the Epistle, the first two being linked to form a unit, by the use of the two cases, the nominative and the dative, while the third forms a separate unit. These first two parts together constitute a non-verbal clause in the Greek, the verb "to write" or "to send" being omitted in the formalized opening.

This unit, then, consists of two propositional clusters, the first identifying the sender and the recipients of the letter, and the second expressing the greeting or blessing. In structure, therefore, it is a paragraph—a compound one, since the two propositional clusters are related by conjoining—and its place in the overall organization of the Epistle is that of the first of the four constituents of the Epistle—the opening, the body, the summary, and the closing.

PROMINENCE AND THEME

There does not seem to be any evidence that either of the two propositional clusters which constitute this paragraph is more prominent than the other, so a theme statement either has to be abstracted or to be made up of information drawn from both halves. The latter course has been followed, since the two halves are diverse in content. In the first cluster, the statement is taken from Heads 1 and 2. In the second cluster, the content is stated in more generic terms with "bless" including both grace and peace, and "God" being used to refer to the Godhead and not just to the Father.

NOTES ON 1:1-2

1:1a.   As is typical of the opening to a letter of this time, there is no verb relating the writer and the recipients, who are identified by the nominative and dative cases respectively. Clearly though, the implied verb is either the verb "to write" or "to send." This is made explicit in the display, as also is "letter."

Sumeōn 'Simon'; this particular spelling of 'Simon', as the name of Peter, is found only in Acts 15:14 besides here.

1:1b.   Peter now describes in further detail who the writer of the letter is. He gives his credentials, so that those to whom he is writing know that they can trust what he has to say. He begins by describing himself as *doulos . . . Iēsou Christou* 'slave of Jesus Christ', and, since the two terms are linked by the genitive construction, the semantic relationship between them needs to be made explicit.

Doulos is used figuratively here of the relationship between Peter and Christ. Whether the word is used in the sense of "servant" or "slave," the fact remains that the one to whom it refers owes complete obedience to his master and must be constantly at his service. The phrase is not used exclusively of apostles (cf. Acts 2:18; 1 Cor. 7:22; Eph. 6:6; Col. 4:12; 2 Tim. 2:24); and, by using the more general term first, before *apostolos* 'apostle', Peter identifies himself with those to whom he is writing, before claiming a hearing by right of his apostleship.

The only other time Peter uses the word *doulos* in this Epistle is in 2:19, when he refers to the false teachers and their followers as *douloi . . . tēs phthoras* 'slaves/servants of corruption', in marked contrast with its usage here.

In the display, the phrase is represented by "(I) who serve Jesus Christ."

Apostolos 'ambassador, delegate, official representative' is, in the New Testament, used predominantly for the twelve "apostles," and for Paul, although it also denoted an official church delegate and officially appointed preacher. (See Arndt and Gingrich)

As with *doulos*, *apostolos* is linked with *Iēsou Christou* by the genitive construction, and the simplest and most obvious meaning is that Peter has been commissioned by Christ to act and speak on his behalf, as an ambassador or envoy acts on behalf of a ruler. By describing himself as such, Peter is making his readers aware of the authority which he has from Christ, which gives him the right to speak to them as he does in this letter. This could be expressed in the display by "an apostle who was appointed by Jesus Christ," or "an apostle who respresents Jesus Christ."

1:1c-e.   Peter now goes on to identify the recipients of the letter as *tois isotimon hēmōn lachousin pistin* 'those who received the same precious faith as ours'. No particular group of Christians in a particular area is designated by this, and the heretical trends which Peter condemns and warns against are common to the church as a whole. We know that the letter was written to those who had received Peter's first letter, or another letter from him, since in 3:1 he says that this is the second letter he has written to them. He tells us in the opening of his first letter that its recipients are believers who have been scattered throughout a number of Roman provinces. Also, in 3:16 of this second letter, we are given to understand that those to whom it is sent accorded Paul's letters the status of Scripture, but there is little else to help us to identify its recipients.

Pistin 'faith, trust' is used here in an active sense which means "believing." Some commentators think that it stands rather for Christian belief as a body of teaching handed down from the apostles; cf. 3:2 and Jude 3, but the former makes better sense in this context. In the display, therefore, it has been expressed as "believe (in Christ)."

The phrase *isotimon hēmin . . . pistin* 'a faith equal in value to/of the same kind as/precious as ours' gives rise to a number of questions:

1. What exactly is the meaning of *isotimon* here?
2. To whom does *hēmin* 'to us' refer?
3. What is the relationship of this phrase to *en dikaiosunē tou theou hēmōn kai sōtēros Iēsou Christou* 'in righteousness of our God and Saviour Jesus Christ'?

According to Arndt and Gingrich, *isotimon* means "equal in value" or "of the same kind." This is its only occurrence in the New Testament. The International Critical Commentary states that its precise sense, rather, is "equal in honour/privileges," and that it is especially used of civic equality, which sense Peter possibly has in mind, i.e., faith makes those to whom he is writing citizens of God's kingdom, of equal standing with those whom he designates by *hēmin* 'to us'. In Acts 11:17, we are told that God bestows 'the same gift' *isēn dōrean* upon the Gentiles, as upon the Jewish Christians. Both have received the same gift of faith; cf. also Acts 15:8-11. This does not seem to be the distinction referred to here, however, since it is not relevant to any of the points handled in the letter. The distinction which would have more relevance would be that between the apostles, who had been eye-witnesses of the original revelation (1:16), and second or third generation Christians, who might feel at a disadvantage and consider their position an inferior one.

It would give good sense, then, for *hēmin* to refer to the apostles. Since all faith is a gift from God, it is all of equal worth, whether, as in the case of the apostles, or, like those to whom Peter was writing, they had not been with Christ personally, but had received their faith since his death and resurrection and ascension. All believe the same precious truth, and all are equally privileged and blessed.

The verb *lagchanō* 'receive, obtain' by lot or divine will, or 'be appointed, chosen' by lot, is used elsewhere in the New Testament only in Lk. 1:9; Jn. 18:24; and Acts 1:17. The implication is that faith is not won or earned by an individual's efforts, but that it has been given by God as he wills. It is a gift of favour or grace.

Two propositions express *tois isotimon hēmin lachousin pistin* in the display. The first, 1:1c, expresses the fact that the apostles and the recipients of this letter believe in Jesus Christ, and that it is God who has granted them the ability to do so. "God" has been made explicit as the agent, and "Christ" as the object of their faith. The pronoun *hēmin* is exclusive, referring to Peter and the other apostles, and not to those to whom the letter is written.

The second proposition, 1:1d, expresses how precious a thing it is to have been given such faith, i.e., how privileged they are. This proposition provides a comment on 1:1c which is the head of the propositional cluster 1:1c-e.

1:1e.   With respect to this proposition, there is some textual variation in the Greek, in that some MSS read *tou theou hēmōn kai sōtēros Iēsou Christou*, while others show the definite article before both *theou* 'God' and *sōtēros* 'saviour'. Accordingly, it may be taken to refer to just one member of the Trinity, i.e., "our God and Saviour, Jesus Christ," or to the Father and the Son, i.e., "God and our Saviour Jesus Christ." Most versions follow the former; cf. NIV, TEV, RSV, NEB, JER, and PHIL, but KJV follows the latter.

Grammatically, if there is only one article, then the occurrence of two substantives under one article gives a strong reason for regarding them as names of the same person; cf. 1 Peter 1:3, *ho theos kai patēr* 'the God and Father'. Also, if Peter had intended to distinguish two persons, it is doubtful whether he would have omitted the article before *sōtēros* 'saviour'.

Peter uses *sōtēr* five times in very similar phrases; cf. 1:11; 2:20; 3:18 *tou kuriou hēmōn kai sōtēros Iēsou Christou*, and 3:2 *tou kuriou kai sōtēros*. He never uses *sōtēr* alone in these, but always under the same article, with another name, and, in each case, the two names almost certainly belong to the same person. This would, perhaps, indicate that this is the case here. However, in the examples just quoted, it is *kurios* 'Lord' which is linked with *sōtēros* 'Saviour', whilst here it is *theos* 'God'. Also, in the next verse, *tou theou kai Iēsou tou kuriou hēmōn* seems to refer to both the Father and the Son.

Although the collocation *ho theos hēmōn* occurs about 12 times in the New Testament, this is a very small proportion of the total occurrences of *ho theos*, whereas *hēmōn* often occurs with *kurios* and *sōtēr*. This would point to Peter thinking primarily of *sōtēr*, i.e., to one person, Jesus Christ, in focus. In the display, therefore, the phrase may be expressed by "Jesus Christ (who is) God whom we(inc.) (worship/serve) and (who is) the one who saves us." Since, in certain languages, the noun "God" may not be possessed, *tou theou hēmōn* has been expressed by "God whom we(inc.) (worship/serve)." It may also be necessary to express *sōtēros Iēsou Christou* as "Jesus Christ . . . (who is) the one who saves us."

There is some discussion amongst commentators as to the sense of *en dikaiosunē tou theou*. Some have suggested that it should be linked with *pistin* 'faith', in the sense of "faith in the justice of God."

Meyer considers that *dikaiosunē* 'righteousness', in harmony with *isotimon*, is that righteousness of God according to which he grants the same faith to all believers without distinction; cf. Acts 10:34-35. According to him, the *en* is akin in meaning to *dia* and brings out more clearly "in what" the obtaining of *isotimon . . . pistin* 'the same precious faith' is grounded.

Alternatively, the righteousness referred to may be that righteousness of Christ which a believer puts on when he trusts in Christ as his Saviour, the righteousness which God gives in Christ, which makes a sinner right with God, and enables him to stand before the righteousness of God.

Peter uses *dikaiosunē* on three other occasions in this letter, (2:5,21; 3:13), and twice in his first letter, (2:24; 3:14). All seem to refer to living in a righteous, godly manner. It seems unlikely, therefore, that here the focus should be upon justice or impartiality, as suggested above. Rather, it seems appropriate that it is because Jesus Christ is righteous that both Peter and those to whom he is writing have been able to put their trust in him for salvation.

A number of versions translate *en dikaiosunē* as "through the righteousness;" cf. KJV, TEV, NIV, NEB, JER. In the display, it has been expressed by a reason proposition.

1:2a-b. The clause *charis humin kai eirēnē plēthuntheiē* 'grace and peace abound/increase to you' is identical with the corresponding greeting in 1 Peter (1:2), but not with that in any other Epistle.

The question to be considered here is how best to represent *charis* 'grace' and *eirēnē* 'peace' in the display.

The noun *charis* 'favour, grace, gracious care' is found, in the sense of "unmerited favour/grace" on the part of God and Christ to sinful mankind, throughout Paul's Epistles. It occurs in fixed formulas at the beginning and end of each of his letters. Peter uses it in a similar way here and in 3:18, and in 1 Peter 1:2 and 5:10.

"Grace" is difficult to represent in a display, since it represents an event in which God or Christ is the agent and man the recipient of the action, but there is no English verb which expresses such an event. When it is given its full theological sense of God giving his blessings freely to those who can in no way merit them, it may be expressed by "act graciously," where "graciously" is marked as a technical term used by the Christian writers of the New Testament in a special Christian sense. If it is regarded as being used in a more general sense, then it may be expressed by "bless," "do good to," "act kindly towards." Since it is a formal greeting, some commentators think it possible that Paul adapted the general Greek word for "greetings," *charein*, to make it a specifically Christian greeting. In a translation, then, an expression which would be appropriate for a greeting should be chosen.

As in Paul's Epistles, this greeting is regarded as a prayer, expressed in a brief and stylised manner. Unlike Paul's Epistles, where there is no verb expressed in the Greek, Peter uses the aorist passive optative *plēthuntheiē* 'be multiplied, increase, abound'. This is expressed by "I pray that God may act very graciously towards you," with *plēthuntheiē* simply intensifying the act, and "you" being those believers to whom Peter is writing the letter. "God" is made explicit as the agent, since he is the one who dispenses all grace.

According to Arndt and Gingrich, *eirēnē* 'peace, harmony', in a literal or figurative sense, may correspond to the Hebrew word for "welfare, health," when used in a greeting, as it is here, and most commentators agree that it is the state enjoyed by those who receive God's grace. It is the state of the whole man which is referred to, his "well-being," "a state of blessedness or prosperity of body and soul," cf. SSA Colossians: Callow. Since God is the source of all grace, he is also the source of the peace which it brings with it, therefore, in the display, God is made explicit as the agent, as in 1:2a, and *plēthuntheiē* 'be increased', which is also understood, is made explicit. The clause is expressed as "I pray that (God) may cause you to be very much at peace."

1:2c. The main point for discussion in the phrase *en epignōsei tou theou kai Iēsou tou kuriou hēmōn* 'in the knowledge of God and of Jesus our Lord' is the sense in which the noun *epignōsis* 'knowledge' is used.

Peter uses both words for knowledge, *epignōsis* and *gnōsis*, in this Epistle. He uses *gnōsis* in 1:5,6, and 3:18, and *epignōsis* here, and in 1:3,8, and 2:20. In his first letter he uses only *gnōsis*, in 3:7. There has been much discussion as to the distinction in meaning between these two words, but no decisive evidence seems to have been put forward as yet as to what exactly that distinction is, or if they are interchangeable, and if so, in what contexts.

Epignōsis is a compound in the Greek, and, according to some commentators, this implies a fuller knowledge. It is difficult though to find an appropriate word for this in English, conveying this stronger sense, even if it is correct.

In an article in *NOT* 63-82, Greenlee suggests that the noun *epignōsis* is almost always used in examples which will bear the intensive meaning, "(true) knowledge." He gives 2 Peter 1:2, 3, 8, and 2:20, amongst other passages which refer to knowing Christ or God, as an example of this use.

According to Greenlee's investigations, there are no instances of this noun being used of false knowledge, nor of knowledge of evil. It is used only in referring to God, Jesus, truth, and good. In addition, it cannot be used, as the verb *epignōskō* can be, in the sense of "recognize." The simple noun *gnōsis*, however, seems to be used of both good or evil knowledge, and true or false knowledge.

Greenlee concludes that *epignōsis* has the intensified sense which the prefix *epi-* implies, but not in the sense of "complete" or "full" knowledge, but with the emphasis on the "truth" of the knowledge involved.

If what Greenlee says is correct, it is difficult to see why Peter uses *gnōsis* in 3:18 and *epignōsis* in 1:2, since each is used in a similar context:

1:2 *charis humin kai eirēnē plēthuntheiē en epignōsei tou theou kai Iēsou tou kuriou hēmōn* 'grace to you and peace be increased in the knowledge of God and of Jesus our Lord'.

3:18 *auxanete de en chariti kai gnōsei tou kuriou hēmōn kai sōtēros Iēsou Christou* 'grow in grace and in the knowledge of our Lord and Saviour Jesus Christ'.

Other commentators (cf. Bigg and Green) suggest that the distinction is between knowing someone personally, (*epignōsis*), and knowing about someone, (*gnōsis*). In the ICC, Bigg suggests that, if we compare verses 5 and 6 with 8, *gnōsis* (5 and 6) appears to denote good sense, understanding, practical wisdom, while *epignōsis* (8) is used of the knowledge of Christ. However, he concedes that, in the New Testament, it is not easy to keep them distinct, and it is difficult again to see how this distinction would apply in 1:2 and 3:18.

Perhaps it is significant that, in 3:18, the immediately preceding context has been concerned with false teaching, and so *gnōsis* should refer to knowledge of the truth about.

In translating this phrase, therefore, the important thing seems to be to ensure that the verb or noun used is one which implies knowledge of a personal nature and not just knowing about someone in an intellectual way. In the display, it has been expressed by 'you (truly/personally) know', with *tou theou kai Iēsou tou kuriou hēmōn* 'God and Jesus our Lord' providing the object of that knowledge. The combination *Iēsou tou kuriou hēmōn* 'Jesus our Lord' is unusual, being found only here and in Rom. 4:24.

The collocation *plēthuntheiē en* is unusual. *En* often indicates accompanying circumstances, but that does not seem appropriate here. It is difficult to find an appropriate relationship, the most suitable being "grounds," although that is not entirely satisfactory.

EPISTLE CONSTITUENT 1:3–3:13
(Part) (Role: Body of the Epistle)

THEME: *Exert yourselves to the utmost to develop a stable Christian character, since false teachers will entice you to behave wickedly, and since the Lord Jesus Christ will certainly come back to judge people; at that time, God will destroy this present world and there will be new heavens and a new earth where only righteous people will live.*

RELATIONAL STRUCTURE	CONTENTS
HEAD1	(1:3–2:22) Exert yourselves to the utmost to develop a stable Christian character, since false teachers will entice you to behave wickedly; God will certainly destroy them.
HEAD2	(3:1-13) Do all you can to behave in a godly manner, since the Lord Jesus will certainly come back to judge people; at that time, God will destroy this present world, and there will be new heavens and a new earth where only righteous people will live.

BOUNDARIES AND COHERENCE

The initial boundary for the body has been discussed in connection with the boundaries of the formal opening of the Epistle. As can be seen from that, it seems preferable to connect 1:3 and 4 with what follows, rather than with verses 1 and 2, and to regard the sentence as an anacoluthon, providing an introduction to the exhortation which follows in 1:5-11. The initial *hōs* has the meaning of 'in the light of' or 'in conformity with', and looks forward to something else. It implies that there is a new/different subject coming up, which is "you" in 1:5; cf. *epichorēgēsate* 'you supply, provide', which is anticipated in 1:4 in *genēsthe* 'you become', and *apophugontes* '(you) having fled'.

The body closes with 3:13, since a new unit is started at 3:14, introduced by the conjunction *dio* 'therefore', the vocative *agapētoi* 'dear ones/friends', and the imperative *spoudasate* 'be diligent/zealous'.

Certain features characterize the body and give it coherence. They are as follows:

1. The occurrence of a group of words to do with the semantic area of knowledge:
   epignōsis 'knowledge' (1:3,8; 2:20)
   gnōsis 'knowledge' (1:5,6)
   ginōskō 'know, understand' (1:20; 3:3)

gnōrizō 'make known' (1:16)
oida 'know' (1:12,14; 2:9)

2. References to stability and instability:
astēriktos 'unstable, weak' (2:14)
bebaios 'reliable, dependable, certain' (1:10,19)
ptaiō 'stumble, fall' (1:10)
stērizō 'establish, confirm, strengthen' (1:12)

3. Frequent references to either true or spurious teaching/messages, transmitted, respectively, by men sent from God, or false teachers. Those to do with the truth are as follows:
phōnēs enechtheisēs . . . *hupo tēs megaloprepous doxēs* 'a voice which came . . . from the majestic glory' (1:17), i.e., the voice of God.
ton prophētikon logon 'the prophetic word' (1:19)
prophēteia 'prophecy' (1:20-21)
hē hodos tēs alētheias 'the way of truth' (2:2)
hagias entolēs '(the) holy commandment' (2:21)
proeirēmenōn rhēmatōn hupo tōn hagiōn prophētōn 'words which were spoken before by the holy prophets' (3:2)
tēs tōn apostolōn humōn entolēs tou kuriou kai sōtēros 'the commandment of the Lord and Saviour through your apostles' (3:2)

Those to do with falsehood are as follows:
sesophismenois muthois 'cunningly devized fables' (1:16)
pseudoprophētai 'false teachers' (2:1)
haireseis apōleias 'destructive heresies' (2:1)
hē hodos tēs alētheias blasphēmēthēsetai 'the way of truth will be evil spoken of' (2:2)
plastois logois . . . *emporeusontai* 'they will deceive . . . by saying what is false' (2:3)
empaigmonē 'scoffing, mocking' (3:3)
empaiktai 'scoffers, mockers' (3:3)

4. Emphasis throughout on living a godly life, and the blessings which will result from this, in contrast with the wicked lives of the false teachers and their adherents, which will result in their destruction. Godly living and the virtues in which it consists are referred to in the following:
eusebeia 'godliness' (1:3, 6, 7; 3:11)
a whole list of virtues to be cultivated (1:5-7)
eutheian hodon 'the right way' (2:15)
tēn hodon tēs dikaiosunēs 'the way of righteousness' (2:21)

and the blessings awaiting those who live holy lives:
plousiōs epichorēgēthēsetai humin hē eisodos eis tēn aiōnion basileian

tou kuriou hēmōn kai sōtēros Iēsou Christou 'entrance will be richly provided for you into the eternal kingdom of our Lord and
Saviour Jesus Christ' (1:11)

oiden kurios eusebeis ek peirasmou rhuesthai 'the Lord knows how to
rescue the godly from temptation/trial' (2:9)

*kainous de ouranous kai gēn kainēn kata to epaggelma autou
prosdokōmen, en hois dikaiosunē katoikei* 'We look forward to a
new heaven and a new earth, which he promised, in which
righteousness dwells'. (3:13)

The lives of the ungodly are described in detail in chapter two, along
with their ultimate judgement and destruction. For the latter see also
3:7.

5. References to effort and perseverance:
spoudēn pasan pareisenegkantes 'making every effort' (1:5)
spoudazō 'be zealous, make every effort' (1:10,15)
speudō 'be zealous, be industrious' (3:12)

These all demonstrate the referential coherence of the body of the
Epistle, with its emphasis on the necessity for believers to make every effort
to live godly, consistent Christian lives, and the close connection there is between achieving stability in this, and dependence on Scripture, for that true
knowledge of God which should guide their actions and enable them to
withstand the wiles of false teachers.

The close connection between perseverance in the Christian life, and a
proper view of the Word of God, is clearly seen in the structure of the body.
Each threat to perseverance is preceded by an exhortation to go back to the
Scriptures. The threat of the false teachers, in chapter two, is preceded by
several verses on the value of the writings of those who are truly inspired by
the Holy Spirit; cf. 1:19-21. The threat of those who seek to undermine the
faith of believers by ridiculing what they believe, in 3:3-4, is preceded by a
reminder, in 3:1-2, of the value of what the Old Testament prophets had said,
and also, the message of the apostle. In Peter's final exhortation and warning
too, Paul's writings are referred to in 3:15-16 when Peter talks of the dangers
of misusing the Scriptures.

STRUCTURE OF THE BODY

Within the body there is a major break between 1:21 and 2:1, where
Peter changes from personally addressing his readers in the final two
paragraphs of chapter 1, and begins to describe the false teachers who will
appear amongst them, their state, their influence on others, and their fate at
the hands of God. In the two paragraphs at the end of chapter 1 he uses
predominantly first person singular and plural verb forms, while in chapter 2
predominantly third person plural verb forms are used, except for third person singular forms when God is the agent.

A second major break comes between 2:22 and 3:1, where Peter ends his description of the false teachers with the two proverbs in 2:22, and once more speaks to his readers personally, addressing them as *agapētoi* 'dear ones'. He also changes to first person singular verb forms and uses the second person pronoun 'you' when addressing his readers.

Despite the break between 1:21 and 2:1 there are features which would suggest that 1:3–2:22 form a single unit.

First, if 1:3–2:22 constitutes a unit, there are obvious parallels between that unit and 3:1-13, in that both consist of a warning to believers concerning those who will try to entice them to do evil and to undermine their Christian beliefs (2:1-22 and 3:1-10), and an exhortation to them to do all they can to live stable, godly lives, in the face of these attacks (1:3-21 and 3:11-13). From this it can be seen that Peter is dealing with the same basic idea twice over, but with different false teaching in focus.

Second, 1:3-21 and 2:1-22 are linked by the conjunction *de* which occurs at the beginning of 2:1. There is no such conjunction linking 2:22 with 3:1. The *de* is contrastive.

Third, there is a tail-head link between 1:19-21 and 2:1, in that Peter closes chapter 1 with statements concerning true prophecy and true prophets, and begins chapter 2 by speaking of the antithesis of this, i.e., false prophets and the heresies they teach. Again, there is no such link between 2:22 and 3:1.

Finally, the respective heads of 1:3-21 and 2;1-22 are in a grounds-conclusion relationship, the latter providing the grounds for the former.

The body then is regarded as consisting of two main units—1:3–2:22 and 3:1-13. Together, they form a chiastic structure, as follows:

A   Exhortation to make every effort to live a godly life (1:3-21)
B   Warning against false teachers (2:1-22)
B'   Warning against those who ridicule belief in Christ's return (3:1-10)
A'   Exhortation to make every effort to live a godly life (3:11-13)

The inner two constituents of the chiasmus, B and B', provide the grounds respectively for the outer two constituents, A and A'

This chiastic structure is reflected in 3:14-18c which provides a summary of the body:

A   Exhortation to live a godly life (3:14)
B   Exhortation concerning doctrinal matters, i.e., the return of Christ (3:15)
B'   Exhortation concerning doctrinal matters, i.e., the danger of error undermining their spiritual stability (3:17)
A'   Exhortation to live a godly life (3:18a-c)

The reminder, in 3:15, that Christ is merciful, in that he has not yet returned to judge people, recalls 3:1-10 and the fact that he will eventually return to judge and to condemn the wicked. The exhortation to be on their guard against those who will try to undermine their Christian beliefs recalls 2:1-22 and the enticements of the false teachers described there.

PROMINENCE AND THEME

In a chiasmus with an even number of constituents it is the outside pair of constituents that is prominent; therefore, the two exhortations, A and A', which form the outer layers of the chiasmus in 1:3–3:13, are naturally prominent. The theme statement for the body then has been based on the heads of these units, which consist of exhortations to holy living in each case.

A large proportion of the body is taken up with warnings against the heresies of false teachers and those who scoff; cf. 2:1–3:10. These warnings provide the grounds for the exhortations which Peter makes, and have therefore been included in the theme statement along with the exhortation.

PART CONSTITUENT 1:3–2:22
(Sub-part) (Role: Head$_1$ of 1:3–3:13)

THEME: *Exert yourselves to the utmost to develop a stable Christian character, since false teachers will entice you to behave wickedly; God will certainly destroy them.*

SITUATIONAL STRUCTURE	CONTENTS
EXHORTATION	(1:3-21) Exert yourselves to the utmost to develop a stable Christian character
GROUNDS	(2:1-22) There will be false teachers who will behave wickedly and will entice you to behave in the same way as they do; God will certainly destroy them.

BOUNDARIES AND COHERENCE

The initial boundary of this constituent has been discussed in connection with the initial boundary of the body, with which it coincides. The final boundary has been discussed in connection with the structure of the body.

PROMINENCE AND THEME

As can be seen from the display, there are two main constituents of 1:3–2:22; an exhortation (1:3-21), and an exposition (2:1-22), with the latter providing the grounds for the former.

Since the theme of a hortatory unit reflects its basic structure of Exhortation and Grounds, the theme statement of this constituent is based on the heads of 1:3-21 and 2:1-22.

SUB-PART CONSTITUENT 1:3-21
(Division) (Role: Head of 1:3–2:22)

THEME: *Exert yourselves to the utmost to develop a stable Christian character.*

RELATIONAL STRUCTURE	CONTENTS
HEAD	(1:3-11) Exert yourselves to the utmost to develop a stable Christian character.
Situational Orienter (Author's intention)	(1:12-21) I intend to keep reminding you very frequently about these matters (i.e., 1:3-11) because they are true.

BOUNDARIES AND COHERENCE

The initial boundary for this unit has been discussed under this heading for the body of the Epistle.

The final boundary is clearly marked, as Peter turns to describing the false teachers and their followers in 2:1, and changes from a personal and hortatory genre to an expository one. This is marked by a change from predominantly first person verb forms in 1:12-21, to predominantly third person plural verb forms in chapter two, which refer to the false teachers and those who follow them.

There is no evidence for a major internal boundary within this unit, since the boundaries marked are clearly ascribably to sections and paragraphs, i.e., lower ranking units. It is therefore analysed as a division consisting of two sections, 1:3-11 and 1:12-21, consisting respectively of two paragraphs each.

Throughout this constituent there are references to the Lord Jesus Christ (1:8, 11, 14, 16); to knowledge (1:3, 5, 6, 8) and its related verb forms (1:12, 14, 16, 20); to striving and effort (1:5, 10, 15); and to stability and firmness (1:10, 12, 19). All of these give coherence to the whole.

PROMINENCE AND THEME

The first of the two sections making up this division, 1:3-11, is hortatory. Peter urges his readers to make every effort to develop those virtues which go to make up a truly Christian character. The second section, 1:12-21, is of a personal nature. Peter tells them why he is writing to them in this way. The hortatory material is naturally the more prominent, and therefore, acts as head of 1:3-21 while 1:12-21 acts as what may be called a "situational" orienter, since it states the author's purpose in saying what he does. The theme statement, therefore, is the theme statement of 1:3-11.

DIVISION CONSTITUENT 1:3-11
(Section) (Role: Head of 1:3-21)

THEME: *Exert yourselves to the utmost to develop a stable Christian character.*

RELATIONAL STRUCTURE	CONTENTS
grounds	(1:3-4) Since God has given us(inc) everything that we(inc) need in order that we(inc) might live eternally and in order that we(inc) might be godly,
HEAD	(1:5-11) exert yourselves to the utmost to develop a stable Christian character.

BOUNDARIES AND COHERENCE

These verses form a unit in that they centre round the theme that Christians should do all they can to develop a stable Christian character, as this is the only appropriate response to the many blessings which God has bestowed upon them, and the only way to confirm that he has chosen them to be his people. Doing the will of God as he has revealed it will supply evidence of salvation.

The initial boundary of this unit has been discussed with reference to the initial boundary of the body of the Epistle, with which it coincides. The final boundary is clearly marked by the start of a new section at 1:12, where there is a change from exhortation to a personal statement by Peter as to why he is writing this letter. This change is marked by the following features:

1. an initial *dio* 'therefore'
2. an orienter, *mellēsō* 'I intend'
3. a change from second person plural to first person singular verb forms; cf. *mellēsō* 'I intend' and *hēgoumai* 'I consider'.

The referential unity of this section lies in the set of words relating to the blessings received by believers from God, and the set relating to those virtues after which beleivers should strive. Belonging to the first set are the following:

> *panta . . . ta pros zōēn kai eusebeian* 'everything . . . necessary for life and godliness' (1:3)
>
> *ta timia kai megista . . . epaggelmata* 'very great and precious promises' (1:4)
>
> *genēsthe theias koinōnoi phuseōs* 'you might partake of the divine nature' (1:4)

pistei 'faith' (1:5)

klēsin kai eklogēn 'calling and election' (1:10)

hē eisodos eis tēn aiōnion basileian tou kuriou hēmōn kai sōtēros Iēsou Christou 'entrance into the eternal kingdom of our Lord and Saviour Jesus Christ' (1:11)

Belonging to the second set are the following:

eusebeian 'godliness' (1:3,6,7)

aretē 'virtue' (1:3,5)

epignōsis 'knowledge' (1:3,8) and *gnōsis* 'knowledge' (1:5,6)

egkrateia 'self-control' (1:6)

hupomonē 'steadfastness' (1:6)

philadelphia 'brotherly love' (1:7)

agapē 'love' (1:7)

The internal structure of this section is not easy to determine. There is no general agreement on paragraph breaks, as can be seen in the various versions:

RSV; JER	3-11
TEV; PHIL	3-9; 10-11
NIV	3-4; 5-9; 10-11
NEB	3-4; 5-7; 8-11

There is some evidence for a break between 1:4 and 5, in that there is a change of genre. Verses 3-4 consist of a statement of the blessings which God has bestowed on believers; then, in verse 5, Peter begins an exhortation to the recipients of the letter to respond by endeavouring to develop Christian virtures in their lives. This is introduced by *kai auto touto de* 'for this very thing', referring to the grounds stated in 1:3-4, i.e., "in the light of all this (1:3-4)." The *kai* indicates the additiion of something further to what has gone before, while the *de* brings out that what is added is a new development relative to what has gone before.

There is also some evidence for a paragraph break between verses 9 and 10 as follows:

1. the introductory conjunction *dio* 'therefore'
2. the vocative *adelphoi* 'brothers/fellow-believers'
3. the imperative *spoudasate* 'strive', marking a return to exhortation.

If these two breaks are accepted then this section may be analysed as consisting of three paragraphs—1:3-4; 1:5-9; and 1:10-11. However, this analysis gives rise to some difficulty as to the relationship between 1:5-9 and 1:10-11. Both have a comand as head:

"Exert every effort to develop a stable Christian character." (1:5-9)

"Do all you can to confirm that God has chosen you to be his people." (1:10-11)

In both cases the exhortation is followed by two motivational grounds introduced by *gar*, thus giving two parallel structures. But what is the relationship between these two commands?

Generally speaking, character is evidence for election, i.e., evidential grounds. Peter seems to be saying, "Establish your election by developing Christian virtues in your life," i.e., a HEAD-means relationship. However, the command in 10-11 seems to be carried forward from 5-9, and it could be said that their purpose in striving to be godly is to make their election sure, which indicates a MEANS-purpose relationship. But the purpose can be said to be marked for prominence by the use of:

> *dio* 'therefore'
> the imperative *mallon spoudasate* 'strive all the more'
> the vocative *adelphoi* 'fellow-believers'

Therefore, MEANS-PURPOSE would seem best, and if 3-4 is also regarded as a separate paragraph then the relational structure for 3-11 would be:

> grounds   (3-4)
> MEANS   (5-9)
> PURPOSE   (10-11)

However, it is also possible to regard verses 5-11 as one paragraph, since they do have a clear unity, which is shown by the following:

1. The theme of striving and effort is to the forefront in both 5-9 and 10-11; cf. *spoudēn pasan pareisenegkantes* 'bringing in every effort' (1:5) and *spoudasate* 'strive' (1:10).

2. Second person plural verb forms are found throughout these verses; cf. *epichorēgēsate* 'provide' (1:5); *spoudasate* 'strive' (1:10); *ptaisēte* 'fall, fail' (1:10); and also the second person plural pronoun; cf. *humōn* 'of you' (1:5,10); *humin* 'in you' (1:8,11).

3. *Tauta* 'these things/matters' occurs in verses 8, 9, and 10, referring to the virtues enumerated in verses 5-7.

As in the alternative analysis, the command in 1:10 and its relationship with that in 1:5-7 is problematic. There are two factors to be considered in this respect.

Firstly, the command in 1:10 is, in a broad sense, a repetition of that in verses 5-7. In urging his readers to do all they can to confirm their election Peter is really urging them, as in 5-7, to do all they can to develop a godly Christian character, since this is evidence of their calling. Following the main command in 5-7 Peter has four uses of *gar*; see verses 8, 9, 10, and 11. In verse 10 he makes a new grammatical start, but not a new semantic start. He does so in order to provide an independent command to which he can attach the second two cases of *gar*.

Secondly, verses 8-11 (two *gar* + two *gar*) follow the main command, supplying a back-up to it. The content of the four *gar* clauses forms a chiasmus, which helps us to see clearly how Peter backs up the main exhortation, which ties up with the rest of the book. The two outside *gar* are prominent, as would be expected. Both are positive, i.e., they speak of the blessings which come from obeying the command. The two inner *gar* are negative.

As was shown above, if verses 5-11 are analysed as two paragraphs, the structures of the two paragraphs are parallel, whereas, if they are analysed as a single paragraph, the structure is chiastic. Since the latter shows a stronger unity, verses 5-11 have been analysed as a single paragraph, with verses 3-4 as a paragraph also.

PROMINENCE AND THEME

The relative prominence of the two commands, 1:5-7 and 1:10, needs to be considered when deciding upon a theme statement for this section. The grounds for them is supplied by 1:3-4.

The repetitive pattern of 1:5-7, with its seven conjoined heads, has a cumulative effect, and gives additional emphasis to the exhortation. Also, Peter's concern throughout this letter is that those to whom he is writing should develop godly characters; cf. also 3:11-13 and 3:14-18c. In doing this they will confirm their calling, but the focus is on their efforts to live godly lives, therefore the theme statement for the section is based on the exhortation in 1:5-7.

SECTION CONSTITUENT 1:3-4
(Paragraph) (Role: Grounds for 1:5-11)

THEME: *God has given us(inc) everything that we need in order that we(inc) might live eternally and in order that we(inc) might be godly.*

BOUNDARIES AND COHERENCE

The initial boundary of this paragraph is also the initial boundary of the body of the Epistle and has been discussed under that heading.

The final boundary is marked by:

1. *kai auto touto de* 'and for this very thing' (1:5), which summarizes the previous paragraph (1:3-4), and introduces the next one.
2. a change from expository discourse in 1:3-4 to hortatory discourse in 1:5, which is introduced by the aorist participle *pareisenegkantes* 'bringing in', which has the force of an imperative, and the imperative *epichorēgēsate* 'furnish, provide'. Apart from the imperative verbs the present tense predominates in 1:5-11.

There is strong relational and referential coherence within this paragraph, with clear grammatical and lexical parallels between the two verses. Both have:

1. the same implied subject, i.e., God, and use the word *theias* 'divine' to refer to his nature/character.
2. the same verb, *dōreomai* 'to give'. They also both use perfect middle

RELATIONAL STRUCTURE	CONTENT
HEAD HEAD	(1:3a) He (God) has given us(inc) everything (that we(inc) need) in order that (we(inc) might) live (eternally) and in order that (we(inc) might) be godly
means1	(1:3b) by means of the power that he has because he is God
means2 HEAD	(1:3c) and by means of our knowing him (God)
description	(1:3d) (who) summoned us(inc) (to be his people) by means of his own glorious and perfect (nature/character).
specific HEAD	(1:4a) By means of this (glorious and perfect nature) he (God) has promised us(inc) (that he will do) very great and precious deeds (for us)
means	(1:4b) in order that, by means of this (what God has promised),
purpose HEAD	(1:4c) you might behave righteously as God behaves righteously,
reason HEAD	(1:4d) (since) you are no longer (morally) depraved
comp. HEAD	(1:4e) (like) those who do not believe in Christ are (morally) depraved,
reason	(1:4f) because (they) desire to do what is evil.

forms; in 1:3 the participle *dedōrēmenēs*, and in 1:4 the finite form, *dedōrētai*.

3. the same beneficiary of the action, *hēmin* 'to us'.

4. *dia* expressing a means; i.e., *dia tēs epignōseōs* . . . 'by means of our knowing' (1:3c), and *di' hōn* 'by means of these' (1:4a).

5. purpose propositions which are closely related semantically, cf. *panta* . . . *pros zōēn kai eusebeian* 'everything (that we need) in order that (we might) live (eternally) and in order that (we might) be godly' (1:3a) (this purpose is implied, within the HEAD), and *hina* . . . *genēsthe theias koinōnoi phuseōs* 'in order that . . . you might behave righteously as God behaves righteously' (1:4c).

Structurally, the head of the paragraph is 1:3a, since all the other clauses are dependent upon it, grammatically as well as semantically.

There are two propositional clusters. The first consists of 3a-d, and the second, 4a-f.

The head of the first cluster is 3a and there are two means propositions in a subordinate relationship to it, i.e., 3b and 3c.

Strictly speaking, *ta pros zōēn kai eusebeian* '(that we need) in order that (we might) live (eternally) and in order that (we might) be godly' identifies *panta* 'everything', and the second means (3c) should be attached to the purpose in 3a. However, it is difficult to represent these two relations in the display, so both have been shown as relating to the HEAD as a whole.

The second propositional cluster has 4a as its HEAD, with 4c providing the purpose for it. The HEAD is in a specific relationship to the HEAD of the first propositional cluster, i.e., 3a, which is therefore HEAD of the paragraph as a whole.

Although 1:3a is the head of this paragraph, it is not an independent finite clause but is in a genitive absolute form, showing that this whole paragraph is subsidiary to the following exhortations in 1:5-11.

Referentially, the use of *theias* 'divine' (twice) and *doxē* 'glory' and *aretē* 'virtue/excellence' brings to our notice the divine nature of the one who makes the gifts which are the subject matter of the paragraph. Also, the use of the adjectives, *timia* 'precious', and *megista* 'very great', to describe the gifts which God makes to believers, contributes to the unity of the paragraph since they belong to the same semantic set.

PROMINENCE AND THEME

Within this short paragraph, prominence is given to the theme of what God has given to believers. This is brought to the fore by the repetition of *theias* 'divine' and *dōreomai* 'to give'.

The permanent nature of what God has given is stressed by the use of the perfect tense in both occurrences of *dōreomai*, i.e., *dedōrēmenēs* (1:3), and *dedōrētai* (1:4). Peter is anxious to make clear that what God has given to believers in his promises, i.e., the means of living eternally and of being godly, is firmly guaranteed, despite the scoffing of those who are seeking to undermine their faith, cf. 1:16 and 3:3ff.

The occurrence of *panta* 'all things', in the prominent position immediately after the conjunction, emphasizes the all-embracing nature of the gift.

The theme is taken from the HEAD, 1:3a.

NOTES ON 1:3-4

1:3a.   Is *hēmin* 'to us' inclusive or exclusive? It may refer to:
1. the apostles (exclusive).
2. Peter and his readers (inclusive).

Those commentators who favour the first of these alternatives stress that the contrast between *hēmin* 'to us', *hēmas* 'us' (1:3d), and the second person plural in *genēsthe* 'you might become', (1:4c) must be preserved. *Hēmin* implies the apostolic circle, who, by virtue of their own experience of the *doxa kai aretē* 'glory and perfection' of Christ, are able to transmit to these readers the great and precious promises of 1:4a.

However, since Peter addresses this letter to *tois isotimon hēmin lachousin pistin* 'those who have obtained faith of equal standing to ours' (1:1), it would seem appropriate here to include those to whom he is writing and make *hēmin* inclusive. There seems to be no reason for Peter to stress the distinction between the apostles and those he is addressing, for what he is saying is applicable to all believers.

The preposition *pros*, with the accusative case of an abstract noun, can mean "in connection with," or can indicate a purpose or result. Here, in the phrase *panta . . . pros zōēn kai eusebeian*, it gives the purpose of *panta* 'everything' and so is expressed by "everything (that we need) in order that."

Most commentators regard *zōēn* 'life' as meaning "spiritual life/eternal life." It contrasts with *phthora* 'corruption' in verse 4. In the display, therefore, the adverb "eternally," has been included to qualify the verb "live."

Peter uses the noun *eusebeia* four times in this Epistle—here in 1:3, and also in 1:6, 7 and 3:11, as he exhorts his readers to live blameless and godly lives in response to the many blessings they have received from God. According to Arndt and Gingrich it has the meaning "piety, godliness, religion" and is used of the duty which man owes to God. They suggest that *ta pros . . . eusebeian* means "what belongs to piety," i.e., what God requires of man with regard to his conduct. It is the opposite to *epithumia* 'lust' (1:4). All that is necessary to enable a man to live in a godly manner and to attain to eternal life is available from God. This contrasts with their previous state of moral depravity, referred to in 1:4, i.e., *tō kosmō en epithumia phthoras* 'the corruption that is in the world through lust'.

The perfect participle, *dedōrēmenēs*, is middle here and not passive, i.e., "having given." Its formal subject is *tēs theias dunameōs autou* 'his divine power', so, in deciding who the subject of *dedōrēmenēs* is, we need to consider the reference of *autou* 'his' (1:3b). In the previous verse Peter has just referred to *tou theou kai Iēsou tou kuriou hēmōn* 'God and Jesus our Lord', so that *autou* could refer to either God or Jesus our Lord. Some commentators think that it refers to Jesus our Lord, since *Iēsou tou kuriou hēmōn* is closest in proximity. Others would refer it to God, since all the effects of the gospel on the human heart are, in the Scriptures, traced to the power of God, mediated to us through Christ.

It would seem more appropriate to refer *autou* to God, since, in addition to the former considerations, *theias* 'divine' is never applied directly to Christ. Apart from here and 1:4, it is used only in Acts 17:29 where it refers to God.

1:3d.   In the New Testament, God is regarded as the one who calls us (cf. 1 Peter 2:9), and, therefore, *kalesantos* 'him who called' has been taken to refer to God. Some commentators consider Christ to be the one who calls, because *epignōsis* 'knowledge' is used in connection with Christ in 1:8 and 2:20. However, in 1:2, it is used to refer to both *tou theou kai Iēsou tou kuriou hēmōn* 'God and Jesus our Lord', and so God is preferred here, in keeping with general New Testament usage.

The use of the verb *kaleō* 'call', in the sense in which it is used in the New Testament, to denote a call to salvation, is figurative, including, not just the outward action but also the inward, spiritual, effective call.

Since the verb "call" generally means either "to shout to/for" or "to give a name to," the verb "to summon" is used here to convey the idea of authority which is a component of the word in this context.

The pronoun *hēmas* 'us' is inclusive as in 1:3a and has the same reference, i.e., himself and his readers; all believers, without exception, are "called" by God.

Some MSS read *dia doxēs kai aretēs* instead of *idia doxē kai aretē*, i.e., "through glory and virtue" as opposed to "by his own glory and virtue," and it is easy to see how the two opening words, *idia* and *dia*, could be confused by scribes. As a result, there are three possible meanings suggested by commentators:

1. to his own glory and virtue (but in this case *eis* would need to be used),
2. by his own glory and virtue (the dative case denoting the agency "by"), and
3. by means of glory and virtue (the preposition *dia* 'by means of, through', with genitive of thing).

The display is based on the second of these, in agreement with the majority of commentators. Calvin considered that it was Peter's object to ascribe the whole praise of our salvation to God, and this reading expresses that most clearly. There is very little difference in meaning, however, between proposals 2 and 3. In 2, "by" equals "by means of" in 3, and the "glory and virtue" of 3 must be "his own" (2), not someone else's. In 3, the means is explicit; in 2, "his own" is stressed.

There is further discussion as to whether this phrase should be connected with:

1. *tou kalesantos* (1:3d)
2. *dedōrēmenēs* (1:3a)

The first of these seems to be favoured by most versions of the New Testament, and is the more natural of the two, since it follows *tou kalesantos* in normal order and is in closest proximity to it. The second would be possible but odd, as it is in the wrong position and is remote from it.

The phrase *doxē kai aretē* has been expressed by "glorious and perfect (nature)" in the display, but it may also be regarded as an example of hendiadys and translated as "glorious perfection" or "gloriously perfect (nature)."

The reference to the Transfiguration, in 1:16-18, is anticipated in the use of *doxa* 'glory', here, and *aretē*, which denotes good quality or excellence of any kind, since it is applied to God here, is expressed in the display by "perfect (nature)."

1:4a. To what does *di' hōn* 'by means of which', refer? There are three possibilities:

1. *doxē kai aretē* 'glorious and perfect (nature)' (1:3d)
2. *panta . . . ta pros zōēn kai eusebeian* 'everything . . . in connection with life and godliness' (1:3a)
3. everything mentioned in the previous verse, i.e., through these arrangements, and to complete them, the promises were made.

The first of these alternatives seems to be the most appropriate, since it immediately precedes *di' hōn*, and because, ultimately, everything depends upon God's glory and virtue. This has been made explicit in the display.

Because of the parallelism, *dedōrētai* 'he has given', is considered to be middle, as is *dedōrēmenēs* in the previous verse. The perfect tense brings out the finality and permanence of the gift. The subject is God, keeping the same reference as *autou* 'of him' and *tou kalesantos* 'who called' in the preceding verse.

The dative pronoun *hēmin* 'to us', is again inclusive, as in 1:3a and 3d. Because of its position, some commentators connect it with *ta timia kai megista epaggelmata* 'promises which are very great and precious to us'. It seems preferable, however, to regard it as the indirect object of *dedōrētai* 'he has given to us', since this provides a parallel with 1:3a, and, with the former view, there would be no expressed indirect object.

The superlative form of *megas* 'great, sublime', i.e., *megista*, occurs only here in the New Testament, although it is found quite frequently in contemporary authors. It is used here in the sense of "very great," qualifying *epaggelmata* 'promises'. This word for "promises" is peculiar to 2 Peter, occurring only here and in 3:13, where it is used in connection with *kainous . . . ouranous kai gēn kainēn* 'new . . . heavens and new earth' in the future. These promises may relate to:

1. the Second Coming of the Lord, and everything associated with it. This looks forward to the third chapter, cf. 3:4; 3:9ff.; 3:12, 13.
2. salvation, i.e., all that had been revealed with regard to the salvation of the people of God; pardon from sin; a glorious resurrection; etc.

The second of these is the more appropriate, in view of the following clause, introduced by *hina* 'in order that' (1:4b), which goes on to elaborate the purpose of these promises. Also, it would include the first.

1:4b. The demonstrative pronoun *toutōn* 'these (things)' may refer to:

1. *epaggelmata* 'promises', which is the last mentioned noun.
2. *doxa kai aretē* 'glory and virtue', resuming *di' hōn* 'through which' (1:4a), so that both these phrases have the same antecedent.

In the display the first alternative has been followed, in view of the proximity of the noun phrase being referred to.

1:4c. What is the best way of expressing the phrase *theias koinōnoi phuseōs* 'partakers of the divine nature'?

According to Peter, believers should be striving to live a completely consistent Christian life, which consists in knowing God and becoming like him. He emphasizes the need of true, personal knowledge of God and Christ; cf. 1:2, 3, 5, 6, 8; 2:20; 3:18. Here, in 1:4c, he tells his readers that they must also become "partakers of the divine nature," i.e., they must become like God. As Dr. D. M. Lloyd-Jones says, a Christian is "one in whom are, essentially, the traits and characteristics of God Himself, the divine life. He is like Christ. The life of godliness, the divine quality of life, the divine characteristics are in him, are being formed in him, and he is manifesting these divine characteristics." He is to be "a new man, a new creation, a new being."

The phrase might be expressed in the display by "you might become like God," or "you might become righteous like God is righteous," or "you might behave righteously as God behaves righteously."

Peter uses *koinōnos* in 1:5 of his first Epistle as well as here; cf. *apokaluptesthai doxēs koinōnos* 'partaker of the glory that shall be revealed'.

1:4d. The aorist participle *apophugontes* 'having escaped' is figurative in meaning, indicating deliverance from the power of corruption, which controls the lives of unbelievers. It is expressed in a nonfigurative way here by "since you are no longer (morally) depraved."

The literal meaning of *phthora* is "decomposition," such as the physical body undergoes after burial. Here it refers to moral deterioration and the ultimate loss of the soul. In chapter 2, particularly verses 12-19, we have a picture of this corruption and the damnation to which it leads. (See notes on 2:12 and 2:19.)

1:4e. What is meant here by *en tō kosmō* 'in the world'? Here, and in 2:20, it seems to mean the "unredeemed" world, i.e., those who do not believe in Christ for salvation; those who are alienated from him by their sins.

1:4f. Peter uses the word *epithumia* four times in this Epistle, and three times in 1 Peter. It has the meaning of "desire, longing" in a bad sense, such as a desire for something forbidden. This has been made explicit in the display.

There is an antithesis between *koinōnoi* 'partakers' (1:4c) and *apophugontes* 'having escaped' (1:4d), and also between *theias . . . phuseōs* 'divine . . . nature' (1:4c) and *en epithumia phthoras* 'corruption in lust' (1:4f).

There is some question as to the relationship between *genēsthe theias koinōnoi phuseōs* 'you might become sharers of the divine nature' and *apophugontes tēs en tō kosmō en epithumia phthoras* 'having escaped from the corruption in the desire which is in the world'. Are they to be regarded as:

1. simultaneous events, i.e., (in this context) reciprocal events. Just as the giving of the promises of God involves their reception, so, as believers turn away from their sins, they come to share in God's moral nature.
2. not simultaneous events, i.e., we share in God's nature after we have turned from our sins.

If the first of these alternatives is preferred, then it would need to be expressed by two coordinate purpose propositions, both dependent on 1:4a; i.e., in order that "you might behave righteously as God behaves righteously" and "in order that you might no longer be (morally) depraved."

If the second alternative is preferred, then the first clause would be expressed as a purpose, directly dependent on 1:4a, and the second clause as reason, i.e., "since you are no longer (morally) depraved," and this would be dependent upon the preceding purpose clause (1:4c).

Some commentators suggest as a further alternative, that the second clause is one of circumstance or time, i.e., "when you are no longer (morally) depraved."

In the display the second alternative has been represented, since the independent form of the verb, the aorist subjunctive *genēsthe* 'you might become', is used in the first clause, while the aorist participle *apophugontes* 'having escaped', is used in the second, and so is subordinate to *genēsthe*.

In the next paragraph Peter goes on to exhort them to do all they can to develop a good Christian character. Here, he seems to be saying that it is only when believers have turned their backs on the habitually sinful way of life they led before they became believers that they can begin to take positive steps towards becoming more righteous, and thus, more like their Lord.

SECTION CONSTITUENT 1:5-11
(Paragraph) (Role: HEAD of 1:3-11)

THEME: *Exert yourselves to the utmost to develop a stable Christian character.*

BOUNDARIES AND COHERENCE

The initial boundary of this paragraph is marked by a change of genre. The preceding paragraph (1:3-4) was a statement of the blessings God has bestowed on believers. Now Peter begins an exhortation to the recipients of the letter to respond by striving to develop Christian virtues in their lives. This is introduced by *kai auto touto de* 'for this very thing', referring back to the motivation stated in the previous paragraph, i.e., in the light of all this (1:3-4). The *kai* indicates the addition of something further to what has gone before, while the *de* brings out that what is added is a new development relative to what has gone before.

The final boundary is marked by the start of a new paragraph in verse 12 where there is:

1. an initial *dio* 'therefore'
2. an orienter *mellēsō* 'I intend'
3. a change from second person plural to first person singular.

There is a strong referential coherence in these verses. The whole thrust of the paragraph is that the Christian life should be one of all out effort to develop a stable Christian character. In the very first verse (1:5) Peter exhorts them to engage in strenuous effort, and again in 1:10. The corollary to such effort will be a life in which Christian virtues will "increase and abound," which will be "useful and productive" (1:8), and will result in God granting a "bounteous entry" into the heavenly kingdom (1:11).

The unity of this paragraph is strengthened by the fact that the qualities enumerated in verses 5-7 belong to the same semantic set, i.e., virtues which Christians should strive to acquire. This is continued throughout the paragraph, with *tauta* 'these things', in verses 8, 9, 10 and *houtōs* 'thus', in verse 11, referring back to the qualities mentioned in verses 5-7.

The repetitive pattern of 1:5c to 1:7b is a unifying factor in the structure of the paragraph. The main verb *epichorēgēsate* 'add, furnish' (1:5c) is implicit in each of the clauses, 1:5d-7b, so that there are seven conjoined heads, each related to the next by the conjunction *de*.

In addition, the coherence is further strengthened by the use of second person plural verb forms referring to the recipients of the letter, cf. *epichorēgēsate* 'add, furnish, provide' (1:5); *spoudasate* 'strive' and *ptaisēte* 'fall, fail' (1:10); and also, second person plural pronouns, cf. *humōn* 'of you' (1:5,10) and *humin* 'in/to you' (1:8,11).

Structurally, this paragraph consists of two commands, *epichorēgēsate* 'add, furnish, provide' (1:5) and *spoudasate* 'strive' (1:10), with each being followed by two statements introduced by *gar*, which are each preceded by an implied condition. (See diagram for details.) The *gar* statements, in each case, provide the grounds for the exhortation which they follow.

PROMINENCE AND THEME

The greatest prominence is on the two aorist imperatives, *epichorēgēsate* 'add' (1:5) and *spoudasate* 'strive' (1:10).

Epichorēgēsate is supported and emphasized by the MEANS proposition *spoudēn pasan pareisenenkantes* 'bringing in every effort' (1:5b), which is itself prominent, since the aorist participle *pareisenenkantes* has the force of an imperative. the introductory *kai auto touto de* 'for this very thing' also contributes to drawing attention to the exhortation which follows, while the exhortation itself is given additional emphasis and urgency by the repetitive nature of its structure and vocabulary, which has a cumulative effect.

Although the exhortation in 1:10a-b is prominent, by reason of the

RELATIONAL STRUCTURE

motivation		
MEANS		
HEAD1		HEAD1
		HEAD2
		HEAD3
		HEAD4
		HEAD5
		HEAD6
		HEAD7
	motivation (positive)	condition
		HEAD
	motivation (negative)	condition
		HEAD
		reason
HEAD2		
purpose		
motivation1		condition
		HEAD
motivation2		condition
		HEAD

imperative *spoudasate* and the vocative *adelphoi*, as has been said in the notes on 1:3-11, it is, in a broad sense, reiterating the command in 1:5. (See notes on 1:3-11 for details.) The theme statement for this paragraph, there-fore, is based on a summary of the heads, 1:5c-7b, i.e., the virtues enumerated there may be regarded as those which constitute "a stable Christian character."

CONTENT

(1:5a) Since God has done all this (1:3-4),

(1:5b) by means of exerting yourselves strenuously/to the utmost

(1:5c) ensure that you not only believe (in Christ) but that you are also upright;

(1:5d) and (ensure that) you are not only upright (but that) you also behave wisely;

(1:6a) and (ensure that) you not only behave wisely (but that) you also control yourself;

(1:6b) and (ensure that) you not only control yourself (but that) you are also steadfast;

(1:6c) and (ensure that) you are not only steadfast (but that) you are also godly;

(1:7a) and (ensure that) you are not only godly (but that) you also love your fellow-believers;

(1:7b) and (ensure that) you not only love your fellow-believers (but that) you love everyone.

(1:8a) If these (qualities) are present in you and if they are increasing (in you),

(1:8b) this demonstrates (that) knowing our(inc) Lord Jesus Christ is effective (in you). [LIT]

(1:9a) If these (qualities) are not present in a person,

(1:9b) he does not realise (that these things (5c-7b) are important)

(1:9c) (because) he has forgotten that (God) forgave him (when) formerly he sinned.

(1:10a) Instead (of acting like the person in 1:9), strive

(1:10b) in order that you confirm (the fact) that (God) has summoned you and that he has chosen you to be his people.

(1:10c) If you do this (i.e., 1:5-7)

(1:10d) you will certainly never sin badly.

(1:11a) If you act like this (i.e., 1:5-7)

(1:11b) (God) will bounteously grant (that) you may enter that place where our Lord and Saviour Jesus Christ will rule (his people) forever.

NOTES ON 1:5-11

1:5a. The *touto* 'this', in the phrase *auto touto* 'for this very thing', may refer to:

1. everything contained in 1:3-4, i.e., everything God has given you and done for you;

2. what immediately precedes in 1:4d-g.

The display is based on the first of these alternatives. The *auto touto* refers back to the *hōs* in 1:3 and has the meaning, "in the light of all this" (1:3-4), i.e., "in the light of all that God has done for you."

1:5b. The clause *spoudēn pasan pareisenegkantes* means literally, "diligence all having brought in," i.e., "(by means that you) exert yourselves strenuously/make every effort." The idea seems to be that God has given us great and precious gifts, so we should respond with no less than all diligence, every effort as we endeavour to develop Christian virtues. This is a prominent theme throughout the letter, as can be seen from such further references as: *spoudasate bebaian humōn tēn klēsin kai eklogēn poieisthai* 'strive to make sure that God has summoned you and that he has chosen you' (1:10); *spoudasō de kai . . .* 'I will be diligent . . . ' (1:15); *spoudasate . . .* 'be diligent . . . ' (3:14).

1:5c. The literal meaning of the verb *epichorēgēsate* is "furnish, provide" at one's own expense. Here it is used figuratively, as it is also in verse 11, where it is used in the sense of "give, grant." There is a correspondence between the two, and also *dōreomai* in verses 3 and 4. A number of commentators emphasize that this verb carries the idea of lavish, generous provision, the expenses incurred by the Christian being in terms of the effort involved (see note on 1:5b).

As this is considered to be a dead figure, it is not used in the display. Instead, it has been represented by "ensure that."

There are two viewpoints expressed with regard to the relationship between the qualities enumerated in verses 5-7:

1. Each of the qualities is built upon, or flows from the previous one, and completes it. They are not separate entities to be added the one to the other, but are interrelated.

2. Each of the qualities is related to faith, but there is no particular inner connection amongst them, and they are not necessarily to be acquired in this particular order.

Neither of these alternatives seems entirely appropriate, although both are applicable to some extent.

With regard to the first alternative, some commentators have tried to show that there is a very definite progression in acquiring these qualities, and that the order in which Peter presents them is significant.

Undoubtedly, the order is not completely random, and certain of the qualities show a direct relationship with that which is next in the list, e.g., exercising self-control helps a person to become more steadfast, and that, in its turn, leads to an increase in godliness. Also, the list does build up to the greatest of virtues, *agapē* 'love'. However, to say that there is a definite line of development from one to the next, so that they should be acquired in that order, seems to be imposing an artificial restriction. They are interrelated in a much more complex manner than either this or the second alternative above, although it is, of course, true that faith is necessary before any of them can develop.

Peter is concerned principally to exhort his readers to acquire all these virtues, rather than to advocate any particular order in which they should be acquired. He is saying, in an emphatic way, that believers should exert themselves in all these aspects of the Christian life, as they are all important in building up an all-round Christian character.

In classical Greek, *aretē* means "excellence" of any kind. Peter has used it in verse 3 when speaking of God and where it is represented by "perfect nature." Here, in relation to the believer, who must strive after this moral excellence, the word "upright" is used.

1:5d. The usual meaning of the word *gnōsis*, in Greek ethical language, is "sagacity" or "practical wisdom." It is used in 3:18 also, but elsewhere Peter uses *epignōsis*, cf. 1:2, 3, 8, and 2:20. This latter is often given the meaning of "full knowledge," but there is some doubt as to whether there is any significant difference in meaning between the two (see note on *epignōsis* 1:2). Here, *gnōsis* is represented by "behave wisely," to reflect the practical nature of this virtue.

1:6a. *Egkrateia* 'self-control' may refer to control over evil inclinations and desires, in general, or to mastery of sexual desires and/or greed. In this list of virtues, the first would seem the more appropriate, i.e., self-restraint in all matters affecting the senses. This contrasts greatly with the licentiousness and greed spoken of in relation to the false teachers and those who follow them, in chapters 2 and 3, and, in particular, in 2:1-3 and 3:3.

1:6b. The noun *hupomonē* 'patience, fortitude, endurance, steadfastness, perseverance' is almost invariably used in the context of affliction, suffering, or persecution.

The idea of being steadfast occurs quite frequently throughout this letter, cf. the following references:

> *mē ptaisēte pote* 'you will certainly never fail' (1:10)
> *estērigmenous* 'established' (1:12)
> *psuchas astēriktous* 'unstable souls' (2:14)
> *stērigmou* 'stability' (3:17)

1:6c. Peter uses *eusebeia* 'piety, godliness, holiness' here and in 1:3. Primarily, it refers to a right attitude to God. This will obviously, then, reveal itself in our attitudes to men. Throughout the letter, Peter stresses that a true knowledge of God will evidence itself in a godly life. This contrasts with those spoken of in the next two chapters, who boast of their knowledge of God but give evidence to the contrary in their lives, by their immoral actions.

1:7a,b. The distinction is made in these two verses, between *philadelphia* 'brotherly love', i.e., love for other Christians, and *agapē* 'love', i.e., love towards all people, regardless of whether they are fellow-believers or not. Yet again, this provides a contrast with the attitudes and actions of the false teachers, as described in chapters 2 and 3.

1:8a. The participles *huparchonta kai pleonazonta* 'being present and increasing/abounding' may be expressed as "since" or "if." The latter has been chosen in the display, as the opposite is assumed possible in 1:9.

The first of these participles, *huparchonta*, has the meaning of "exist (really), be present, be at one's disposal," and is, according to some commentators, a strong expression, stressing the permanence and reality of these qualities in the life of a believer.

There is some discussion as to whether *pleonazonta* is used here in the sense of "being present in abundance," or "increasing." Lenski points out that, since the qualities enumerated in 1:5-7 do not come about in a day, in order to abound, they must increase. The difference is one between the process and the final state. The meaning "increasing" has been used in the display, as this appears to be the consistent meaning elsewhere in the New Testament (see Rom. 5:20, 6:1; 2 Cor. 4:15; Phil. 4:17; 2 Thess. 1:3).

1:8b. The basic meaning of *argos* is "unemployed, idle, with nothing to do," but it can also mean "useless," which seems appropriate here.

The literal meaning of *akarpos* is "unfruitful, barren," with reference to trees and plants, etc., but here it is used in a figurative sense to mean "useless, unproductive."

The expression *ouk argous oude akarpous* 'not useless or unproductive' is best understood as a litotes, and can be expressed positively as "useful and productive." In addition, it is likely that it is a doublet, since the two terms are functionally synonymous in this context (see Moore, *NOT* 43). It has, therefore, been expressed as "effective."

The clause *ouk argous oude akarpous kathistēsin eis tēn tou kuriou hēmōn Iēsou Christou epignōsin* presents certain difficulties with respect to the verb *kathistēsin* and the preposition *eis*.

The verb *kathistēsin* may be used in the sense of "make, cause someone to become something." As used here, with *argous* and *akarpous*, it would mean "cause to be effective."

Taking the *eis* in the sense of "towards," this would give the goal towards which the virtues listed in verses 5-7 lead, i.e., *tēn tou kuriou hēmōn Iēsou Christou epignōsin* 'the knowledge of our Lord Jesus Christ'. This knowledge is acquired by actively striving to fulfil his will. This would be represented in the display by "they (the virtues of verses 5-7) effectively cause (you) to know our Lord Jesus Christ (very well)."

This gives rise to a problem, however, for, in 1:3, we have *epignōsis* described as the means by which we can receive the divine gifts, while here it is presented as the goal to which we attain. This is not necessarily contradictory. As J. P. Lange says, " . . . there is an admirable fitness, in that the knowledge of Christ, which consists of different gradations, is first described as the source and afterwards as the fruit of these virtues. (Christ is the Author and Finisher of our faith.)"

There is, however, another possibility which seems more appropriate in the context, and this has been represented in the display.

Another sense of *eis* is "with respect to," cf. Arndt and Gingrich, meaning 5, here, "with respect to knowledge of our Lord Jesus Christ." Also, *kathistēsin* can have the sense "constitute, classify." It is used in this sense in Romans 5:19 and James 4:4.

If these senses are understood, then the clause in question has the meaning "they (i.e., the virtues of verses 5-7) constitute you as (being) effective with respect to knowledge of our Lord Jesus Christ." This has been represented in the display by "this (1:8a) demonstrates (that) knowing our(inc) Lord Jesus Christ has been effective (in you)."

In the context, this is more appropriate, in that it provides the motivation for verses 5-7 and does not contradict 1:3c.

1:9a. With the use of *hō* 'in whom, whoever', there is a change from second person plural "you" to third person singular "he to/in whom," thus distinguishing between those true believers he is addressing in the letter, to whom verse 8 will apply, and those who are in error. The *mē* 'not' is used here with the indicative, where *ou* would be expected, because the relative clause has a hypothetical sense, i.e., "if these qualities are not present."

1:9b. *Tuphlos estin muōpazōn* 'is blind, being short-sighted' is a figurative expression, used of mental and spiritual blindness. The one who does not cultivate Christian virtues in his life, i.e., *hō . . . mē parestin touto* 'the one in whom those (virtues) are not', is blind in that he has no understanding of their importance in demonstrating the reality of his faith. Their presence distinguishes between one who truly believes and one who merely professes to do so.

The present participle *muōpazōn* 'being short-sighted' is found only here in Scripture. In the figurative sense in which it is used here, it is generally understood to mean that such a person is so spiritually undiscerning that he only considers immediate, earthly matters, and not spiritual matters. His understanding is so circumscribed that he has no grasp of the implications of being a Christian.

The question has been asked, "How can someone be both blind and short-sighted?" The more definite term following the general may explain the kind of blindness. Possibly it has the meaning that he is so short-sighted that he is as good as blind. Someone who is physically extremely short-sighted often functions as a blind person does because his vision is so limited. The same can be said of someone who is spiritually blind. His understanding may be so limited that he has no vision of the glorious scope his life can have as a Christian. His thoughts and actions are so circumscribed that his knowledge of Christ has little possibility of increasing. Another possibility is that *tuphlos estin muōpazōn* is a doublet, since, in the context, the two terms are used in the same sense, i.e., lack of spiritual understanding. This seems very probable, and, since this figure of spiritual blindness is such a commonly known one, it has been treated as a dead metaphor and represented by "he does not realise (that these things (5c-7b) are important)."

1:9c.   An explanation of, or reason for, this state of spiritual blindness is introduced by the aorist participial phrase *lēthēn labōn* 'forgetfulness having taken'. The fact that he has forgotten what Christ has done for him, i.e., cleansed him, forgiven his sins, is the reason for his present lack of spiritual discernment. Peter's aim in writing this letter is to stir up their memories about such things; cf. 1:12-15; 3:1-2, as well as references such as *mē lanthanetō* 'do not forget' (3:8).

Katharismou 'purification' is used of the external ceremonial washing of the Jews. Here, it is used figuratively of the internal cleansing from the defilement of sin. Not to cultivate these qualities as a believer is equivalent to being in a state in which sin has not been dealt with.

1:10a.   The introductory *dio mallon* 'therefore rather/all the more' needs some discussion. (See notes on Boundaries and Coherence for Section 1:3-11 for *dio*.)

The comparative adverb *mallon* 'more, rather' may indicate intensification or antithesis.

The readers have been exhorted in 1:5 to strive after Christian virtues, *spoudēn pasan pareisenegkantes* 'bringing in every effort', but two additional motivations have been given in verses 8 and 9, hence *mallon* 'all the more' to reinforce the repeated exhortation in verse 10.

On the other hand, *mallon* may be used here in the sense of "rather," introducing an antithesis, i.e., rather than behaving as the person described in verse 9 and forgetting that they have been cleansed from their sins, they should do all they can to make sure that God has called them and chosen them, by giving evidence of Christian virtues in their lives.

Although both of these alternatives are possible, the second makes slightly better sense, in that he has already exhorted them to make every effort, which implies that they can do no more than that. Also, the second alternative refers back to the immediately preceding verse and so follows on naturally. It has been represented in the display by "instead of."

Some commentators consider that the use of the aorist tense, *spoudasate* 'make every effort', is a means of stressing the urgency of his appeal.

1:10b.   When used literally, *bebaian* is used of such things as a root or an anchor, to mean "strong, secure, firm, permanent." When it is used figuratively, as here and 1:19, it has the meaning of "reliable, dependable, certain, sure." It is used here with the middle voice of *poieō* 'to make/do', which has the meaning of "to do something for oneself or of oneself"; the combination thus means "to make sure" or "to confirm."

The recipients are to confirm *tēn klēsin kai eklogēn* their "calling and election," for, although both are completely God's doing, and, therefore, sure on his part, they need to prove to themselves and others that they are "called and chosen," by the evidence of Christian virtues in their lives.

In the display, "God" has been made explicit as the agent in the process of calling and choosing. (See note on the use of the verb "summon" instead of "call" in verse 3.)

The first motivation for complying with this exhortation is introduced by *gar*.

1:10c. The demonstrative pronoun, *tauta* 'these things', refers to the virtues of verses 5-7.

The present active participle, *poiountes*, is best understood as conditional, i.e., "if you do these things."

1:10d. The double negation, *ou mē* 'by no means', and the *pote* 'ever', placed finally, strengthen the statement, and have been expressed emphatically as "certainly never."

The verb *ptaiō* means literally "stumble, fall," but used figuratively, as here, it can mean "make a mistake, go astray, sin, be ruined, be lost." The same word is translated "offend" in James 2:10 and 3:2, and as "stumble" in Romans 11:11. Some commentators think that it means to be "ruined" or "lost," in the sense of losing our salvation. However, the most suitable sense here seems to be that believers will not sin in a really serious manner, if they strive continually to cultivate the virtues of verses 5-7. Obviously, it does not mean that believers will never sin at all, for in this sense we all stumble (cf. James 3:2). Perhaps we might refer to it as backsliding.

1:11. The second motivation for responding to the exhortation in 1:10a-b is also introduced by *gar*. This is the final *gar* in a series (1:8, 9, 10b, 11) building up strong grounds for the exhortation to live a holy life.

1:11a. The *houtōs* 'so, thus, in this way', in a sense, summarizes what has gone before, i.e., the doing of these things represented by *tauta* in verses 8, 9, and 10, and referring back to the virtues of verses 5-7.

1:11b. The adverb *plousiōs* means "richly, abundantly." It needs to be considered with the verb *epichorēgēthēsetai* 'furnish, provide', which it qualifies. (The same verb is used in verse 5 when believers are exhorted to develop Christian virtues.) In this context, the sense is of an action which is unreserved, unstinting, generous, i.e., Christ will enable believers to enter his kingdom freely and fully. As has been said previously, this is the opposite to *molis* 'scarcely' in 1 Peter 4:18. They will not enter by a miserably small margin, but gloriously, because the Lord has enabled them to persevere and develop Christian graces in their lives.

This idea corresponds with *spoudēn pasan* 'all diligence, every effort' (1:5), and *pleonazonta* 'abounding, increasing' (1:8), in that the degree of effort and the resulting fruit in the life of the believer will be more than matched by the gracious welcome he will have into the kingdom of God.

Tēn aiōnion basileian tou kuriou hēmōn kai sotēros Iēsou Christou 'the eternal kingdom of our Lord and Saviour Jesus Christ' is understood to refer to the kingdom of heaven which the believer will enter when he dies, or when the Lord returns to gather up those who are his, and not the kingdom of heaven here on earth. The reasons for this are the following:

1. the future tense of the verb *epichorēgēthēsetai* 'will be granted'.
2. Peter is addressing people who are already believers and are, therefore, already part of the kingdom of Christ here on earth.

God is considered to be the agent of this event and *tēn aiōnion basileian* 'the eternal kingdom' has been expressed by the phrase "that place where he will rule (his people) forever."

DIVISION CONSTITUENT 1:12-21
(Section) (Role: Situational orienter for 1:3-11)

THEME: *I intend to remind you very frequently about these matters (1:3-11), because they are true.*

RELATIONAL STRUCTURE	CONTENTS
HEAD	(1:12-15) I intend to remind you very frequently about these matters (1:3-11).
reason	(1:16-21) You can be sure that these matters are true because we ourselves (exc) witnessed that our(inc) Lord Jesus Christ is supremely great, and because what the prophets say about him is completely reliable also.

BOUNDARIES AND COHERENCE

The evidence for 1:12 being the start of a new unit has been discussed in connection with the boundaries of 1:3-11, and the final boundary, at 1:21, has been discussed in connection with the final boundary of 1:3-21.

The personal nature of this unit, as shown in the preponderance of first person verb forms, sets it apart from what immediately precedes and follows it. Peter here explains to his readers the urgency he feels, which compels him to remind them as often as he can about the important matters he sets before them in this letter. He also stresses the sure basis he has for what he says, i.e., that the message of the Old Testament prophets and of Christ himself, are both completely reliable, since both come from God.

PROMINENCE AND THEME

This section consists of two paragraphs, 1:12-15 and 1:16-21. The second of these is introduced by the conjunction *gar* and is in a subordinate relationship to the first. In the first, Peter makes a statement as to what he is going to do, and in the second, he gives the reason for his action. In 1:12-15 he tells them that he intends to remind them, as often as he can, about the matters in 1:3-11, i.e., the necessity of doing all they can to live godly lives in response to all that God has done for them. Then in 1:16-21 he tells them that his reason for doing so is that everything he teaches them is based on what the Old Testament prophets and Christ himself taught, and is therefore completely trustworthy.

These two paragraphs, therefore, are in a Head-reason relationship. Because the theme of 1:16-21, i.e., the true and reliable witness of the apostles and the Old Testament prophets, is an important theme of the whole letter, (cf. also 3:1-2 and 3:17), a concise form of the reason is included in the theme statement for the section, along with the head.

SECTION CONSTITUENT 1:12-15
(Paragraph) (Role: Head of 1:12-21)

THEME: *I intend to keep reminding you very frequently about these matters (1:3-11).*

BOUNDARIES AND COHERENCE

The boundaries of this paragraph are very clearly defined. Initially there is an introductory *dio* 'therefore' (1:12) and a transition from second person plural orientation in the preceding paragraph (1:10-11) to first person singular orientation in this paragraph. The final boundary is marked by a change to first person plural orientation in the next paragraph, which begins 1:16.

This paragraph forms a distinctive unit with strong referential coherence, in that Peter is in the role of first person agent throughout. We see this in the use of the first person singular verb forms in each of the main clauses:

> *mellēsō* 'I intend' (1:12a);
> *hēgoumai* 'I consider' (1:13a);
> *spoudasō* 'I shall endeavour' (1:15a);

and also in the use of the first person singular pronouns *mou, moi* (1:14) and *emēn* (1:15). The second person pronoun *humas* is used throughout for those addressed (1:12,13,15).

RELATIONAL STRUCTURE			CONTENT
HEAD	HEAD		(1:12a) I intend to keep on reminding you very frequently about these (matters, i.e., 1:3-11) [HYP]
	concession₁		(1:12b) even though you (already) know (these matters)
	concession₂		(1:12c) and even though you are firmly convinced that these (matters) are true.
reason	HEAD	HEAD	(1:13a) I consider it right that I should stimulate you (to think about these matters)
		means	(1:13b) by means of (my) reminding (you about them)
		time	(1:13c) as long as I am alive, [EUP]
	reason	HEAD	(1:14a) because I know that I shall die soon, [EUP]
		comp.	(1:14b) just as our Lord Jesus Christ clearly revealed this (14a) to me.
equiv.	HEAD		(1:15a) Moreover, I shall make every effort to enable you to recall these (matters, i.e., 1:3-11) at all times
	time		(1:15b) after I will have died. [EUP]

Further referential coherence is found in the repetition of words with the component of "remembering":

hupomimnēskein 'to remind' (1:12a);

diegeirein . . . hupomnēsei 'to stimulate by way of remembrance' (1:13a);

mnēmēn poieisthai 'to recall to mind' (1:15a).

Also, references to Peter's own death, each in a euphemistic expression, give unity to the paragraph:

eph' hoson eimi en toutō tō skēnōmati 'while I am still alive' (1:13b) (with the implication that he may soon not be);

tachinē estin hē apothesis tou skēnōmatos mou 'I will suddenly/soon die' (1:14a);

meta tēn emēn exodon 'after I will have died' (1:15b).

The relational coherence of this paragraph is not obvious. The clearest evidence would seem to be the structural parallelism of the grammar. There are three parallel units, each consisting of:

1. a first person singular orienter:
   mellēsō 'I intend' (1:12a)
   hēgoumai 'I consider' (1:13a)
   spoudasō 'I shall make every effort' (1:15a)

2. a present tense infinitive:
   hupomimnēskein 'to keep on reminding' (1:12a)
   diegeirein 'to stimulate' (1:13a)
   echein . . . mnēmēn poiesthai 'to enable . . . to remember' (1:15a)

3. second person plural personal pronoun in the accusative case:
   humas 'you' (1:12a,13a,15a)

4. a time word/phrase acting as a modifier:
   aei 'constantly', i.e., very frequently (1:12a)
   eph' hoson eimi en toutō tō skēnōmati 'while I am still alive' (1:13c)
   hekastote 'at all times' (1:15a)
   meta tēn emēn exodon 'after I will have died' (1:15b)

The second two units also have the conjunction *de*, which, along with the parallel structure, possibly indicates that something more on the same point is being said.

PROMINENCE AND THEME

Prominence is given to the topic of "remembering/reminding" by the number of references made to it, but since the relationships between the three sentences which make up this paragraph are not clear, it is difficult to say exactly how one is more prominent than the others. However, the following arguments would indicate that verse 12 is the head.

1. The second and third sentences have the conjunction *de*, which, along with the parallelism in the structure, probably indicates the introduction of further material on the same point as 1:12.

2. The fact that 1:12 and 1:15 have more features in common with each other than the middle sentence (1:13-14) is probably also significant. They both have: future tense where 1:13-14 has the present; *toutōn* 'these (matters)'; adverbs of time, cf. *aei* 'constantly' (1:12) and *hekastote* 'always, at all times' (1:15).

This indicates that 1:12 and 1:15 contain the main information, with 1:15 being more or less equivalent to 1:12. The first says "I intend to go on reminding you" and 1:15 says "I shall make every effort to enable you to recall." The latter confirms the former, and this would make 1:12 the more prominent of the two, since 1:15 is repeating it, probably for purposes of prominence, as Peter seeks to emphasize his statement.

These arguments would point to the main statement being in 1:12, so that 1:12a, the head of 1:12, constitutes the theme of the paragraph.

NOTES ON 1:12-15

1:12a. *Mellēsō* with the present infinitive, as here, *hupomimnēskein* 'to remind', denotes intended action, i.e., "I intend, propose, have in mind." Sometimes, in a weakened sense, it serves simply as a periphrasis for the future. This is probably the case in 2 Peter 2:6 where we have the participle *mellontes*.

The adverb *aei* is used of a frequently recurring action or situation, with the meaning "constantly, always." Here it is being used hyperbolically, in that Peter was not reminding them every moment of the day and night. Probably it is equivalent to "very frequently." It should be construed with the infinitive *hupomimnēskein*, and is emphatic.

There would seem no reason to limit the reference of the deictic *toutōn* 'these (matters)' to the *tauta* in 1:10, which in turn refers back to 1:5-9. This would be to remind them of what they are to aim at (1:10-11), and the means they are to employ (1:5-9), but would not bring to their minds the grounds on which they base their actions, i.e., that God has given them everything necessary to live a godly life, etc., (1:3-4). It would seem best, therefore, to regard *toutōn* as referring to all that precedes in 1:3-11.

1:12b. The implicit object of *eidotas* 'know' is *tauta*, which refers to the *peri toutōn* 'about these (matters)' of the previous clause.

1:12c. The passive participle *estērigmenous en* 'established in', is a dead metaphor, and has the meaning here "firmly convinced about." Peter uses the related noun *stērigmos* 'stability, steadfastness' in 3:17, and we find the verb in 1 Peter 5:10. In contrast we have *astēriktous* (2:14) and *astēriktoi* (3:16) "unstable," describing those who are not firmly grounded in the truth.

The participle *parousē* is from the same verb, *pareimi*, as *parestin* in 1:9. It has the meaning of "have, be present, be at one's disposal." Here, it is used to qualify *alētheia* 'truth' and means "the truth that you have." It has been represented in the display by "these matters are true," referring to the same matters as *toutōn* in 1:12a.

1:13a. *Dikaion* here means "right," in the sense of doing one's duty, fulfilling one's obligations.

The infinitive *diegeirein* has the literal meaning "to wake up, arouse" someone who is asleep. Here, however, it is used in a figurative sense "to rouse, stir up." It is followed by the accusative case, which here is *humas* 'you'. To complete the sense, it is necessary to supply a purpose for the verb. What is Peter stimulating them to do? From the immediate context and from the preceding paragraphs, it would seem that he wants to stimulate them to think about, and to call to mind, the truths they already know, and which he has been speaking about in 1:3-11. He has said in 1:12 that he intends to remind them about these truths. Here he says that he does so because he considers it his duty, and because he will soon be dead and unable to do so. Then in 1:15, he says that he will do all he can to ensure that they will continue to think about them after he is dead.

1:13b. The use of *en hupomnēsei* is probably instrumental, i.e., "by means of my reminding (you about these matters)." It is used in conjunction with *diegeirō* again in 3:1.

1:13c. The clause *eph' hoson eimi en toutō tō skēnōmati* 'as long as/while I am in this tent', is a figurative expression in which the body is compared to a *skēnōma* 'tent'. The comparison of the human body to a dwelling place is common in literature. The use of *skēnōma* 'tent' signals the idea of "temporary," "mortal," or "short-lived." Since the comparison is not developed further, it can be considered to be a dead metaphor and has been expressed in the display by "as long as I am alive."

1:14a. *Hē apothesis tou skēnōmatos mou* 'the removal of my tent' is a euphemism for his death. Peter again uses the figure of a tent, which he used in 1:13, this time in connection with *hē apothesis* 'the removal, the getting rid of'. He uses *apothesis* 'removal' also in 1 Peter 3:21 when he speaks of the removal of dirt in baptism—again a figurative use.

It is difficult to decide what *tachinē* means here. The same word is used in 2:1, when Peter speaks of the destruction of the false teachers, but nowhere else in the New Testament. It may mean "coming soon, swift, imminent," and is translated as "soon" in most versions. However, by reason of its position, immediately following *hoti*, emphasis falls on *tachinē*, which would lead one to expect that this is what Jesus told him, cf. 1:14b. But Jesus told him that he would die a **violent** death (John 21:18ff), not that it would be soon. Some commentators posit that there was a further revelation which indicated that his violent death would be soon, but we have no evidence for this.

The general concensus, that it is used in the sense of "soon," seems most appropriate here. Peter is exhorting them to remember these important matters, because he knows that there is not much time left in which he will be able to do so, because he will soon die. In support of this is the use of the related adverb *tachu* 'without delay, soon', and the noun *tachos* 'speed, quickness' used with *en*, i.e., *en tachei* to mean "speedily, without delay, soon," quite frequently throughout the New Testament; cf. 1 Tim 3:14, Rom 16:20, Rev 1:1, 22:6, 7, 12, 20.

1:14b. Since *kathōs kai* 'just as' indicates comparison, and since the content of *eidōs* 'I know' (1:14a) is the same as what Jesus revealed to him, which would be comparison, this clause is represented in the display as comparison (of equality).

1:15a. The *de* here is considered to be parallel with the *de* in verse 13, linking the clause to what has preceded, while the *kai* has an adverbial function and is expressed as "moreover."

We have one of several references to striving or effort here in *spoudasō* 'I shall make every effort'; cf. also 1:5, 1:10, and 3:14.

In the display, 1:15a-b has been related to the head cluster (1:12a-c), as it seems to be making an equivalent statement to it. An alternative analysis would be to make 1:15 a contraction of 1:13-14.

It is difficult to know whether *hekastote* 'always, at any time' should go with *spoudasō* 'I will strive' or with *echein* 'to enable, etc.' Most versions favour the second alternative and I have followed the general view in the display. It seems appropriate, in view of his concern for the future, when false teachers and scoffers will come, that what he has to say should be available "always, at any time," whenever needed.

The use of *echein* here is in the sense of "to have the possibility, to be able," and of *poieisthai* "to make, do something for/of oneself." In conjunction with *humas* and *mnēmēn* 'remembrance, memory', the meaning is "to enable you to recall." What they are to recall is supplied by the genitive *toutōn* 'these things'. This probably refers to the same matters referred to by *toutōn* in 1:12, i.e., the truths stated in 1:3-11, and, by extension, the rest of the letter. Some commentators suggest that it refers to the Gospel of Mark, which Peter is said to have superintended, or even to further Epistles he intended to write. Neither of these, however, seems plausible in view of his soon/sudden death. It is much more likely that he would be referring to the letter he is writing now.

1:15b.   As in 1:13 and 1:14, Peter uses a euphemistic expression when talking of his death. There he refers to it as "the removing of my tent," while here he speaks of "my departure."

SECTION CONSTITUENT 1:16-21
(Paragraph) (Role: Reason for 1:12-15)

THEME: *You can be sure that these matters are true, because we(exc) ourselves witnessed that our(inc) Lord Jesus Christ is supremely great, and because what the prophets say about him is completely reliable also.*

BOUNDARIES AND COHERENCE

The initial boundary of this paragraph is marked clearly by a change of person and a change of tense.

In the preceding paragraph (1:12-15), the first person singular and the future tense are used throughout. In verse 16, there is a change and we have *egnōrisamen* 'we made known', which is first person plural and aorist tense.

This marks a change from Peter giving personal reasons for exhorting them, to giving the grounds on which he and the other apostles based their teaching about Christ, i.e., personal testimony based on their being eyewitnesses, and the testimony of the Old Testament prophets.

The final boundary is marked by a change of subject matter, when, in 2:1, he begins to speak of *pseudoprophētai* 'false prophets', and *pseudodidaskaloi* 'false teachers', who deny the power of Christ, and lead others astray by the heresies they teach. This is in contrast with the true prophets, who are inspired by the Holy Spirit to speak the words of God (1:21).

In some versions, verses 20 and 21 of chapter 1 are attached to 2:1 and begin a new paragraph, with *touto prōton ginōskontes* (1:20) translated as "first of all you should know this," and going on to talk of true and false prophets. This is a possible alternative, but, in the display, these verses have been analysed as relating back to *prosechontes* 'pay attention, heed' in verse 19, because of the rhetorical bracketing of verses 16 and 21.

Verse 16 begins with a negative statement introduced by *ou gar*, which is followed by a contrasting positive one introduced by *alla* 'but', and referring to the apostles as eyewitnesses. The subject of personal testimony is then elaborated upon in 1:17 and 18, followed by comments on the testimony of prophecy in verses 19 and 20. The unit then closes, as it began, with a negative statement followed by a positive one, also introduced by *ou gar* and *alla* (1:21). This gives a sandwich structure, with verses 16 and 21 both consisting of a rejection of what is false, and from man, and a statement of what is reliable and true, and from God.

The unity of this paragraph is maintained by references to divine power and glory, and other vocabulary belonging to the same semantic set:

> *dunamin* 'power'; *megaleiotētos* 'majesty' (1:16)
> *timēn* 'honour'; *doxan* 'glory'; *megaloprepous doxēs* 'the excellent glory' (1:17)
> *ouranou* 'heaven'; *hagiō orei* 'holy mountain' (1:18)
> *heōs hou hēmera diaugasē kai phōsphoros anateilē* 'until the day dawns and the morning star rises' (1:19) which probably refers to Christ's glorious return.

There is unity also, in that all three persons of the Trinity are referred to; cf. *tou kuriou hēmōn Iēsou Christou* 'our Lord Jesus Christ' (1:16); *theou patros* 'God the Father' (1:17) and *theou* 'God' (1:21); *pneumatos hagiou* 'Holy Spirit' (1:21). The message of the apostles and prophets centered on Christ, and was transmitted from God to man by means of the Holy Spirit.

Further, since this paragraph is concerned with the reliability of the Gospel message, there are references throughout to the means of communicating this message:

> *egnōrisamen* 'we made known'; *epoptai genēthentes* 'being eyewitnesses' (1:16)
> *phōnēs enechtheisēs . . .* 'a voice borne . . . ' (1:17)

RELATIONAL STRUCTURE

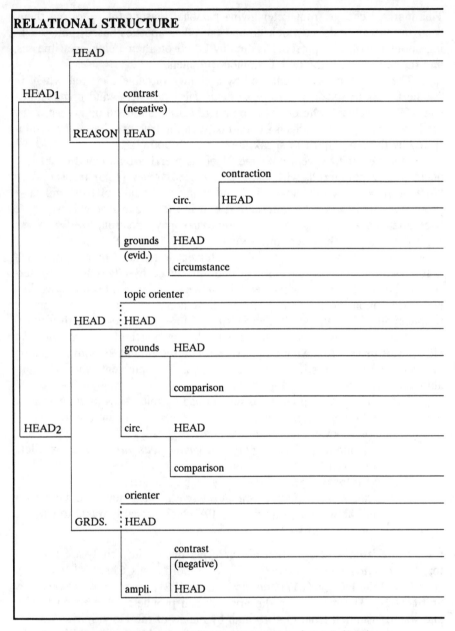

tautēn tēn phōnēn . . . 'that voice we heard . . . ' (1:18)
ton prophētikon logon 'the prophetic word' (1:19)
prophēteia graphēs 'prophecy of Scripture' (1:20)
prophēteia 'prophecy'; elalēsan apo theou anthrōpoi 'men from God
    spoke' (1:21)

CONTENT

(1:16a) We(exc) told you that our(inc) Lord Jesus Christ is powerful and that he (will) come back,

(1:16b) not because we(exc) based (what we told you) on stories which (people/we(exc)) had cleverly invented,

(1:16c) but because we(exc) ourselves saw with our own eyes that he (our(inc) Lord Jesus Christ) is supremely great.

(1:17a) When God, our(inc) Father, greatly honoured him (our(inc) Lord Jesus Christ),

(1:17b) (that is), when God who is supremely great (said) this/in this way, "This (person) is my Son, whom I love very much. I am very pleased with him."

(1:18a) We(exc) ourselves heard (God) say (this, i.e., 17b) from heaven,

(1:18b) when we(exc) were with him (our(inc) Lord Jesus Christ) on the holy/sacred mountain.

(1:19a) We(inc) have what the prophets wrote (long ago), which is completely reliable.

(1:19b) You should heed this (i.e. what the prophets wrote)

(1:19c) since it (what the prophets wrote) enables (you) to discern whether what is taught is true or whether it is false,

(1:19d) like a lamp which is shining in a dark place enables (a person) to see where he is going. [SIM]

(1:19e) (You should heed it) until our(inc) Lord Jesus Christ comes back, and (until he) enables you to know/understand God fully,

(1:19f) which (19e) is like when the day dawns and the morning star rises. [SIM]

(1:20a) It is important that you should realise that

(1:20b) nothing that the prophets wrote in Gods book originated with the prophet himself.

(1:21a) The prophets never wrote anything because a human being decided (that it should be written);

(1:21b) on the contrary, holy men, (who belonged to) God, spoke because it was the Holy Spirit who caused them to do (so).

ou . . . sesophismenois muthois exakolouthēsantes 'not based on cleverly-invented stories' (1:16)

The repeated use of the verb *phero* 'bring, bear', in connection with the *phonē* 'voice' of God from Heaven (1:17 and 18), and the *prophēteia* 'proph-

ecy' (1:21), gives further unity to the paragraph, and serves to keep to the fore
the divine origin of the message.

This unit (1:16-21) has been analysed as a double-headed paragraph,
with verses 16-18 comprising one propositional cluster, of which the head is
16a, and verses 19-21 comprising a second propositional cluster, of which the
head is 1:19b.

Alternatively, it would be possible to analyse these verses as two
separate paragraphs, on the basis that verses 16-18 have as their topic the
eyewitness account, by the apostles, of Christ's transfiguration; and verses 19-
21 are concerned with the written witness of the prophets.

In favour of this analysis is the fact that the first person plural and the
aorist tense is used throughout verses 16-18, while, apart from the initial first
person plural, *echomen* 'we have' in 1:19, second and third person plural are
used in verses 19-21. However, there is such strong referential coherence in
verses 16-21, as noted above, that this, along with the sandwich structure of
verses 16-21, makes it seem preferable to regard this as one paragraph. A
third alternative would be to analyse verses 16-21 as a (compound) paragraph
cluster, i.e., two paragraph-like units, closely linked, and functioning as a
single unit in a section.

In the case of the first head, an initial negative statement (1:16b),
together with a positive one (1:16c), provide the reason for the head (1:16a),
while the *gar* in verse 17 indicates that what follows in verses 17 and 18
provides the evidential grounds for what has just been said in verse 16.

There is a problem in relating verses 17 and 18, in that Peter seems to
break off what he is saying, after *eudokēsa* 'I am very pleased' (1:17b), and
we do not know how he intended to complete it. However, we have the aorist
indicative *ēkousamen* 'we heard', preceded by *kai* in 18a, and, as this would
presumably be in a coordinate relationship to the missing verb, it has been
analysed as the main statement of this subordinate group of clauses, i.e., 1:17-
18b.

The participial verb forms:
    labōn 'having received' (17a)
    enechtheisēs 'having been borne' (1:17b)
    enechtheisan 'having been borne' (1:18a)
    ontes 'being' (1:18b)
mark subordinate relationships to *ēkousamen* 'we heard' (1:18a).

The *kai*, at the beginning of 1:19, marks a coordinate relationship between the two clusters of propositions, 1:16-18, and, 1:19-21, and hence, between HEAD 1 and HEAD 2.

The second head consists of two propositional clusters, 1:19a-19f, and 1:20a-
21b. The head of the second of these, 20b, provides the grounds for the head of
the first, 19b; and 19a, c, and e are in a subordinate relationship to it.

There is some discussion as to whether the clause introduced by *heōs
hou* 'until' (1:19e), should be related to *phainonti* 'shining' (1:19d), or to

prosechontes 'you should heed' (1:19b). (See notes.) In either case, the relationship is a subordinate one of circumstance.

As has been mentioned previously, verses 20 and 21 are regarded by some commentators as belonging to the following section, and attached to 2:1. However, they seem to be closely related to *kalōs poieite prosechontes* 'you do well to heed' (1:19b), the head of the preceding propositional cluster, and provide the grounds for it.

The *touto prōton ginōskontes* 'you should realise this above all' (1:20a) directs the attention of his readers to the point which demands their special attention, i.e., the words following, introduced by *hoti* (1:20b). This is further emphasised by 1:21a and 21b, which provide an amplification for 1:20b in negative and then positive terms.

PROMINENCE AND THEME

The use of an unusual noun, *epoptai* 'eyewitnesses' (1:16b), draws attention to the subject of personal testimony, and it is given further prominence by its position, following immediately after *alla* 'but, rather', which introduces the positive element of a negative/positive contrast. This emphasis is maintained by the use of the aorist indicative, *ēkousamen* 'we heard' (1:18a), accompanied by no less than four participles, viz. *labōn* 'having received' (1:17a); *enechtheisēs* 'having been borne' (1:17b); *enechtheisan* 'having been borne' (1:18a); *ontes* 'being' (1:18b). The personal pronoun *hēmeis*, accompanying *ēkousamen*, stresses the personal nature of their testimony.

The emphatic statement, *echomen bebaioteron ton prophētikon logon* 'we have more sure the prophetic message' (1:19a), with the present indicative of the verb, and the comparative of the adjective preceding the phrase to which it relates, brings the topic of the testimony of the prophets to the fore, and the exhortation following, *hō kalōs poieite prosechontes* 'which you do well to heed' (1:19b), indicates its importance.

Prominence is given to verses 20 and 21, by the *touto prōton ginōskontes*, which introduces them and draws attention to what is to come, i.e., that true prophecy is from God and not man. The two strong negatives in 20b and 21a *pas . . . ou*, and *ou . . . pote*, stress that it does not originate in the will of man, while the positive side.of the contrast gains emphasis by its position following *alla* (cf. 16b), concluding the paragraph.

Furthermore, the *hupo pneumatos hagiou* 'by the Holy Spirit', is forefronted, stressing the divine agent behind the *elalēsan* of the "holy men of God," and in contrast to *thelēmati anthrōpou* 'the will of man'. Thus, we are left with the positive idea that it is God who speaks, although he may use man as the vehicle for what he wants to say.

As we saw in the section on coherence, vocabulary pertaining to the power and glory of God and Christ is used throughout this paragraph, so that the subject matter of what is testified by the apostles and the prophets is kept before us.

The theme is based on the heads of the two propositional clusters, i.e., 16a and 19b, plus the subordinate clauses 16c and 20b.

NOTES ON 1:16-21

1:16b The word *muthois* 'myths, fables, tales', is found only here in the New Testament, and in the pastoral Epistles. Paul uses it twice in his first letter to Timothy, in 1:4 and 4:7, and once in the second letter, in 4:4. The only other occurrence is in Titus 1:14.

On each occasion, as here, it is used in connection with false teachers, who present man-made fables to believers, seeking to deceive them and turn them from the truth.

We cannot be sure that a particular body of tales is referred to here, or whether this is just a general reference, but it seems quite likely that it could be the former, in view of the references in Timothy and Titus. Clearly, such fables existed and were in circulation at the time of the early church, and were made use of by those seeking to undermine the faith of believers.

The phrase, *sesophismenois muthois* 'cleverly-devised/cunningly-contrived stories' may imply that someone had accused Peter and the apostles of basing their message on such tales, or, that Peter is accusing the false teachers of doing this. The second of these seems more likely, again, in view of the references to such in the letters of Timothy and Titus.

Peter goes on to contrast the reliable authorities on which the teachings of the apostles are based with these misleading tales.

The phrase anticipates the *pseudoprophētai* 'false prophets' and *pseudodidaskaloi* 'false teachers' of 2:1, who, in contrast to the apostles, lead astray some believers with their *plastois logois* 'false words' (2:3).

The verb *exakoloutheō* means "to follow, obey" an authority, which may be personal or impersonal. It is used figuratively here, and the authority followed is impersonal. It is expressed in the display by "based upon."

It is used also in 1 Peter 2:2 and 15 but nowhere else in the New Testament.

1:16a. The personal pronoun "we" in *egnōrisamen* 'we made known/told' is exclusive, since Peter is speaking only of himself and those apostles who were present when Christ was glorified, and not of believers in general.

The subsequent *genēthentes* 'having become' (1:16), and *ēkousamen* 'we heard' (1:18) refer to the same subject as *egnōrisamen*.

There are two opinions regarding the phrase *dunamin kai parousian* as follows:

1. It is a hendiadys, i.e., it is equivalent to "his powerful coming," or "his coming in power."
   This is possible since the two terms have only one article and so might constitute one idea, i.e., the power which will be evident when Christ comes again to judge the world; cf. 3:10-13.
2. There are two different but closely related ideas, i.e., Christ will show

his power when he comes again, but he has given a foretaste of it at his transfiguration.

The second of these seems the more appropriate, since Peter has already spoken of the divine power which bestowed gifts upon believers (1:3), and then gives further evidence of it in chapter 2, in God's dealings with righteous and unrighteous men.

The *parousia* referred to here is Christ's second coming and not his first. Peter is introducing the subject matter of chapter 3 where he refutes the heresies taught by the false teachers about Christ's second coming.

1:16c. *Epoptai* 'eyewitnesses' is not found elsewhere in the New Testament, although Peter uses the related verb, *epopteuo* 'observe, see' in 2:12 and 3:2 of his first Epistle. In other literature, it is used in a technical sense of initiation into particular mysteries of religions. Here, it indicates close, intense observation.

In the New Testament, the noun, *megaleiotēs* 'grandeur, sublimity, majesty', is used only to describe divine glory and power. It is used in Luke 9:45 to describe the power Jesus displayed when he healed the boy who had the unclean spirit; and in Acts 19:27, referring to the goddess Diana. Here, it refers to Christ at his transfiguration, and is indicative of his supreme power and majesty. It has been expressed in the display by "supremely great."

1:17-18. The *gar* in 1:17 introduces a justification (evidential grounds) of Peter's assertion, that he (along with James and John) had witnessed Christ's glory at his transfiguration. This justification extends to the end of verse 18.

1:17a. The subject of *labōn* 'having received' is Christ.

When used with the genitive of a person, as here, *para* 'from (the side of)' indicates that something proceeds from this person; it occurs after verbs of taking, accepting, receiving. In the display, God has been made the subject, and Christ, the beneficiary of the action.

When used with the dative case, as in 2:11, *para* has the figurative meaning of "before someone's judgement seat," and in 3:8, "in the sight or judgement of someone."

Timēn kai doxan 'honour and glory' is probably an intensive doublet, i.e., "greatly honoured."

1:17b. The events represented by the aorist participles *labōn* 'having received' and *enechtheisēs* 'was borne' would seem to be concurrent, and so 17a has been analysed as a contraction of 17b.

In the genitive absolute *phōnēs enechtheisēs autō* 'a voice was borne to him', the passive form of the verb is understood to have God as the agent, and this has been expressed by "God said," in the display, since *hupo*, with a passive verb and the genitive case of *tēs megaloprepous doxēs* means "by the majestic glory, the divine majesty." In agreement with some commentators, I have taken this to be a periphrasis for God. Others think it refers to the bright cloud overshadowing Christ at his transfiguration. The phrase has been represented in the display by "(God) who is supremely great."

The demonstrative adjective *toiasde* 'such as this, of this kind' occurs only here in the New Testament. It may refer to "what" the voice said, i.e., what follows, or to the "kind" of voice it was, i.e., emanating from God. The first of these has been expressed in the display by "thus/in this way."

The verb, in the phrase *eis hon egō eudokēsa*, although aorist, is best expressed in English by the present tense, i.e., "I am very pleased with him." This is the only occurrence in the New Testament of this verb with *eis* 'toward'.

1:18a. The Greek construction breaks down after *eudokēsa*, and the subject changes from Jesus to the apostles who were with him at his transfiguration. There is no finite verb to complete the sentence, and it is not possible to know how Peter intended to complete it. (See note in section on coherence.)

Here, the pronoun *hēmeis* 'we' is exclusive, i.e., the apostles Peter, James, and John. It is used for emphasis, almost in the sense of "we ourselves."

The repetition of *phōnēn* 'voice' and *enechtheisan* 'was borne', from the previous verse, is by way of emphasis, whilst *ex ouranou* 'from heaven' further reinforces the divine origin of the voice and its message. It is represented by "we heard God speak from heaven."

1:18b. *Sun autō ontes* 'being with him' states the circumstances in which they heard God speak from heaven, i.e., when they were with him *en tō hagiō orei* 'on the sacred/holy mountain'. It is not known definitely to which mountain this refers. The important fact is that it was described as holy because God had manifested himself there at the transfiguration of his Son.

1:19a. The opening *kai* is taken to mean "and," i.e., "in addition to," "further to what I have just said." It indicates that the information in verses 19-21 is conjoined to that in verses 16-18.

The pronoun "we" in *echomen* 'we have' may be regarded as referring to:

1. believers in general;
2. all the apostles who had preached about the power and the Second Coming of Christ;
3. those who were with Christ at his transfiguration, i.e., Peter, James, and John.

The first of these seems the most likely, since the prophecies of the Old Testament were for everybody, and not just the apostles. The pronoun here, then, is regarded as being inclusive.

The phrase, *ton prophētikon logon* 'the prophetic word', is used only here and in Romans 16:26, in the New Testament. It is generally regarded as referring to the Old Testament prophecies, and particularly those pertaining to the power and second coming of Christ.

The adjective *bebaios* is used figuratively here, and in 1:10, to mean "sure, reliable, certain"; (see note on 1:10). Here, the comparative, *bebaioteron*, may indicate either:

1. that the prophetic word is a more reliable testimony than the voices from heaven; or,
2. that the transfiguration of Christ, as witnessed by the apostles, confirms the truth of the Old Testament prophecies in its fulfilment of them; or,
3. that the prophecies of the Old Testament authenticate the witness of the apostles and the gospel they preach, since, if anyone doubts the truth of what they say, it can be verified from the Old Testament Scriptures.

The KJV seems to follow the first of these, but most versions follow the second.

A further possibility, suggested by Arndt and Gingrich (cf. *bebaios*, (2)), is that the comparative should be expressed by "altogether reliable." The sense would then be that, not only do we have the apostles' testimony to Christ, but we also have all the prophecies of the Old Testament, which are *bebaioteron*, i.e., "very reliable," as the apostles' testimony is. This last alternative has been followed in the display.

1:19b. The relative pronoun *hō* 'to which' refers to the immediately preceding *ton prophētikon logon* 'the prophetic word'. It is in the dative case since it is collocated with *prosechontes* 'paying attention to, giving heed to'.

The "you," in the phrase *kalōs poieite* 'you do well', refers to the recipients of the letter. Followed by the participle *prosechontes*, it has the meaning "you do well to heed, you do well if you heed." It is a gentle kind of exhortation and warning because some of them were being led astray by the teachings of those who misused the Scriptures. The imperative is expressed by "you should heed."

1:19c-d. The *hōs* 'as' introduces a comparison which points out the nature and significance of *ton prophētikon logon* 'the prophetic word'. What the prophets have written is compared with *luchnō phainonti en auchmērō topō* 'a lamp shining in a dark place'. This simile occurs elsewhere in Scripture; cf. Psalm 119:105. Since this appears to be a live figure, the nonfigurative meaning has been stated in 1:19c and the comparison made explicit in 1:19d.

There is some discussion amongst commentators as to the meaning of *auchmēros*, which occurs only here in the New Testament. Although it is translated as "dark" in most versions, some commentators say that its usual meaning is "dry" and therefore it would be more correct here to use "a dirty/waste place." The comparison would then be, that as a light reveals all the dirt in a place, so Scripture makes Christians conscious of sin.

I have followed the majority view and taken *auchmēros* to mean "dark," since a light is usually thought of as a means of lighting a path so that we can avoid obstacles as we walk, or lighting up a house or room so that we can see what we are doing, and this would point to "a dark place" as being more appropriate than "a dirty/waste place." Scripture, and in particular here, what the Old Testament prophets wrote, gives us spiritual illumination, so that we can discern truth from error, and hence not be deceived by false teaching, no matter how plausible.

The "dark place" is regarded by some to be referring to this present wicked world, and by others, to the hearts of Peter's readers. In either case, only the Word of God can enlighten, and therefore should be heeded.

1:19e. The clause which *heōs hou* 'until' introduces is best taken with *prosechontes* 'paying attention to heeding', rather than with *phainonti* 'shining', as some commentators suggest. As Meyer says, "it would be a somewhat superfluous adjunct' if it were not also applied to *prosechontes*. Therefore, in the display, it is shown as being dependent on 19b rather than 19d.

Peter continues to speak figuratively until the end of verse 19, and we have a further figure now in *heōs hou hēmera diaugasē* 'until the day dawns'.

I have taken this to refer to the Second Coming of Christ in glory and in judgement. As the daylight disperses the darkness of night, so the return of Christ to the earth will reveal the truth which has been hidden by sin. This interpretation keeps the usual meaning of *hēmera* 'day', and foreshadows the description of Christ's Second Coming in 3:10-11.

Some commentators suggest that it refers to a change in spiritual life, from a state of nature to a state of grace, when the revelation of the holiness and justice of God enables a man to see his own sinful state clearly. But this does not make good sense, for it implies that there will be a stage in a believer's life when he will not need the Scriptures.

The word *phōsphoros* 'morning star' usually refers to the planet Venus, which appears just before the dawn. Here, it is used figuratively and may refer to:

1. Christ
2. Christ's Second Coming
3. a change in spiritual life, i.e., inner illumination by the indwelling of the Holy Spirit.

I have taken this to refer to Christ, since there are a number of other examples in Scripture where star imagery is used when speaking of him; cf. Num. 24:17; Rev. 22:16; Luke 1:78.

Some commentators have pointed out that this involves an inaccuracy, in that the morning star precedes and does not follow the dawn. Probably, however, Peter, having mentioned the Parousia, wishes to refer now to Christ himself, and does so by representing him as the morning star, in keeping with well-known prophecy and imagery.

There is some discussion as to whether *en tais kardiais humōn* 'in your hearts' should be connected with:

1. *anateilē* 'rises'
2. *diaugasē* 'dawns' and *anateilē* 'rises', together
3. *prosechontes* 'paying attention to'

The last of these involves a long parenthesis, from *hos luchnō* to *anateilē* and seems an unnatural construction.

The first of these seems the most appropriate in this context. The image of the day dawning applies then to the objective aspect of Christ's coming, and that of the morning star rising applies to the subjective aspect, i.e., the spiritual illumination believers will have on that occasion. The use of the words *en tais kardiais humōn* 'in your hearts' indicates that Peter was thinking of the spiritual implications of that day, rather than its outward splendours.

The picture which Peter paints here is that of a world in a state of spiritual darkness, apart from the revealed truth of God in the Old Testament Scriptures and the teachings of the apostles. These give a degree of enlightenment to believers until the Lord returns, and gives them complete spiritual knowledge, when they shall see him as he is.

Since there are several related figures in verse 19, this would seem to be a live figure and so both figurative and nonfigurative expressions are given in the display, in 1:19c, d, e, and f.

1:20a. The demonstrative pronoun *touto* 'this' refers to the clause following, which is introduced by *hoti* 'that' and gives emphasis to the *hoti* clause.

Although *prōton* can mean "first" in time, here, in the neuter case, it is more likely that it is being used adverbially to mean "above all, especially," i.e., first in importance; cf. also 3:3.

The present participle *ginōskontes* 'knowing, understanding, realising' should be closely connected to *kalōs poieite prosechontes* 'you do well to heed' (1:19b). He is directing his readers to the point which should have their closest attention, i.e., the content of the clause introduced by *hoti*, which provides the grounds for 19b. In the display, therefore, 1:20a is the orienter and what follows is the content.

The relationship of verses 20 and 21 to what precedes and what follows is discussed in the section on coherence.

1:20b. The phrase *prophēteia graphēs* 'prophecy of Scripture' is generally regarded as referring to Old Testament prophecies, and so can be equated with *ton prophētikon logon* in verse 19. In the New Testament, *graphē* 'writing' is used exclusively of the Holy Scriptures. The prophecies referred to here contrast with those alluded to in 2:1, which are put forward by false prophets.

The *pasa . . . ou* 'every . . . not' is probably a Hebraism for *oudemia* 'no' and is here applied to *prophēteia graphēs* 'prophecy of Scripture'.

The present indicative, *ginetai* 'comes from, is a matter of, is the result of', used with the genitive case, implies a "relation of dependence, and in such a way that the genitive denotes that on which something else depends" (Meyer). Here, it occurs with the genitive *idias epiluseōs*, which refers back to the subject *pasa prophēteia*, and means "private interpretation," i.e., of the one who utters the prophecy.

This word for "interpretation," *epilusis*, is found nowhere else in the New Testament, but the verb *epiluō* 'set free, release' is used in a figurative sense in Mark 4:34, to mean "explain, interpret," and in Acts 19:39 to mean "decide, settle" a dispute.

The whole clause, *pasa prophēteia graphēs idias epiluseōs ou ginetai* 'no prophecy of Scripture is of any private interpretation', gives rise to several points of view as to its meaning. The three main ones are as follows:

1. no prophecy of Scripture is of any private impulse or invention, i.e., it does not originate in the will of man;
2. no prophecy of Scripture is of private interpretation, i.e., is not to be interpreted according to the fancies of men but according to the Word of God and the guidance of his Spirit;
3. no prophecy of Scripture is of self-interpretation, i.e., is its own interpreter.

From the context, the first of these seems to be the most applicable, since it is the origin and authenticity of what the apostles have been teaching with which Peter is concerned, not how such teaching should be interpreted.

He has stated in verses 16-18 that what they taught was not based on "cleverly contrived stories" but on personal testimony concerning what God himself had spoken. Now, he is speaking of the testimony of the prophets, which is also very reliable because, again, it is God speaking and not men. This is stated in verse 20 and then explained/amplified negatively in 21a, and positively in 21b, i.e., prophecy did **not** come from the will of man; it **did** come from the Spirit of God.

The *touto prōton ginōskontes* 'you should realise this as important' draws attention to what follows in verses 20 and 21 as being of some importance, and this would also support the view that it is the origin of Scripture which is being spoken of here, since that is a matter of prime importance.

1:21a. The *gar* introduces an explanation of what has been said in verse 20. (See note on 20b.)

After a negative, as here, the adverb *pote* 'at some time or other, once, formerly', means "not . . . ever, never."

Peter's use of *ēnechthē* 'was brought', with reference to *prophēteia* 'prophecy', is probably deliberate here, to remind us of its use in verses 17 and 18 in connection with the voice from heaven. It points to the divine origin of prophecy, i.e., just as that voice came from God, so does what the prophets say.

The phrase *thelēmati anthrōpou* 'by the will of man', is a dative of cause, i.e., the act of willing or desiring on the part of man does not result in prophecy.

1:21b. Here, *alla* 'but' introduces the positive side of the explanation, i.e., what prophecy **is**, in contrast to what it is **not** (21a). As is usual, this second unit is the more prominent of the two. This is an amplification of 1:20b.

The preposition *hupo* 'by' with the genitive case, i.e., *pneumatos hagiou* 'the Holy Spirit', and a passive verb, i.e., *pheromenoi* 'being brought', denotes the agent. The same verb is used in verses 17 and 18; cf. 21a above.

The Majority Text reads *hagioi* and couples it with *anthrōpoi*, giving "holy men." In either case, the Holy Spirit is the driving force behind any prophecy, and this is kept to the fore.

SUB-PART CONSTITUENT 2:1-22
(Division) (Role: Grounds for 1:3-21)

THEME: *There will be false teachers among you who will behave wickedly and will entice you to behave in the same way as they do; God will certainly destroy them.*

RELATIONAL STRUCTURE	CONTENTS
HEAD	(2:1-3) There will be false teachers among you, who will behave wickedly and will entice you to behave in the same way as they do; God will certainly destroy them.
amplification	(2:4-22) Because these false teachers will act like this (2:1-3), God will destroy them.

BOUNDARIES AND COHERENCE

The boundaries of this unit have been discussed when considering 1:3–2:22.

The unity of this constituent of the letter is very strong, in that it is taken up completely with a description of the wicked lives of the false teachers and those who follow them, and God's dealings with them. The vocabulary obviously reflects this, with many words used which are descriptive of sin and destructiion; eg., *aselgeia* 'licentiousness', *asthesmos* 'lawless, unprincipled' (2:7); *epithumia* 'lust', *miasmos* 'pollution, corruption' (2:10); *akatapaustous hamartias* 'restless for sin' (2:14); *phthora* 'destruction', *phtharēsontai* 'they will be destroyed' (2:12) etc.

Also, throughout these verses, predominantly third person plural verb forms are used, referring to the false teachers and their adherents. The exception to this is the use of third person singular forms when God is the agent.

PROMINENCE AND THEME

Verses 4-22 give a more detailed exposition of what has been stated already in verses 1-3. In them, Peter gives further examples of the depravity of the false teachers, and restates their inevitable destruction at the hands of God, if they continue their evil way of life. (For further details of the development of the theme of 2:1-3 refer to the notes on 2:4-22).

Verses 1-3, therefore, are regarded as the head of this unit, with verses 4-22 being an amplification of that head. The theme statement therefore, is based on the theme statement of 2:1-3.

DIVISION CONSTITUENT 2:1-3
(Paragraph) (Role: Head of 2:1-22)

THEME: *There will be false teachers among you, who will behave wickedly and will entice you to behave in the same way as they do; God will certainly destroy them.*

RELATIONAL STRUCTURE			CONTENT
	comparison		(2:1a) Just like there were false prophets among the (Israelite) people
HEAD1	HEAD		(2:1b) (so) there will also be false teachers among you,
	generic	HEAD	(2:1c) who (the false teachers) will teach (insidiously) what is false,
		result	(2:1d) and, as a result, (they will be) destroyed* (by God).
desc.of "false teachers"	HEAD	HEAD	(2:1e) In particular, they will even deny (that) the Lord (Jesus Christ died in order that he might) redeem them,
		result	(2:1f) and (as a result of 1e) they will soon be destroyed* (by God).
	conjoined HEAD		(2:2a) And many (of you) will behave in an extremely immoral manner, imitating the extremely immoral manner in which they (these false teachers) behave,
		result	(2:2b) and, as a result of 2a, (people) will discredit the Way which is the true one.
		reason	(2:3a) Because (the false teachers) are covetous,
		means	(2:3b) and by means of (their) saying what is false,
HEAD2	HEAD		(2:3c) they will exploit you.
HEAD3			(2:3d) (God decided) long ago (that he would) condemn them, and (he will most certainly) destroy* them.

BOUNDARIES AND COHERENCE

The initial boundary of this paragraph is also the initial boundary of a new section of the Epistle, and has been discussed under Sub-part Constituent 2:1-22. The main feature is a change from hortatory to expository genre.

The final boundary is marked by the following features:

1. A change of subject matter.

   In 2:1-3 the false teachers are introduced, then in 2:4 Peter begins to give specific examples of how God deals mercifully with the righteous, but condemns the unrighteous, including the false teachers and their followers, to eternal punishment.

   The initial *gar* 'for' of 2:4 introduces this list of examples which forms the grounds for the statement made at the end of 2:3, concerning the fate of the false teachers, i.e., *hois to krima ekpalai ouk argei, kai hē apōleia autōn ou nustazei* 'whose judgement for a long time is not idle, and whose destruction does not sleep'.

2. A change of agent.

   In 2:4 the agent changes from *pseudodidaskaloi* 'false teachers' to *ho theos* 'God', with a resulting change of person in the verb, from predominantly third person plural in verses 1-3 to third person singular in the next paragraph.

3. A change of tense.

   In verses 1-3 all the finite verbs are future tense, except for the first one and the two final ones. The first, *egenonto* 'there were', is aorist and refers to *pseudoprophētai* 'false prophets' (2:1), looking back to the true prophets referred to at the end of chapter 1 and forward to the *pseudodidaskaloi* 'false teachers' he is about to introduce, thus providing a tail-head link between the two. The final two are present tense, *ouk argei* 'is not idle', and *ou nustazei* 'does not sleep', but they are part of a figure of speech and actually refer to the future punishment of the false teachers. In verse 4 there is a change to aorist tense.

There is strong referential coherence in the paragraph due to the following:

1. Numerous references to the *pseudodidaskaloi* 'false teachers', chiefly by the use of pronouns. They provide the topic, not only of this paragraph, but of the whole chapter. The following references to them are found in these verses:

   2:1 *pseudodidaskaloi* 'false teachers'; *hoitines* 'who'; *autous* 'them'; *heautois* 'themselves'.

   2:2 *autōn* 'of them'; *di' hous* 'because of whom'.

   2:3 *hois* 'for whom'; *autōn* 'of them.

2. The use of *apōleia* 'destruction', twice in verse 1, and once in verse 3. This forms a lexical sandwich, along with *krima* 'judgement' (2:3), which also refers to the punishment of the ungodly. There is also a group of words referring to vice or wickedness which forms the filling: *aselgeiais* 'vices' (2:2); *blasphēmēthēsetai* 'will be blasphemed/reviled' (2:2); *pleonexia* 'greed' (2:2).

3. The use of words belonging to the same semantic set of words, pertaining to deceit and falsehood:
   pseudoprophētai 'false prophets' (2:1); *pseudodidaskaloi* 'false teachers' (2:1); *pareisaxousin* 'they bring in (secretly)' (2:1); *haireseis* 'heresies' (2:1); *plastois logois humas emporeusontai* 'they will exploit you with deceitful words' (2:3).

Structurally, the paragraph is in three parts, corresponding to the three verses, the latter two of which are linked to the first by *kai*. Within each part, the grammatical form is remarkably parallel, with a relative clause following the independent clause(s) in each case.

In the first verse, grammatically, the main statement would seem to be 2:1a, *egeneto de kai pseudoprophētai en tō laō* 'there were also false prophets among the people', since this is an independent clause containing a finite verb. However, semantically the emphasis lies in the grammatically subordinate clause *hos kai en humin esontai pseudodidaskaloi* 'as there will be false teachers amongst you' (2:1b), and this has been analysed as head of this verse, with 2:1a as a clause of comparison. The rest of the verse (1c-1f) is a propositional cluster providing a description of the false teachers, and is related to *pseudodidaskaloi* by the relative pronoun *hoitines* 'who' (2:1c).

Within this subordinate cluster (1c-1f), grammatically the head is 2:1c, by virtue of the finite verb *pareisaxousin* 'they will bring in'. However, semantically the prominence is on 2:1e, which is a specific example of one important aspect of the false teaching referred to in generic terms in 2:1c. Peter is drawing our attention to it, cf. 'in particular', therefore, 2:1e is the head.

The *kai* at the beginning of verse 2 marks a coordinate relationship with what precedes. The two propositions, 2a and 2b, are related to each other by the relative pronoun *di' hous* 'because of whom'.

There are three result clauses in verses 1 and 2, i.e., 1d, 1f, 2b, and, in each case, the normal prominence is reversed, with the result clause playing a subordinate role to its accompanying reason clause. This is because each of the reason clauses, i.e., 1c, 1e, 2a is more closely related thematically with the first head (1b); (See notes) and also, in 2:1c the verb *pareisaxousin* 'they will bring in' is a finite verb, while 2:1d is a genitive construction and therefore subordinate to it.

The *kai* at the beginning of verse 3 also marks a coordinate relationship to what precedes. It consists of two main clauses, 3c and 3d, preceded by two subordinate clauses, 3a and 3b, which give respectively the reason and means of 3c.

PROMINENCE AND THEME

Verses 1 and 3 are more prominent than verse 2 because they deal directly with the topic, *pseudodidaskaloi* 'the false teachers'. Both refer to the false teaching and the destruction of the false teachers.

The motif relating to the destruction of the false teachers increases in prominence as the paragraph progresses. When it is first referred to in 2:1d, it is in a genitive construction, *haireseis apōleias* 'heresies of destruction'. The next reference is in the participial clause 2:1f, i.e., *epagontes eautois tachinēn apōleian* 'bringing on themselves soon destruction'. Finally, in 2:3d, it is referred to in a finite clause which is the fourth head of the paragraph and part of the theme statement.

This is a descriptive paragraph with three heads, 2:1b, 2:3c, and 2:3d. Since there is no marked prominence on any of these heads, a more generic theme has been formulated, based on the three heads.

NOTES ON 2:1-3

2:1a. The *de* 'but' introduces the *pseudoprophētai* 'false prophets', in contrast to the true prophets and true prophecy of verses 19-21, which immediately precede. The *kai* 'and, also' indicates that there were false prophets in Israel as well as the true prophets.

The *pseudoprophētai* 'false prophets' were those who claimed to be prophets of God, but who prophesied falsely, i.e., their predictions were not fulfilled.

The word *laos* 'people' is commonly used by the New Testament writers with the specific meaning "the people of God," referring to the people of Israel. It is used here in that sense.

2:1b. The *hōs kai* 'just as' introduces a subordinate clause, grammatically, but one which is thematic in meaning, for this paragraph. (See section on Boundaries and Coherence.) Peter has probably stated it in this way in order to bring out the contrast between true and false prophets. In the display, 2:1b has been made primary in form in order to represent the meaning more closely, i.e., just as there used to be false prophets among the people in the past, so now there will be false teachers among them.

The *pseudodidaskaloi* are those who claimed to be teachers of God's truth and way, but who taught falsehoods. There are references to this latter point in this chapter, giving details of the false teaching which they would propagate, i.e., the liberty they promise (2:19) and also, in chapter 3, if those who scoff are assumed to be the same people, their implied denial of the return of Christ.

2:1c. The verb *pareisaxousin* 'they will bring in', i.e., introduce into the church, is not used elsewhere in the New Testament, but, in other literature, it has the connotation that it is done secretly or maliciously. The false teachers would corrupt the church from within, insidiously and subtly, by introducing false doctrine and living according to it. It has been expressed by "will teach (insidiously)."

Hairesis can mean "sect, party, school," or "opinion, dogma"; the latter seems the more appropriate in this context, since the emphasis is on false teaching, and so *haireseis* has been expressed by "what is false."

Peter uses *apōleia* 'destruction, ruin', or its related verb *apollumi* 'destroy, ruin' seven times, in this letter—twice in 2:1; then also in 2:3; 3:6, 7, 9, 16. He also uses a number of semantically related items:

> *phthora* 'ruin, destruction, dissolution, deterioration, corruption' (1:4; 2:12,19)
>
> *phtheirō* 'destroy, ruin, corrupt, spoil' (2:19)
>
> *luō* 'break up, destroy' (3:10,11,12).

The idea of ruin or destruction in a physical sense is common to each of these in some contexts; cf. 2:1; 2:12; 3:10-12. The false teachers will be destroyed when Christ returns in judgement, if not before then, and the fabric of this present universe will also be destroyed at that time. This destruction is not complete annihilation, but rather dissolution or disintegration of this present earth and heavens and those who live there. Those who are righteous will then inhabit the new heavens and earth which will then begin to exist, and those who behave wickedly will suffer eternal punishment in darkest hell (2:17 and 3:13).

The sense in which Peter uses *luō* seems to be limited to the idea of physical destruction; cf. 3:10-12. He describes the disintegration of this present world into its component parts. He also uses *parerchomai* in this sense in 3:10.

In the case of *apōleia* and *apollumi* there is a sense of spiritual as well as physical destruction; cf. 2:1-3 and 3:7, 9, 16. When the Lord Jesus Christ returns in judgement, as well as being destroyed in the final conflagration on that day, the wicked will suffer spiritual destruction, in that there will no longer be any hope for them to repent and be saved; their souls will be utterly lost.

In 2:12 *phthora* has the sense of 'destroyed', but in 1:4 and 2:19 it is generally taken to refer to the moral corruption which follows as a result of wilful indulgence in sinful actions. In all three usages it also conveys the sense of spiritual deterioration leading to final condemnation and the eternal loss of the soul.

Although 'destroy' has been used in the displays for *apōleia* and *apollumi*, no English word seems completely appropriate to express the sense of the Greek. There is no exact equivalent. All the occurrences, except possibly 3:6, refer to the destruction of people, but in English "destroy" is used principally to refer to things and not people. The verb "kill" is more usually used in relation to people. Occurrences of "destroy" have been marked with an * therefore, to show that it is used in a special sense. It will be necessary to make sure that the word used in the RL is one which can be used in relation to people or things as indicated by the context in each case.

2:1d. The genitive *apōleias* 'of destruction' is best understood as expressing a result, i.e., "heresies which cause destruction." The heresies they taught destroyed doctrine and character, and resulted in eternal destruction for those who believed them, but here it probably refers to the actual physical destruction of the false teachers, in view of the following:

1. *epagontes eautoi tachinēn apōleian* 'bringing on themselves soon destruction' (2:1f).
2. *hois to krima ekpalai ouk argei, kai hē apōleia autōn ou nustazei* 'for whom judgement has not been idle and whose destruction has not slept' (2:3d)
3. the next paragraph (2:4-10c), in which Peter gives examples of those who have behaved in an ungodly manner in the past and whom God has destroyed because of this.

These seem to point to a more immediate retribution than that on the final day of judgement, although ultimately it does refer to that, cf. 2:9.

God is understood to be the agent of their destruction and this has been made explicit in the display.

2:1e. The *kai* 'even' highlights one outstanding example of the false teaching which brought destruction. It has been expressed by "in particular."

The verb *arneomai* means "to deny, repudiate, disown." Here the object is *ton agorasanta autous despotēn* 'the Master/Lord who bought them'. The use of the participle *arnoumenoi* 'denying' puts this clause into a subordinate relationship with 1c but, thematically, it is more prominent and has, therefore, been made head of this subordinate cluster of propositions (see section on Boundaries and Coherence).

The verb *agorazō* 'to buy' is used to refer to ordinary transactions of buying in a number of places in the New Testament, e.g., Matt. 13:44, 46; 14:15; and Mark 6:36, 37. Here, however, it refers to Christ "purchasing" believers with his blood; cf. also 1 Corinthians 6:20; 7:23; and Revelation 5:9 and 14:3, 4 where it is rendered "redeemed" in most versions. In 1 Peter 1:18-19, the verb *lutroō* 'redeem' is used rather than *agorazō*, but it is probable that, by then, the terms had become synonymous in the context of Christ's death on the cross; see *agorazō* 2 (Arndt and Gingrich) and *exagorazō* in Galatians 3:13; 4:5.

Despotēs 'Master/Lord' occurs in the New Testament only in the following places and in the following senses:

1. A secular sense, referring to a "lord" or "owner," in contrast to slaves. It has the implication of unlimited authority or power in this realm, cf. 1 Timothy 6:1, 2; Titus 2:9; 1 Peter 2:18: Christian slaves are told to please God by obeying their masters.

2 Timothy 2:21: a figure in which Christians are compared with dishes which are fit for their master to use.

2. God is referred to as *despotēs*, cf. Luke 2:29: Simeon in the temple addresses God as *despota*; Acts 4:24: the believers addressing God in prayer on the release of Peter and John from prison.

3. Christ is referred to as *despotēs* here in verse 1 and in Jude 4. It is surprising, however, that it is used rather than *kurios* 'Lord' which is more commonly used to refer to Christ. Because of this, some commentators suggest that it refers to God the Father, since God bought them, in the sense that he was the author of the plan of redemption and caused them to be redeemed.

Possibly *despotēs* is used rather than *kurios* to suggest the function of Jesus "as the one who commands and exercises influence and power," and emphasises "His right to His own by virtue of His saving act." (Theological Dictionary of the New Testament Ed. by Gerhard Kittel: Vol. 2, p. 44ff. 1964.) Christ is master and owner of those whom he has purchased by his blood, and Peter speaks of these false teachers in this way to stress that they not only deny that Christ is Lord, but also deny the act by which he became their Saviour.

2:1f. The verb *epagō* 'bring on' is used only figuratively in the New Testament with the meaning of "cause something to happen to someone" (usually in the sense of something bad). It is used again in verse 5 when referring to God bringing the flood upon the earth. The denial that Christ died in order to save them results in their (the false teachers') destruction.

The use of the present participle, *epagontes* 'bringing on', has been expressed as a result of 2:1e, i.e., it is because of their denial of Christ and his redeeming power that they will be destroyed.

Although this clause and the previous one, 2:1e, are both participial, and the result clause would normally be expected to be the more prominent of the two, 2:1e is the head by virtue of Peter picking out this specific example of false teaching upon which to focus our attention. (See section on Boundaries and Coherence.)

In the phrase *tachinēn apōleian* 'soon destruction', we have the second of three references in the paragraph to the destruction of the false teachers. The others are in 1d and 3d. Here, Peter uses *tachinē* 'coming soon, imminent, swift' to describe the destruction. It is the same adjective as that used in 1:14 to refer to his death. There it was used in the sense of "soon" and it could be used in that sense here also.

The destruction referred to is generally assumed to be the final, utter destruction awaiting the ungodly when the final day of judgement comes, but it could also be temporal judgement which is referred to. In the latter case, the destruction could be physical, or it might mean that their power and influence would be destroyed. (The former is understood here, but the latter would accompany it.) (See note on 2:1d.)

2:2. The *kai* 'and' marks a coordinate relationship between this verse and verse 1.

2:2a. The *polloi* 'many' probably refers to believers, since they are told in verse 1 that the false teachers will come *en humin* 'amongst you', i.e., the body of believers. Also, in 2b, Peter talks of *hē hodos tēs alētheias blasphēmēthēsetai* 'the way of truth shall be reviled', presumably because of the immoral behaviour of those who profess to be believers.

The same verb, *exakoloutheō* 'follow, obey', is used here as was used in 1:16, and again the use is a figurative one. Many will believe the heresies taught by the false teachers and consequently will live the immoral sort of life which they condone.

Peter uses the noun *aselgeia* 'licentiousness, debauchery, sensuality' three times in this letter, in 2:7 and 18 and here. He also uses it in 4:3 of his first letter. It refers to all types of immorality and extremes of wicked behaviour. It is a strong word for reckless and hardened immorality, and is the complete antithesis of the behaviour demanded of those following "the Way of truth." In the display, it is expressed by "they live/behave in an extremely immoral manner."

2:2b. The *di' hous* 'on account of whom' may refer to the false teachers, or those they have deceived and who are imitating their behaviour, or both. However, since it is the behaviour of these people which is discrediting "the Way of truth," it has been expressed by "as a result of (2a)," referring to the preceding proposition which describes the immoral behaviour.

Blasphēmēthēsetai is the future indicative passive of the verb *blasphēmeō*. This verb occurs three times in this chapter, in verses 2, 10, and 12. Peter also uses it in 4:4 of his first letter, and its related adjective *blasphēmos* is used in verse 12 of 2 Peter 2. The verb is used quite frequently in the New Testament, but the adjective is found in only a few places. (See note on 2:12).

Blasphēmeō refers to speech which is directed against a person's claims, opinions, or teachings, rather than against a person himself. It is also directed against what is good rather than evil.

The range of meaning covered by *blasphēmeō* is quite wide. It means "insult, defame, revile, injure the reputation of, deride, blaspheme." In English there is no one word which covers this wide range of meaning, as can be seen from the following examples:

> *en hois agnoousin blasphēmountes* 'things about which they know nothing (i.e., divine, spiritual things) ... speaking disparagingly about' (2 Peter 2:12).
> This is a relatively mild statement, dismissing these things as unimportant although they know nothing about them.
> *hē hodos tēs alētheias blasphēmēthēsetai* 'the way of truth will be discredited' (2 Peter 2:2)

doxas ... blasphēmountes 'the glorious ones ... insulting' (2:10)
This is directed more against their position and power than against
their persons.

eblasphēmoun auton 'ridiculing/deriding him (Christ)' (Matt. 27:39)
This is directed at what Christ had said concerning rebuilding the
temple in three days, and what that implied, as we can see from the
following verse which gives us the content of their derisive remarks.

tō de eis to hagion pneuma blasphēmēsanti ouk aphethēsetai 'to him who
blasphemes the Holy Spirit it shall not be forgiven' (Luke 12:10).
This is at the other end of the scale to a mere disparaging remark,
and implies a complete denial of the power and work of the Holy
Spirit.

The expression *hē hodos tēs alētheias* 'the way of the truth' is figurative
and denotes Christianity, including both doctrine and practice. This could
possibly be expressed in a nonfigurative way by "what those who believe in
Christ teach," but it has been represented in the display by "the Way which
is the true one," which, although still figurative, should not pose a problem
in translation, since this use of "way" is not uncommon.

2:3. The conjunction *kai* 'and' introduces the third clause cluster. It returns
to describing the activities of the false teachers, rather than those of their adherents.

2:3a. The literal meaning of *pleonexia* is "a desire to have more." With the
preposition *en*, it probably has the meaning "because they are greedy." This
is their motivation to exploit/deceive people, either for financial gain, or for
the sake of gaining more adherents to their teaching and way of life. The
reference to Balaam in verse 15, *misthon adikias ēgapēsen* 'he loved the
reward of unrighteousness', in relation to the money Balak would have given
him for cursing Israel, makes it likely that financial gain is referred to here.
Peter uses the same word in verse 14 where it has the meaning of un-
restrained desire for illicit things.

2:3b. *Plastos* means "forged, fabricated, invented." It is used only here in
the New Testament, in the expression *plastois logois* 'with invented words'. It
refers to the false teachings which the false teachers are propagating in their
attempts to win over Christians to their way of life. It reminds us of the
sesophismenois muthois 'cleverly contrived tales' of 1:16 which are in opposition to the truth of the gospel and the Old Testament teachings.

Both *muthoi* and *plastoi logoi* are apparently heretical alternatives to the
gospel. They stand in antithesis to the *logos* of the gospel and are spread by
teachers who satisfy the *epithumia* 'lusts' of man.

We are not told a great deal in this chapter about the actual content of
what the false teachers say, in either the "destructive heresies" (2:1) or the
"invented words," except for 2:1e where we learn that they deny that Christ

died to save them. However, the fact that they cause others to live extremely immoral lives in imitation of their own, gives some idea of the emphasis which their teaching took.

The phrase *plastois logois* has been expressed in the display by the clause "by means of their saying what is false," since it states the means by which the false teachers exploit those who follow them.

2:3c. The verb *emporeuomai* 'to buy, sell, to trade in' is used only here and in James 4:13 in the New Testament. In James, it is used in this literal sense but here, in Peter, *emporeusontai* is used in the sense of "they will exploit/cheat." It very rarely, as here, has the person as object, cf. *humas* 'you'.

This contrasts with the reference, in 2:1e, to Christ purchasing our salvation with his blood, and foreshadows the comparison with Balaam in the illustration at the end of the next paragraph, cf. 2:15-16.

2:3d. The pronoun *hois* 'with respect to them' refers to the false teachers.

Most commentators agree that *ekpalai* 'for a long time, long ago' should be understood adverbially with the following verb, *ouk argei* 'is not idle'.

The whole of this statement is a figure, with *krima* 'judgement, condemnation' and *apōleia* 'destruction' being personified, the first being described as *ouk argei* 'is not idle', and the second as *ou nustazei* 'is not asleep'. The decision to condemn the false teachers was taken long ago and proceeds inexorably towards their destruction, as we see from the examples in the next paragraph and also 2:1 and 3:7 and 16.

The phrase *plastois logois* has been expressed in the display by the clause "by means of their saying what is false," since it states the means by which the false teachers exploit those who follow

Both halves of 3d use the figure of a litotes, saying with a double negation what is true positively. Moore, in *NOT* 43, suggests that this rhetorical parallelism is a doublet, taking *krima* to include not only the sentence of condemnation but also the subsequent punishment. This is certainly possible, but, in the display, I have retained the two separate ideas of the passing of sentence and its actual performance, in view of the references in this chapter and chapter 3 to God "keeping" the ungodly "for/until judgement"; see the following examples:

  2:4 *eis krisin tēroumenous* 'being kept for judgement', referring to the angels who sinned.

  2:9 *eis hēmeran kriseos kolazomenous tērein* 'to keep, while being punished for the day of judgement', referring to the unrighteous.

  3:7 *tēroumenoi eis hēmeran kriseos kai apōleian* 'being kept until the day of judgement and destruction', i.e., of the ungodly.

The present tense of the two verbs, *argei* 'is idle' and *nustazei* 'slumbers', represents the future referentially, i.e., refers to their future judgement. The Majority Text has the future for the second verb, i.e., *nustaxei*. The present tense is probably used because the idea is being conveyed that their judgement is actively waiting now, though it will fall later.

The meaning is expressed in a nonfigurative way in the display, with God made explicit as the agent of their judgement/condemnation and their ultimate destruction.

DIVISION CONSTITUENT 2:4-22
(Section) (Role: Amplification of 2:1-3)

THEME: *Because these false teachers will behave wickedly and will entice others to behave in the same way as they do, God will destroy them.*

RELATIONAL STRUCTURE	CONTENTS
grounds	(2:4-10c) It is certain that God knows how to rescue those who are godly, and that he knows how to keep those who are unrighteous until the time when he will punish them
HEAD	(2:10d-22) Because these false teachers will behave wickedly and will entice others to behave in the same way as they do, God will destroy them.

BOUNDARIES AND COHERENCE

The initial boundary for this constituent has been discussed in connection with the boundaries of 2:1-3, and the final boundary has been discussed when dealing with the boundaries of 1:3–2:22.

The unity of this constituent consists largely in its subject matter, i.e., the behaviour of ungodly people, and in particular, of the false teachers, and God's dealings with them. This can be seen clearly in the preponderance of words belonging to those semantic sets referring to wicked behaviour, punishment, and destruction. For more details on this refer to the appropriate notes on the individual paragraphs which make up this section of the Epistle.

In 2:4-10c the focus is on God as agent, and the verb forms are predominantly third person singular. In 2:10d-22 the focus is on the false teachers and their followers, and the verb forms are predominantly third person plural. These features indicate a boundary between 2:10c and d. This is discussed further in connection with 2:10d-22.

PROMINENCE AND THEME

The two constituents of this section 2:4-10c and 2:10d-22, are in a grounds-conclusion relationship. The head, 2:10d-22, is therefore prominent, and the theme statement for the section is based on the theme statement of this constituent.

SECTION CONSTITUENT 2:4-10c
(Paragraph) (Role: Grounds for 2:10d-22)

THEME: *It is certain that God knows how to rescue those who are godly, and that he knows how to keep those who are unrighteous until the time when he will punish them.*

BOUNDARIES AND COHERENCE

The initial boundary of this paragraph is marked by the following features:

Gar 'for' which introduces a long conditional sentence, giving the grounds for the immediately preceding statement in 2:3 concerning the certain judgement God will pass on the unrighteous.

A change of tense from future and present to aorist.

A change of agent, from the *pseudodidaskaloi* 'false teachers' and their followers, to *ho theos* 'God', with an accompanying change of person from third person plural to third person singular.

The final boundary is marked by a sudden change of focus from the broad and general indictment of ungodliness, illustrated by the various examples, to a more particular aspect, which is described in the next paragraph (2:10d-16), and to which attention is drawn by the adverb *malista* 'especially', at the end of this paragraph in verse 10.

In the second half of verse 10, the construction alters suddenly to a description of the wicked persons who were the object of the preceding sentence, and there is a change of agent from God, to the lawless and lascivious men Peter goes on to describe. This is accompanied by a change of person from third singular to plural.

There is strong referential coherence in the paragraph, not least in the references to God as agent which occur throughout. At the beginning we have *ho theos* 'God' (2:4) and at the end *kurios* 'the Lord (God)' (2:10), whilst it is implicit in each verse that he is the agent.

This unity is further strengthened by two groups of words belonging to two distinct semantic sets as follows:

Those referring to the godly:

dikaiosunēs 'righteousness' (2:5); *dikaion* 'righteous' (2:7); *ho dikaios* 'the righteous' (2:8); *psuchēn dikaian* 'righteous soul' (2:8); *eusebeis* 'godly' (2:9).

and those referring to God's attitude to the godly:

ephulaxen 'he guarded, protected' (2:5); *errusato* 'he rescued' (2:7); *ruesthai* 'to rescue' (2:9).

In contrast we have those referring to the unrighteous:

aggelōn hamartēsantōn 'the angels who sinned' (2:4); *kosmō asebōn* 'the world of the ungodly' (2:5); *asebein* 'to be living ungodly' (2:6); *tēs tōn athesmōn en aselgeia anastrophēs* 'the licentious way of life of lawless men' (2:7); *anomois ergois* 'unrighteous deeds' (2:8); *adikous* 'the unrighteous' (2:9); and indeed the whole of 10a-c.

and those expressing God's attitude to the unrighteous:
ouk epheisato 'he did not spare' (2:4,8); *seirais zophou tartarosas paradōken eis krisin tēroumenous* 'cast them into Tartarus and chained them in darkness being kept for judgement' (2:4); *kataklusmon . . . epaxas* 'brought on a flood' (2:5); *tephrōsas katastrophē katekrinen* 'condemned to extinction by burning to ashes' (2:6); *eis hēmeran kriseos kolazomenous tērein* 'to keep for the day of judgement, in the meantime punishing' (2:9).

Grammatically, this paragraph is related by the initial *gar* to the immediately preceding statement at the end of 2:3. This is discussed under Section Constituent.

In the Greek, this paragraph consists of one long sentence made up from a series of coordinate clauses, each linked to the next by *kai* 'and', and each providing a grounds for the concluding statements of 2:9-10c.

Each of these grounds is very similar in structure in that:
1. each is introduced by *ei* 'since', explicitly in verse 4 and implicitly in verses 5, 6, and 7.
2. each is linked by *kai*, cf. verses 5, 6, and 7.
3. each has a main statement containing a verb in the aorist tense and following a subordinate clause which is in an equivalent relation to it, cf. 4a, b; 6a, b. Verse 7 is the exception in that the equivalent clause (8a) is related to 7b, rather than to the head (7a).

In 2:9-10c, we have the conclusion to the grounds stated in verses 4-8. There is a slight difficulty, in that Peter seems to set off in 2:4 to stress particularly the punishment that God will certainly mete out to the ungodly, as we see by the *gar* 'for' which relates the paragraph to the final statement of verse 3. However, he introduces the subject of God's mercy to the righteous in the examples, and so ends with a two-pronged conclusion in 9a and 9c, referring to the righteous and the unrighteous respectively.

PROMINENCE AND THEME

The way in which the various grounds are stated in a repetitive pattern in verses 4-8 has a cumulative effect which gives weight to the conclusion (2:9-10c) and prominence to the two heads, 9a and 9c.

Further emphasis is given to it, by the use of the perfect tense with present meaning, in *oiden* 'he knows (how)' (2:9a), in contrast to the aorist tense which predominates in the preceding clauses.

RELATIONAL STRUCTURE

grounds$_1$	HEAD		
(example)	ampli.	HEAD	
		purpose	
grounds$_2$	HEAD		
(example)	ampli.	HEAD	
		circ.	
grounds$_3$	HEAD	HEAD	
(example)		equiv.	
	result		
grounds$_4$	HEAD		
(example)	circ.	HEAD	HEAD
			reason
		equiv.	HEAD
			means
			time
HEAD$_1$	HEAD		
	circumstance		
HEAD$_2$	HEAD	HEAD	
		time	
	specific	HEAD	
		ident. of "ungodly people"	HEAD$_1$
			HEAD$_2$

CONTENT

(2:4a) God destroyed [LIT] the angels who sinned,

(2:4b) that is, he (God) cast (them) into Tartarus and confined (them there) [MET] in darkness

(2:4c) (in order that) they should be kept (there by God) until (he will) judge (them).

(2:5a) He (God) also destroyed [LIT] (the people who lived in) the ancient world,

(2:5b) that is, he saved (only) eight (people) including Noah, who was a righteous preacher,

(2:5c) (when) he (God) destroyed with a flood (all) the ungodly people (who lived in) that world.

(2:6a) He also condemned the cities (which were named) Sodom and Gomorrah,

(2:6b) that is, he destroyed them by means of his burning (them) completely to ashes,

(2:6c) and (by doing this (6a-b)) he warned (those who) afterwards (would) live in an ungodly manner.

(2:7a) He also rescued Lot, (who was) a righteous (man),

(2:7b) (when) he (Lot) was greatly distressed

(2:7c) (because) lawless (men) behaved so corruptly;

(2:8a) that is, that righteous (man Lot) was tormenting his righteous soul day by day

(2:8b) by (means that) he (Lot) saw and heard those wicked men behave (in such a) lawless (manner),

(2:8c) (when he was) living amongst them.

(2:9a) (Since God acted like this (verses 4-8)), (you can be sure that) the Lord (God) knows how to rescue godly (people)

(2:9b) (when) they are being tested,

(2:9c) and (he knows how) to keep ungodly (people) (who are even now) being punished,

(2:9d) until the time (when) he will (finally) condemn (them).

(2:10a) In particular, (he will keep) those (ungodly people)

(2:10b) who indulge their bodies by (doing those deeds which they) lust after (and which) defile (them);

(2:10c) and who despise (all beings who) rule (over them).

The *ho theos* 'God' at the beginning of the paragraph, and *kurios* 'Lord (God)' at the end, together with the repeated references to him throughout the paragraph keep God to the forefront as the protagonist in all that is described.

At the same time, each example of the Lord's judgement in the past is focused upon, in turn, by being forefronted to a position preceding the verb, cf. *hamartēsantōn ouk epheisato* 'the sinning angels he did not spare' (2:4a); *archaiou kosmou ouk epheisato* 'the ancient world he did not spare' (2:5a); *Nōe ... ephulaxen* 'Noah ... he saved' (2:5b); *poleis Sodomōn kai Gomorras . .. katekrinen* 'the cities of Sodom and Gomorrah ... he condemned' (2:6a); *dikaion Lōt ... errusato* 'righteous Lot ... he rescued' (2:7a).

The theme is taken from the two heads 9a and 9c.

NOTES ON 2:4-10c

2:4.   The *gar* 'for' relates this paragraph to the immediately preceding statement in 2:3, i.e., *hois to krima ekpalai ouk argei, kai hē apōleia autōn ou nustazei* 'whose judgement is not idle and whose destruction does not sleep'. This speaks of the certain punishment of the false teachers, and now we are to hear the grounds upon which this is based.

2:4a.   The conjunction *ei* 'if, since' introduces a protasis of which the apodosis does not occur until 2:9. It is to be understood also in 5a, 6a, and 7a. Its meaning throughout the paragraph is "since," as it is introducing grounds preparatory to a conclusion.

Ho theos 'God' is the agent in this clause and is the implied agent in each of the other protases, i.e., 5a, 6a, 7a. Its initial position in this opening clause marks it as the topic also. Peter switches focus from the false teachers to God and his activities.

The phrase *aggellōn hamartēsantōn* 'the angels when they sinned/who sinned' possibly refers to the angels described in Genesis 6:1-4 or Jude 6, but their particular sin is not specified here. The verb *hamartanō* is used of offences against the religious and moral law of God. The participle here could represent either the circumstances in which God did not spare the angels, i.e., "when they sinned," or it might identify the angels referred to, i.e., "who sinned." The second alternative is preferred, since the reference throughout is to those who are punished, and not when they are punished.

The verb *ouk epheisato* 'he did not spare' is a litotes and means "he destroyed," cf. also 2:5a.

2:4b.   The conjunction *alla* 'but' introduces a fuller statement of the brief remark *ouk epheisato* 'he destroyed' (2:4a) and is, therefore, shown as being in an amplification relationship to 4a.

This pattern, of a formally negative statement, followed by a formally positive one introduced by *alla*, is repeated in 2:5a and b. In both cases, the negative statement is the head and the positive one is in an amplification relationship to it.

The participle *tartarōsas* 'cast into Tartarus' has God as the agent and the "angels who sinned" as the object. Tartarus was thought of by the Greeks as a subterranean place lower than Hades where divine punishment was meted out. It was so regarded in Jewish apocalyptic literature as well. The verb is formed from this name and is used only here in the New Testament. Some commentators regard it as the equivalent of Hades or Gehenna but others disagree, since these are places of final punishment, whilst this seems to be a place of "preliminary custody."

The clause *seirais zophou paredōken* 'committed (them) to chains of darkness' is echoed in verse 17 by *ho zophos skotous tetērētai* 'black darkness/gloomy hell has been reserved for them'. *Zophos* is used in Greek writing of the "deep gloom" of the underworld. The "chaining" is considered to be a metonymy for "confined/imprisoned," since fallen angels (presumably) do not have bodies. The verb has the implied idea of punishment.

Moore, in *NOT* 43, suggests that the verbal part of *tartarōsas* 'cast into Tartarus' and *paredōken* 'he committed' form a near-synonymous doublet. However, I have kept the two terms separate, (see display) since the first seems to carry with it the idea of actually putting them into Tartarus while the latter, in conjunction with *seirais zophou* 'chains of darkness', has more the sense of confining and ensuring that they stay there.

2:4c.   The participle *tēroumenous* 'being kept' refers to "the angels who sinned." It has the meaning of being kept for a definite purpose or a suitable time, in this case, the final judgement, cf. *eis krisin* 'for judgement'. It might be preferable to use 'guard' instead of 'keep' in a language where the latter is only used when referring to things.

2:5.   The conjunction *kai* introduces a second grounds coordinate with that in 2:4 and following the same pattern; see note on 2:4.

2:5a.   *Archaiou kosmou* 'the ancient world' denotes the world before the deluge; cf. also 3:6. In this context, it probably refers not so much to the earth as to the people who lived there.

2:5b.   *Ogdoon Nōe* 'Noah as the eighth (person)' means "eight people, including Noah." Some commentators suggest that the numeral has been put in a prominent position in the sentence to stress the small number saved, in contrast to *kosmō asebōn* 'the world of the ungodly'.

The expression, *dikaiosunēs kēruka* 'a preacher of righteousness', may be either an objective or a qualitative genitive, i.e., either "a man who preached righteousness" (as a way of life), or "a righteous preacher." It seems more likely that it refers to Noah's own righteousness, since the emphasis throughout the paragraph is that those who live godly lives will be saved, and those who behave in an ungodly way will be destroyed; cf. verse 9.

2:5c. The aorist participle *epaxas* '(he) brought upon' here implies that this action was simultaneous with *ephulaxen* 'he saved, protected' (5b). It states the circumstances that existed and from which God saved Noah and his family.

In the phrase *kosmō asebōn* 'a world of ungodly (people)', the emphasis is probably on "a whole world of ungodly people," in contrast to the eight saved. See also 2:6 and 3:17.

The noun *kataklusmon* 'flood, deluge' is only used of the flood in Noah's time, by which God destroyed the world.

2:6. The conjunction *kai* introduces the third example of how God punishes the ungodly, and the second, of his deliverance of the righteous. The construction still depends on the *ei* of verse 4.

2:6a. The verb *katekrinen* 'he (God) condemned', along with *katastrophē* 'ruin, destruction' means "he condemned them to be destroyed," i.e., the cities of Sodom and Gomorrah; cf. Genesis 19:29 where the same word is used in the Septuagint of the overthrow of the cities.

2:6b. The participle *tephrōsas* 'having reduced to ashes' has God as agent and states the means which he used to destroy the two cities. As in the two previous grounds, this second clause provides an equivalent statement to the head.

2:6c. The abstract noun *hupodeigma* 'an example' is used here in the sense of "a warning," and gives the result of the overthrow of the cities.

The particple *mellontōn* 'coming, future', when used with the infinitive as here with *asebein* 'to be living ungodly', has the meaning "any who should afterwards live in an ungodly manner."

2:7. The conjunction *kai* again introduces a coordinate statement, with the *ei* 'since' of verse 4 still implicit. Here we have another illustration of God's merciful dealings with the righteous, in the person of Lot.

2:7a. *Dikaion Lōt* 'righteous Lot' refers to Lot, the son of Haran, nephew of Abraham, who lived a righteous life in the midst of the wickedness of the two cities.

2:7c. The reason for Lot's great distress is given by *hupo tēs tōn athesmōn en aselgeia anastrophēs* 'the behaviour of the lawless in licentiousness', i.e., "because lawless men behaved so corruptly."

2:8a. The *gar* 'for' may introduce the reason for 7a, i.e., why God needed to rescue Lot, or it may explain further his great distress (7b). Since it clearly further describes his distress, in strong terms, the latter view is preferred, and puts it in an equivalent relationship with 7b.

The verb *basanizō* originally meant "to test in order to prove something genuine." Used figuratively, as here, it describes any severe distress. The imperfect form, *ebasanizen* 'he was being tortured, tomented', is used to show the continuing nature of the distress.

2:8b. *Blemmati ... kai akoē* 'by what he saw ... and heard' goes with *psuchēn dikaian ... ebasanizen* 'his righteous soul ... he was tormenting'. It is expressed by a means clause, with the sense being completed by *anomois ergois* 'lawless deeds', i.e., by means of his seeing and hearing those wicked men behave in such a lawless manner.

2:8c. The participial clause *egkatoikōn en autois* 'living amongst them' states the time of 8a, with *en autois* 'amongst them', referring to "the unrighteous/wicked men."

2:9-10c. These verses provide the conclusion to the preceding clause, beginning with *ei* 'since', in 2:4, and which stated the grounds. The conclusion is that the Lord saves the righteous and punishes the unrighteous.

2:9a. The verb *rhuomai* means "save, rescue, deliver, preserve someone or something" for a definite purpose or a suitable time; cf. also 2:7a. The infinitive *ruesthai* is used here following *oiden* 'he knows how, is able'. The object *eusebeis* 'righteous people' precedes the verb because it is in contrast with *adikous* 'the unrighteous' in the following clause.

2:9b. *Ek peirasmou* 'out of testing/trial' states the circumstances from which God delivers the righteous, i.e., when they are being tested by the excessive wickedness of those around them.

2:9c. The conjunction *de* introduces God's dealings with the unrighteous which contrast with his mercy to the righteous.

Oiden kurios 'the Lord knows how is able' is understood and so is made explicit in the display as "(he is able)."

As in 2:9a, the object precedes the infinitive because of the contrast, *adikous ... tērein* 'ungodly people ... to keep'. Note that the *tērin* 'to keep' repeats the *tēroumenous* 'being kept' of 2:4.

The participle *kolazomenous* 'being punished' implies, that whilst awaiting their final punishment, they are already under punishment. Some versions have "to be punished," i.e., in the future, but, since the present participle is used, the first alternative seems preferable.

2:9d. The expression *eis hēmeran kriseōs* 'until the day of judgement' is also used in 3:7, while, in 3:10, we have *hēmera kuriou* 'the day of the Lord', and, in 3:12, *hē tou theou hēmera* 'the day of God'. Also, in 2:4c, there is the briefer expression *eis krisin* 'until judgement'.

The time when God will finally condemn all ungodly people is indicated by this expression.

2:10a. The superlative adverb *malista* 'especially, particularly' introduces those whom God singles out particularly as objects of his wrath.

2:10b. The *tous* 'them' refers to the ungodly people of 2:9c and d. Peter has been talking in general terms of the ungodly in the previous verses, but now he goes on to describe *tous opisō sarkos . . . poreuomenous* 'those who after the flesh . . . follow', i.e., those who indulge their fleshly lusts.

The participle *poreuomenous* with *opisō* 'going, proceeding, traveling after' is here used figuratively, in the sense "seek a close relation with, indulge" themselves in all sorts of carnal lusts.

The noun *sarkos* 'flesh' literally means the material that covers the bones of a human or animal body. Sometimes it is used of the physical or sinful side of man as opposed to the spiritual, and this seems to be the case here. These people are indulging the physical side of their nature to an excessive degree.

The genitive construction *en epithumia miasmou* 'in the lust of uncleanness' involves two abstract nouns, both representing events. The second event is the result of the first event, i.e., they are defiled as a result of their lusting after those things which are evil. The same construction occurs in 2:1 with *haireseis apōleias* 'false teachings of destruction', i.e., "those things which are false and result in destruction."

Since it is apparent that these false teachers not only desired what is sinful but acted according to their desires, as we see in the next paragraph, this clause has been expressed by "by (doing those deeds which they) lust after (and which) defile (them)."

This clause and 2:10c provide identification of the "ungodly people" in 2:10a.

For *epithumia* 'lust', see also 1:4, 2:18, and 3:3.

2:10c. *Kuriotētos* means "ruling power, lordship, dominion" and especially the power that the *kurios* 'lord' wields. Here it probably means both divine and earthly power and authority. These ungodly people flout the authority of the church and of the state, and, by doing so, despise divine authority, since all these people rule because God has ordained that they should do so. It has been represented by "(all beings who) rule (over them)," to include both earthly and heavenly authority.

SECTION CONSTITUENT 2:10d-22
(Paragraph cluster) (Role: Conjoined Heads of 2:4-22)

THEME: *Because these false teachers will behave wickedly and will entice people to behave in the same way as they do, God will destroy them.*

BOUNDARIES AND COHERENCE

The initial boundary of this unit is marked by a sudden change of construction in the middle of 2:10. The wicked persons who were the ob-

RELATIONAL STRUCTURE	CONTENTS
HEAD1	(2:10d-16) Because these false teachers will behave wickedly God will destroy them.
HEAD2	(2:17-22) Because these false teachers will entice people to behave wickedly God has reserved darkest hell for them.

ject of the preceding sentence now become the subject, as Peter goes on to describe their behaviour in more detail. There is also a change of person, from third singular to plural, since God is no longer the agent, as he had been in the preceding paragraph.

There is also a change of focus in 2:10d. In 2:4-10c there was a general indictment of ungodly behaviour, but now our attention is drawn to a particular type of ungodly person by *malista* 'especially', at the end of 2:4-10c, i.e., to those who follow their own corrupt desires and who flout all authority. These, then are described in detail in 2:10d-22.

The final boundary is marked by the two proverbs in 2:22, and by Peter once more addressing his readers directly as *agapētoi* 'dear ones', in 3:1, with an accompanying change of verb forms to first person singular.

The boundary between the two paragraphs which constitute this para graph cluster is not clearly defined grammatically, but there is a change of focus in 2:17, which, coupled with the illustration of Balaam in 2:16 and the two figures in 2:17, indicates the start of a new paragraph. (For further details, see notes on paragraph 2:10d-16.)

The false teachers are the subject of both these paragraphs, and they are referred to throughout. In 10d-16 the focus is on their licentious behaviour, and in 17-22 it is on the ultimate consequences for them, and all who follow them, of such behaviour.

There are a number of parallels between the constituents 10d-16 and 17-22, which support their being analysed as a paragraph cluster, i.e., a pair of paragraphs which functions as a unit parallel with a single paragraph. They are as follows:

1. In both, the false teachers and their followers are the agents.
2. In both, the false teachers are compared to animals; cf. 2:12 and 2:22.
3. In both, they are described as having known the right way and then turned aside from it; cf. 2:15 and 21.

PROMINENCE AND THEME

Neither of these paragraphs is marked for prominence and so the theme statement for 2:10d-22 is based on the theme statements for both.

PARAGRAPH CLUSTER CONSTITUENT 2:10d-16
(Paragraph) (Role: Head₁ of 2:10d-22)

THEME: *Because these false teachers will behave wickedly, God will destroy them.*

BOUNDARIES AND COHERENCE

The initial boundary of this paragraph has been discussed with reference to the final boundary of the previous paragraph. (See section on Boundaries and Coherence 2:4-10c.)

There seem to be no clear grammatical signals marking the final boundary of this paragraph. It is, rather, its referential coherence which marks it off as a unit, and only a change of subject matter enables a boundary to be drawn. Even then, the change is not complete, in that Peter is still talking about the false teachers, but the focus changes, from their greed, lasciviousness, and lack of respect for authority, to the deceitful nature of what they teach, cf. 2:17 where this is introduced in two figures of speech.

At the beginning of verse 17, Peter switches from the illustration of Balaam with which this paragraph (2:10d-16) closes, back to the false teachers, cf. *houtoi* 'they', and the use of an illustration may be an indication of closure, since he has something similar at the end of the next paragraph in the two proverbs he quotes in verse 22.

In this paragraph (2:10d-16), as in all the paragraphs of this section, the false teachers are the subject and are referred to repeatedly throughout. They are mentioned in every verse until the illustration of Balaam begins in 2:15d. This, along with the consistent use of the present tense throughout (only changing to aorist with the illustration of Balaam), is a unifying feature of the paragraph.

Peter strongly denounces the false teachers, as he builds up a vivid picture of their unlicensed behaviour by the use of largely figurative language. All the images evoke strongly the insatiable and defiling nature of their lusts, as we see from the following:

> *aloga zōa gegennēmena phusika eis halōsin kai phthoran* 'unreasoning beasts born for capture and destruction' (2:12)
>
> *spiloi kai mōmoi* 'blots and blemishes' (2:13)
>
> *ophthalmous echontes mestous moichalidos* 'having eyes full of adultery' (2:14)
>
> *deleazontes psuchas astēriktous* 'luring/enticing unstable souls' (2:14)
>
> *kardian gegumnasmenēn pleonexias echontes* 'having hearts trained in greed' (2:14)

The illustration of Balaam, in verses 15 and 16, with its reference to *misthon adikias ēgapēsen* 'he loved the reward of unrighteousness' reminds us of *misthon adikias* 'the reward of unrighteousness' in 2:13, and further strengthens the referential unity of the paragraph, as does other related vocabulary such as the following:

blasphēmountes 'blaspheming, insulting, speaking disparagingly of' (2:10 and 12)

blasphēmon krisin 'a railing, insulting accusation' (2:11)

tolmētai, authadeis 'presumptuous, arrogant' (2:10)

kataras tekna 'accursed children' (2:14)

The only references to anything outside the realms of vice and wickedness seem to be to *doxas* 'glorious ones' (2:10d) and to *aggeloi* 'angels' (2:11a).

With regard to the structure of this paragraph, Peter seems to be carried away by his denunciation of the false teachers, and piles up participle after participle. In verses 13 and 14, there are nine participles in succession, and in the whole paragraph, excluding the illustration about Balaam, there are only five finite verbs as opposed to fourteen participles. There are also few conjunctions, only one, *kai*, occurring between the *de* in 12a and the illustration at the end of the paragraph.

In this descriptive paragraph, there are five heads, with Head 4 consisting of three conjoined heads.

There is a certain parallelism about the first three heads, in that each of them is preceded by a clause of reason, cf. 2:10d and 10e; 2:12c and 12d; 2:13c and 13d. The fifth head also has a subordinate reason proposition related to it, but following it and not preceding it.

Heads 1 and 2 have finite verbs, cf. *ou tremousin* 'they are not afraid' (2:10e); *phtharēsontai* 'they will be destroyed' (2:12d); but Heads 3 and 5 are both exclamatory clauses consisting of two nouns and having no explicit verb, while Head 4 consists of three participial clauses. However, despite the presence of the finite verbs in Heads 1 and 2, all Heads seem to be given equal prominence.

Semantically, there seems to be a type of sandwich structure, consisting of an alternation of heads referring to the vices of the false teachers, with those referring to the punishment meted out to them by God. It is as follows:

A   *doxas ou tremousin blasphēmountes* 'they are not afraid to insult important beings (who rule over them)' (2:10e) (i.e., they despise authority, cf. 2:10c)

B   *phtharēsontai* '(as a result) they (the false teachers) will be destroyed (by God)' (2:12d)

A'   *spiloi kai mōmoi* '(these false teachers) disgrace and shame (you)' (2:13d) and 14a to 14c (i.e., they indulge their bodies by lusting after those things which defile, cf. 2:10a and b)

B'   *kataras tekna* 'they (the false teachers) are people whom (God) has cursed' (2:14d)

As can be seen, A and A' refer back to the two particular examples of wicked behaviour specified at the end of the previous paragraph, and B and

RELATIONAL STRUCTURE

	reason			
HEAD₁	HEAD			
	contrast	HEAD		
		concession		
		reason	HEAD	
			compar.	
	reason	HEAD		
HEAD₂	HEAD	HEAD		
		compar	HEAD	
			desc.	
	equiv.	HEAD		
		reason		
		reason		
HEAD₃	HEAD	HEAD		
	equiv.	HEAD		
		circ.		
	HEAD₁			
HEAD₄	HEAD₂			
	HEAD₃			
HEAD₅	HEAD	HEAD		
		reason	HEAD	
			ampli.	HEAD
				reason

(Continued)

CONTENT

(2:10d) Because (these false teachers are) extremely arrogant [DBL]

(2:10e) they are not afraid to insult important beings (who rule over people).

(2:11a) In contrast, angels do not insult them (the false teachers) when they accuse (them) before the Lord (God),

(2:11b) (even though) they (the angels) are much more powerful [DBL] (than the false teachers are powerful).

(2:12a) (Because) these (false teachers are irrational)

(2:12b) like animals are irrational [DBL]

(2:12c) they (the false teachers) speak disparagingly about things concerning which they know nothing.

(2:12d) (As a result) they (the false teachers) will be destroyed (by God)

(2:12e) like irrational animals (are destroyed by man),

(2:12f) (which animals) are born in order that they should be captured and destroyed;

(2:13a) (that is), they (the false teachers) will be punished

(2:13b) (because) they have acted unrighteously.

(2:13c) Because it pleases them that they should indulge themselves in the daytime

(2:13d) (these false teachers) disgrace (you) greatly, [DBL]

(2:13e) (that is) they (the false teachers) indulge themselves as they please

(2:13f) (while) they (the false teachers) feast with you.

(2:14a) They (the false teachers) want to commit adultery constantly,

(2:14b) and they never stop craving opportunities in order that they might sin.

(2:14c) They (the false teachers) entice people who are unstable (spiritually, to join them).

(2:14d) They (the false teachers) are people whom (God) will curse

(2:14e) (because) they have become more and more greedy (for material gain).

(2:15a) They behaved (wickedly) like this (14e)

(2:15b) because they rejected good moral standards.

(Continued)

RELATIONAL STRUCTURE   (continued)

illus.	HEAD				
	ampli.of	HEAD			
	content of "imitated"	contra-	HEAD	HEAD	
		expect.			reason
			equiv.	HEAD	
					means

B' refer to the punishment these people will receive as a result of their evil behaviour.

Martens (1975) suggests that the two ideas introduced in 2:10a-c are developed in a chiastic way in 2:10d-16, i.e., *kuriotētos katatphronountas* 'despising (all beings who) rule' [2:10c] is developed in 2:10d-13b and *opisō sarkos en epithumia miasmou poreuomenous* 'indulging their bodies by (doing) (those deeds which they) lust after (and which) defile (them)' [2:10a-b] is developed in 2:13d-16.

On the basis of this, he posits two paragraphs rather than one, although he admits that there is no clear-cut boundary between them. He does, however, put forward several other reasons in support of this analysis, as follows:

1. Peter uses two plays on words; in 12d, *en tē phthora outōn kai phtharēsontai* 'in their destruction they will be destroyed', and in 13a, *adikoumenoi misthon adikias* 'suffering wrong as the wages of wrong'. These belong together, both expressing the result of their insubordinate attitude.
2. *hedonēn hegoumenoi tēn en hēmera truphēn* 'it pleases them that they should indulge themselves in the day time' (2:13c) is the first mention of the false teachers' immoral behaviour.
3. Beginning a paragraph at 13c places the phrase *misthon adikias* 'wages of unrighteousness' near the end of both paragraphs, cf. 13a-b and 15d.

It would be possible to analyse these verses in this way, but it seems preferable to regard them as one paragraph, since the likeness of the false teachers to the *aloga zōa* 'irrational animals' is not only evidenced in their despising authority but also in the behaviour described in 13c-16, which demonstrates that they are completely controlled by their physical desires. Also, although the illustration of Balaam focuses on his greed, it also has

---

CONTENT (continued)

(2:15c) They imitated (what) Balaam the son of Bosor (did).

(2:15d) He (Balaam) desired that he should be paid because he had acted unrighteously.

(2:16a) (Although he desired to be paid) he (Balaam) was rebuked (by God)

(2:16b) because he (Balaam) had done that which was wrong;

(2:16c) that is, a dumb donkey hindered the prophet (Balaam), when he (Balaam) would have behaved very foolishly,

(2:16d) by means of it (the donkey) speaking like a person (speaks).

---

relevance with regard to his attitude to authority, and so to the first part of this paragraph.

The exclamatory expression, *Tolmētai, authadeis* 'Presumptuous, arrogant' (2:10d), referring to the false teachers, is prominent by reason of its position at the beginning of the paragraph and sets the theme and tone of it, i.e., the exceedingly wicked behaviour of the false teachers.

Two other exclamatory expressions, *spiloi kai mōmoi* 'blots and blemishes' (2:13) and *kataras tekna* 'accursed children' (2:14), further emphasize the theme and intensify the denunciatory nature of the paragraph, which stems from the strength of Peter's feelings about these false teachers. There is particular emphasis on *kataras tekna* because of its position following the long string of participial clauses in verse 14.

This emphasis on the extreme wickedness of the false teachers is maintained and strengthened by the number of expressions used in the paragraph which are doublets, or which may possibly be considered to be such; cf. Moore in *NOT* 53. There are seven such, in verses 10c-16, and, of these, only one is not referring to some vice or its resulting destruction. They are as follows:

> *Tolmētai, authadeis* 'bold, arrogant' (2:10a)
>
> *ischui kai dunamei* 'might and power' (2:11b)
>
> *aloga zōa ... phusika* 'unreasoning animals ... creatures of instinct' (2:12)
>
> *en tē phthora autōn kai phtharēsontai* 'in the destruction of them they will be destroyed' (2:12)
>
> *spiloi kai mōmoi* 'blots and blemishes' (2:13d)
>
> *entrouphontes ... suneuochoumenoi* 'reveling ... as they feast' (2:13e-f)
>
> *kataleipontes ... eplanēthēsan* 'leaving behind ... they go astray' (2:15a-b)

For further details see notes.

As this is a descriptive passage with a number of heads, a more generic theme has been presented.

Heads 1, 3, and 4 describe the wickedness of the false teachers, while Heads 2 and 5 state the result of their inordinately wicked way of life, i.e., God will destroy them. The theme statement, therefore, has been based on these two general statements.

NOTES ON 2:10d-16

2:10d.   *Tolmētai* 'bold, audacious' and *authadeis* 'self-willed, stubborn, arrogant' describe the understood subject of the following verb *ou tremousin* 'they are not afraid', i.e., "the false teachers." This has been made explicit in the display, and so also has "because," to show that this clause provides the reason for the following statement 2:10e.

The two words probably constitute a doublet, since they are nearly synonymous in the context. Only one term need be used, therefore, but it is preceded by an intensifier, "extremely," so that the force of Peter's statement is not lost.

Tolmētai is used nowhere else in the New Testament and *authadeis* only here and in Titus 1:7.

2:10e.   The verb *tremo* means "tremble, quiver" but when used figuratively, as here, it means "be afraid." The construction *ou tremousin blasphēmountes* 'they are not afraid while/when insulting' consists of a present indicative, followed by a present participle, and is like that in 1:19, *kalōs poieite prosechontes* 'you do well to pay attention'; it is expressed in English by an indicative followed by an infinitive, i.e., "they are not afraid to insult." (See note on 2:2 for *blasphēmountes*.)

There is some discussion concerning *doxas* 'the glorious ones', which is ambiguous here and in Jude 8. It may refer to:
1. angels or spiritual powers: these men despise those spiritual agencies by means of which God conducts the government of the world. Some commentators even regard them as being the fallen angels mentioned in 2:4.
2. men of exalted rank such as emperors, magistrates, or even the rulers of the church.

The very fact that the expression is so indefinite would seem to indicate that it is meant to be taken generally, and, therefore, to be applied to any beings, whether spiritual or earthly, who are ordained by God to have authority over men, to a greater or lesser degree. In the display, therefore, it has been represented by "important beings who rule over people."

2:11a.   The conjunction *hopou* 'where' is a particle denoting place, but can take on a causal and temporal meaning (Arndt and Gingrich). Here it is used figuratively to state a situation in which the angels do not insult; cf. Jude 9 for a particular example of this. Sometimes it is translated "whereas," but here it has been represented by "in contrast," since it introduces a contrast between the attitude of the false teachers with that of the angels.

The verb *pherousin* 'bring, utter, make' is usually used with "word, speech, announcement, charge," etc. Here it is used with *blasphēmon krisin* 'a slanderous/insulting judgement'. The Greek adjective *blasphēmos* 'slanderous, defaming, blasphemous' has a wider application than in English, since it can be applied not only to God and to things directly connected with him but also to men, cf. Acts 6:11 where it is used in connection with Moses, and here with reference to "the false teachers." The only other places it is used in the New Testament are 1 Timothy 1:13 and 2 Timothy 3:2.

The *kat' auton* 'against them' may refer to the *doxas* 'glorious ones' or to the false teachers. The latter seems preferable, since it emphasizes the great contrast between the angels and the false teachers. While these sinful, degenerate men do not hesitate to slander those who are higher and holier than they are, the angels would not presume to slander them before the Lord, who is the only righteous judge.

The preposition *para* 'at/by the side of, beside, near, with' is followed by the genitive *kuriou* 'Lord'. "(God)" has been provided here to show that the first person in the Trinity is referred to.

2:11b. The phrase *ischui kai dunameis* is probably a doublet, since *ischui* 'might, strength, power' and *dunameis* 'might, strength, power, force' are synonymous in the context, although it has been suggested that *ischus* emphasizes the outward, physical manifestations of power, and *dunamis* the inward, spiritual, or moral virtue. It has been expressed in the display by "much more powerful," in order to maintain the idea of the great gulf that exists in this respect between the angels and the false teachers.

The comparative adjective *meizones* 'greater' is used figuratively here. It is from *megas* 'large, great' and is used of rank or dignity. The comparison may be with the *doxas* 'important beings' of the preceding verse, or the false teachers who are being described in this paragraph. The second of these seems the more appropriate. Angels have the right to complain to God of the behaviour of the false teachers by virtue of their greater power and holiness, but they, nevertheless, would not revile them.

Peter uses this same adjective in 1:4 when speaking of the great and precious promises God has given to believers.

The participle *ontes* 'being', expresses the idea "even though they are." This is one not uncommon form in which a concession is expressed in the Greek New Testament, i.e., with a present participle preceding the main verb.

2:12a. The conjunction *de* may introduce a contrast to the angels just mentioned, but is better considered to signal that the preceding *houtoi* 'these' refers to the false teachers, not the angels just mentioned; the *de* indicates the switch of reference, since the *houtoi* is potentially ambiguous here.

This clause has been included to make explicit the point of the comparison between the wild beasts described in this verse, and the false teachers.

2:12b. The conjunction *hōs* 'like' introduces the comparison between the false teachers and the *aloga zōa* 'unreasoning animals'. In this simile, various points of comparison are made explicit in 12a-f.

Apart from the parallel passage in Jude 10, *alogos* 'unreasoning' is only used in one other place in the New Testament, i.e., Acts 25:27.

Phusika 'natural, in accordance with nature', i.e., "creatures of instinct" along with *aloga zōa* 'irrational animals', is probably a doublet. (See Moore, *NOT* 53.) Both mean that these men acted according to their instincts and passions rather than to reason or conscience. The only other place it is used in the New Testament is in Romans 1:26, 27.

2:12c. The participial clause *en hois agnoousin blasphēmountes* 'reviling, speaking disparagingly about those matters concerning which they are ignorant' refers presumably to divine, spiritual matters which the false teachers cannot understand, since, like unreasoning beasts, they respond only to their physical desires.

This clause has been brought forward in the order since it is closely connected to 12a, which provides the reason for it. It demonstrates the irrational nature of these people that they would speak in a derogatory manner about matters concerning which they know nothing. The three clauses, 12a-c, represent that part of the figure to do with the behaviour of the false teachers, while 12d-f deals with the result of their behaviour.

2:12d. *Phtharēsontai* 'they will be destroyed' is the main statement in this group of clauses. The participants in the action are supplied in the display, i.e., "the false teachers" and "God," who is the agent.

It is difficult to define the function of the *kai*, but Bigg (ICC) and Green (Tyndale New Testament Commentaries) suggest that it is there for emphasis, i.e., to stress the truth of the statement, and so might be expressed by "indeed," "certainly," "surely."

2:12e. Commentators differ as to the meaning of *en tē phthora autōn* 'in their destruction/corruption'. It may mean:

1. they will be destroyed "through their corruption," taking *phthora* to mean "corruption" and *autōn* to refer to the false teachers. Their own evil behaviour will bring about their downfall.

2. they will be destroyed "like the animals are destroyed," taking *phthora* to mean "destruction" and *autōn* to refer to the animals. Since they behave like animals, following their natural appetites without restraint, then they will be destroyed in the same way.

Both of these seem reasonable interpretations, but the second has been chosen for the display, following Kittel (Theological Dictionary of the New Testament) and Meyer in his commentary on 2 Peter.

Kittel agrees that the first of these is possible, i.e., "they will perish in their conduct, which destroys faith and morality," but he considers the second to be more appropriate. As the animals perish, "so the false teachers will perish too, as all things must perish in the Last Judgement, apart from those who are rescued for a new world."

Meyer understands *phthora* as "destruction" rather than "moral corruption," because it is used in that sense in this same verse, cf. *eis halōsin kai phthoran* 'for capture and destruction', and he considers it preferable to keep the same sense here.

Moore (*NOT* 43) suggests that *phthora* and *phtharēsontai* form a noun-verb doublet but this is not possible if the second alternative above is followed, since they refer to different groups, i.e., *zōa* 'the wild animals' and "the false teachers."

As in 12d, the agent has been made explicit. In this case, it is "man."

2:12f. The clause *gegennēmena eis halōsin kai phthoran* means "having been born for capture and destruction," with the abstract nouns being understood passively. The reference is to the capture of the animals with the purpose of killing them for food.

This is the only occurrence of *halōsis* 'capture' in the New Testament.

Peter uses *phthora* 'destruction, deterioration, corruption', or its related verb, five times in this letter, in 1:4; 2:12; 2:19. In this verse, we have the noun twice and the verb once, emphasizing the inevitability of their destruction (see note on 2:1d).

2:13a,b. There are alternative readings for the statement expressed in these two propositions, i.e., *adikoumenoi misthon adikias* 'suffering wrong as the reward of wrongdoing', or *komioumenoi misthon adikias* 'receiving the reward of wrongdoing'.

The expression is a figurative one, since *misthon* means literally "pay, wages" for work done. Whichever reading is preferred, the basic meaning seems to be that the destruction which is foretold for the false teachers is their just punishment for all the wicked and unrighteous deeds they have performed. This has been expressed in the display in a nonfigurative way in the two propositions 13a and 13b, which together provide the equivalent of 12d.

2:13c. The participle *hēgoumenoi* 'thinking, regarding, considering', is the first of a string of participles extending to the end of verse 14, all enumerating various ways in which the false teachers seek to satisfy their lusts. It takes a double accusative here, the two accusatives being *hēdonēn* 'pleasure, enjoyment' (in the New Testament used only in a bad sense, i.e., sensual gratification, cf. Tit 3:8; Jas 4:1,3; Lk 8:14), and *truphēn* 'indulgence, reveling'.

The false teachers consider reveling a pleasure. The only other occurrence of *truphē* in the New Testament is in Luke 7:25.

The statement is qualified by *en hēmera* 'in the day', which may be understood literally to mean "daylight, daytime," or may imply a contrast between this present moment and the future, and the transitory nature of the pleasure.

It has been understood as the former, since there seems little reason not to accept a literal interpretation here, and it emphasizes the shameless nature of these people, in that they indulge themselves so blatantly, making no effort to hide their disgraceful behavior under the cover of darkness.

2:13d. The nouns, *spiloi* 'blots, stains, blemishes' and *mōmoi* 'blemishes, defects', are used figuratively here to describe the false teachers who, by their evil behaviour, bring disgrace upon true believers by their association with them, spoiling their witness in the same way that spots and blemishes disfigure a person or thing.

Spiloi is found only here and in Eph 5:27 in the New Testament, while *mōmoi* is found only here.

Moore, in *NOT* 53, classifies these two terms as a doublet, since the literal meanings are very close and the figurative meanings are identical. A single term can, therefore, be used in a translation, and, as the figure is a dead one, the meaning can be stated nonfiguratively as, "(these false teachers) disgrace (you) greatly," with the qualifying adverb "greatly" helping to maintain the intensity of Peter's denunciation.

2:13e. The participle, *entruphōntes* 'reveling, carousing, luxuriating', looks back to *truphēn* 'reveling, indulgence' earlier in the verse. The verb generally denotes complete wantonness. It only appears here in the New Testament.

The phrase, *en tais apatais autōn* 'in their deceits/lusts', still refers to the false teachers. There is some disagreement, however, as to whether it should read *apatais* 'deceits/pleasures' or *agapais* 'love-feasts', although the first of these is the more commonly accepted alternative; (both UBS 3 and Majority Text). These people disgrace other believers by openly indulging their lusts even while associating with Christians, either at love-feasts or possibly just ordinary social occasions.

2:13f. The participial clause, *suneuōchoumenoi humin* 'while feasting with you', is subordinate to the previous clause, stating the circumstances in which it occurred. The only other occurrence of the verb in the New Testament is in Jude 12.

Moore suggests that *entruphōntes* 'reveling' and *suneuōchoumenoi* 'feasting' form a doublet but, in the display, they have been expressed separately, since the former seems to have more the idea of indulgence than the latter. The New Bible Commentary suggests that the latter is a more neutral word and possibly implies merely sitting down to eat together.

2:14a. The adjective *mestous* means "full" literally, but here it is used figuratively. It is followed by the genitive case, *moichalidos* 'an adulteress', or, in some versions, *moicheias* 'adultery'. In either case, the meaning is that these men are so completely engrossed in satisfying their sensual desires that they cannot look at any woman without wanting to commit adultery with her. This has been expressed nonfiguratively.

2:14b. The adjectival phrase, *kai akatapaustous hamartias* 'and unceasing restless/insatiable for sin', is still referring to the eyes of the false teachers, continually looking for new opportunities for indulging in sin. No matter how often they seek to gratify their lusts, they remain unsatisfied and continue to crave opportunities to sin.

This is the only occurrence in the New Testament of the adjective *akatapaustos*.

2:14c. The participle, *deleazontes* 'luring, enticing', when used in its literal sense, is applied to catching animals with bait, but is a dead figure here. It is used figuratively to describe the way in which the false teachers try to persuade others to indulge in the same sinful way of life as their own, using deceitful means to do so, cf. also verse 18.

The only other occurrence of this verb in the New Testament is in Jas 1:14.

The *psuchas astēriktous* 'unstable souls' are those who are spiritually weak or unstable because they do not have a firm foundation for their faith and so are easily deceived by false teaching, cf. also 3:16, the only other occurrence of *astēriktos* in the New Testament.

2:14d. The exclamatory *kataras tekna* 'accursed children' describes the state of the false teachers as destined for or worthy of damnation. It is connected with 14e which provides the reason for this accursed state, and also with what follows in verses 15 and 16, which illustrate how they came to this state by citing the example of Balaam which they have followed. "God" has been supplied as the agent of the cursing, and "the false teachers" as the recipients of the curse.

2:14e. The verb *gumnazō* 'to exercise/train in/by something' is usually used of an athlete training for the games, but can be used figuratively of training one's mental or spiritual powers, cf. also 1 Tim 4:7; Heb 5:14 and 12:11. It contrasts with *astēriktous* 'unstable', in the previous clause. This perfect passive participle applies to the hearts of the false teachers, which have been well trained in *pleonexia* 'greediness, avarice, covetousness', cf. also 2:3. They have so gratified every desire as they have felt it, that they have conditioned themselves to desire more and more. As soon as one craving has been satisfied, another takes its place.

It has been expressed nonfiguratively in the display by "they have become more and more greedy."

In verses 15 and 16, Peter compares the false teachers to the false prophet Balaam.

2:15a. The aorist indicative, *eplanēthēsan* 'they have gone astray', is the main verb in this cluster of propositions, describing the likeness of the false teachers to Balaam. It is used figuratively to mean that they have ceased to obey the Lord's teaching and so no longer behave in a godly and righteous way. It is expressed in a nonfigurative way in the display.

2:15b. The present participle, *kataleipontes* 'forsaking', is in some versions replaced by the aorist participle, *katalipontes* 'having forsaken', which is in keeping with *eplanēthēsan* (aorist indicative) and *exakolouthēsantes* (aorist participle). It is used here with *eutheian hodon* 'the right/straight way/road' which is a common metaphor in Scripture for upright conduct and obedience to God's commandments.

In verse 2, Peter uses a similar expression, *hē hodos tēs alētheias* 'the way of truth', to describe the Christian way of life and its teaching. As with *eplanēthesan*, this has been expressed nonfiguratively in the display.

Moore suggests that *eplanēthēsan* and *kataleipontes* form a positive-negative doublet, but there would seem to be an element of the meaning missing if only one term was used, since "forsaking" seems to imply something deliberate, cf. 15c "they rejected good moral standards," and it was when they did this that they began to behave in such an extremely wicked manner.

2:15c. The participial clause, *exakolouthēsantes tē hodō tou Balaam tou Bosor* 'having followed the way of Balaam the (son) of Bosor', picks out one particular example of their wicked behaviour. Instead of living their lives according to Christian principles, they have been imitating the way in which Balaam behaved.

This again is a figure of speech which needs to be expressed in a nonfigurative manner in the display.

The verb *exakolentheō* is also used in a figurative sense in 1:16 and 2:2.

There seems to be no satisfactory explanation as to why Peter uses the form Bosor here when, in the Hebrew and the Septuagint, the form is Beor; cf. Numbers chapter 22.

2:15d. The pronoun *hos* 'who' refers to Balaam.

The clause, *misthon adikias egapēsen* 'he loved the reward of wrongdoing', makes it clear that Balaam consciously and willingly did wrong, hoping that he might profit from it. The statement recalls that of 2:13 which refers to the false teachers, i.e., *misthon adikias* 'the reward of (their) wrongdoing'. As in verse 13, the expression is a figurative one and so is stated in a nonfigurative manner in the display.

This is regarded by some commentators to refer to the counsel which Balaam gave to the Midianites for the corrupting of the Israelites, but, according to verse 16, the reference is rather to the intended cursing of the people of Israel which Balaam wanted to do for the sake of the reward he would get (Numbers 22).

2:16. The conjunction *de* introduces a statement of what happened when Balaam sought to gain financially from acting contrary to God's command. Instead of gaining what he wanted, all he received was a rebuke from the Lord.

2:16a. *Elegxin ... eschen* 'a rebuke ... he received' refers to Balaam. The agent of the rebuking was "a donkey." Both participants are stated in the display. The noun *elegxin* is used only here in the New Testament.

2:16b. *Idian paranomias* 'for his own transgression/evil doing' indicates that, although he knew that it was the will of God that he should not curse Israel, he still cherished some hope of gaining Balak's promised reward.

This is the only occurrence of *paranomia* in the New Testament.

2:16c. *Hupozugion aphōnon* 'a dumb donkey' is used in the sense that the donkey was able to bray but not to speak.

The only other occurrence in the New Testatment of *hupozugion* is in Matthew 21:5.

Ekolusen 'hindered, prevented, restrained' refers to Balaam's insatiable desire for money. The experience with the donkey (and the angel) restrained his greed, but did not prevent him from continuing on his journey. He did, in fact, continue on his way, but only because the angel instructed him to do so.

Paraphronia 'madness' indicates that Balaam was acting contrary to reason, as indeed he was, in fighting against God. The meaning would seem to be that he acted "foolishly" or "unreasonably" rather than in a mad or crazy manner.

2:16d. The participial clause, *en anthrōpou phōne phthegxamenon* 'spoke with the voice of a man', is the means by which the prophet was restrained. The donkey rebuked Balaam for his brutal striking of her and his perverse temper, i.e., the donkey rebuked him for his wicked and irrational behaviour. Also, it was the donkey's behaviour that saved Balaam from being killed by the angel.

The verb *phtheggomai* is used in verse 18 of the false teachers. The only other occurrence is in Acts 4:18.

PARAGRAPH CLUSTER CONSTITUENT 2:17-22
(Paragraph) (Role: Head₂ of 2:10d-22)

> **THEME:** *Because these false teachers will entice people to behave wickedly, God has reserved darkest hell for them.*

BOUNDARIES AND COHERENCE

In the preceding paragraph (2:10c-16), Peter has been declaiming against the lasciviousness and greed of the false teachers, and their insolent

RELATIONAL STRUCTURE

HEAD   HEAD

comp.1

comp.2

RESULT

means

ampli.   HEAD

means1

means2   HEAD

concess.   HEAD   HEAD

comp.

concess.   HEAD

means

reason   HEAD

ampli.   HEAD

ampli.   HEAD

time

comp.   HEAD   HEAD

desc.

orienter

comp.1

comp.2

illus.   HEAD

CONTENT

(2:17a) These (false teachers delude/entice/mislead people by promising what they cannot perform/ appearing to be what they (are not),

(2:17b) (like) dried-up wells/springs (delude people, by causing them to expect water from them although the wells are empty),

(2:17c) and (like) clouds (which are) blown along by strong winds (delude people by causing them to expect rain, but no rain falls).

(2:17d) (Therefore God) has reserved darkest hell for them (the false teachers).

(2:18a) (By means of) boasting proudly/in a futile manner,

(2:18b) they (the false teachers) entice those (people who have) recently ceased to behave like those (people who) act according to wrong principles;

(2:18c) (they entice them (those people in 18b) by encouraging them) to indulge their sinful nature by (doing those) evil deeds (which they) lust after (doing)/so greatly desire (to do).

(2:19a) They (the false teachers) promise them (those people in 18b) (that) they (those in 18b) can do whatever they want to do,

(2:19b) (even though) they themselves can only do those sinful deeds which are according to their sinful nature/which their sinful nature causes them to do,

(2:19c) (like) a person (who has been) defeated by someone becomes enslaved by the one who defeated him.

(2:20a) (Although) they (the false teachers) stopped doing those deeds which are pagan/heathen, and which defile/corrupt (people spiritually),

(2:20b) by (means of) knowing our(inc) Lord and Saviour Jesus Christ,

(2:20c) they (the false teachers) began doing again (those deeds (20a)), with the result that they can do nothing else except such deeds.

(2:20d) (Since they have done this (20c)) they are in a worse state (now) than (that state in which they were) before (they knew our(inc) Lord and Saviour Jesus Christ).

(2:21a) It would have been better for them (the false teachers) if they had never known about what it means to behave in a' righteous manner,

(2:21b) than, after they had done so (i.e., known how to behave in a righteous manner)

(2:21c) (that) they (should have) rejected those things which God commanded that (people) should do,

(2:21d) which (the apostles) told/taught to them.

(2:22a) That (which) has been said in the proverb (is) true concerning them (the false teachers):

(2:22b) (like) a dog (which) returns to (eat) its vomit,

(2:22c) and (like) a sow (which has) washed and then wallows (again) in the mud,

(2:22d) (so these false teachers are behaving again in an evil manner).

attitude to all authority, which will lead ultimately to their destruction. The illustration of Balaam brings the paragraph to a clear conclusion, and the initial boundary of the next paragraph, verse 17, is marked by a change of focus, as Peter turns his attention to the way in which they deceive people by what they say, and the way they behave. This is introduced by the means of two figures, 17b and 17c.

The final boundary of the paragraph is also the final boundary of the Sub-part 1:3–2:22 and has been discussed in connection with the constituent.

The false teachers are still the topic of this paragraph, as they were of the previous one, and are referred to initially by the demonstrative pronoun *houtoi* 'these', then successively by *hois* 'for whom' (2:17); *autoi* 'they themselves' (2:19); *autois* 'for them' (2:20, 21, 22).

There is strong referential coherence in the paragraph in the many lexical items used in relation to the false teachers. At the very beginning Peter compares them to *pēgai anudroi* 'dried-up springs/wells', and to *homichlai/ nephelai hupo lailapos elaunomenai* 'mists/clouds blown along by strong winds' (2:17), i.e., they raise false hopes, enticing people to follow them in their evil ways, by making promises which they are powerless to fulfil. He then goes on, in the rest of the paragraph, to reinforce this picture of the false teachers, by using vocabulary which puts into contrast the specious nature of what they teach and that which is true:

> *huperogka* 'haughty, boastful things' (2:18)—they speak as though they have something about which they can be justifiably proud, when in reality they have not.
> *mataiotētos* 'emptiness, futility' (2:18)
> *deleazousin* 'they entice' (2:18)

In contrast with these are:

> *en epignōsei tou kuriou hēmōn kai sōtēros Iēsou Christou* 'in the knowledge of our Lord and Saviour Jesus Christ' (2:20)
> *epegnōkenai tēn hodon tēs dikaiosunēs* 'to have known the way of righteousness' (2:21)
> *hagias entolēs* 'the holy commandment' (2:21)
> *tēs alēthous paroimias* 'the true proverb' (2:22)

Similarly, there are two contrastive sets of words relating to "slavery" and "freedom." On the one hand, there are those relating to "slavery":

> *douloi* 'slaves' (2:19)
> *hēttētai* 'he has been overcome/defeated' (2:19)
> *dedoulōtai* 'he is enslaved' (2:19)
> *emplakentes* 'being entangled' (2:20)
> *hēttōntai* 'they have been overcome' (2:20)

In contrast, we have those relating to "freedom":

> *apopheugontas* 'escaping' (2:18)
> *eleutherian* 'freedom' (2:19)

apophugontas 'having escaped' (2:20)

The referential coherence of the paragraph is strengthened further by the set of words relating to the wicked way of life of these people:

en epithumiais sarkos 'in lusts of the flesh' (2:18)

aselgeiais 'debaucheries' (2:18)

en planē anastrephomenous 'living in error' (2:18)

phthoras 'corruption, destruction' (2:19)

miasmata tou kosmou 'defilements of the world' (2:20)

and their ultimate condition:

hois ho zophos tou skotous tetērētai 'for whom shades of darkness are reserved' (2:17)

ta eschato cheirona tōn prōtōn 'their last state is worse than their first' (2:20)

In the Greek, this paragraph consists of five sentences, i.e., 2:17, 2:18-19, 2:20, 2:21 and 2:22, with all but the last linked to the one preceding by the conjunction *gar*. This gives a grammatical sandwich structure which coincides with the lexical one, since the first and last sentences are figures of speech which illustrate aspects of the behaviour and condition of the false teachers. These are explained and amplified in verses 18-21, which provide the filling to the sandwich.

Alternatively, it might be said that the paragraph divides into two halves, with the specious promises of the false teachers being described in 2:17a-19a, and the depraved state of the false teachers in 2:19b-22d. Grammatically this cuts across the sentence structure, but is supported by the occurrence of *autoi* 'they themselves' in 2:19b, which is one of only two nominative pronouns in the paragraph which refer to the false teachers, the other being *houtoi* 'these' in 2:17a. The one introduces their false promises and the other the teachers themselves.

PROMINENCE AND THEME

There are two finite verbs in verse 17, *eisin* 'they are', and *tetērētai* 'it has been reserved'. The first of these is the more prominent, since the second occurs in a relative clause. Also, although 2:17d may be regarded as the result of 17a, it is not the head of the propositional cluster 17a-d, since the focus here is on the behaviour of the false teachers rather than on their future punishment. However, throughout chapter 2, and also in chapter 3, the judgement and destruction of the false teachers and all ungodly people is referred to repeatedly, so that clearly it is an important theme. The theme statement for this paragraph, therefore, is based on both 2:17a and 17d.

The other finite verbs in this paragraph are not associated with prominent information. *Deleazousin* 'they entice' (2:18b) introduces an explanation/amplification of the preceding figures, which is developed in the following verses.

The final sentence is introduced by the finite verb *sumbebēken* 'it has been said', which is an orienter for the two proverbs in 2:22, which comment on the final condition of the false teachers by providing an illustration.

The other finite verbs in 2:19-21 occur in a relative clause or an "if" clause, with the exception of *en* in 2:21.

The theme statement of the paragraph, therefore, is taken from the head, 2:17a, which is the (nonfigurative) meaning of the two metaphors used in 17b and c, and on the RESULT clause, 2:17d.

NOTES ON 2:17-22

2:17a. The demonstrative pronoun *houtoi* 'these' is used to emphasize persons already mentioned, i.e., the *pseudodidaskaloi* 'false teachers' of 2:10-16.

2:17a-c. The figure *pēgai anudroi* 'dried-up wells/springs' is used only here in the New Testament, although in Jude 12 we have *nephelai anudroi* 'clouds without water'. According to Arndt and Gingrich, it is an expression used typically of sinners.

The noun *pēgē* means literally "spring, fountain," but it is used a number of times in the New Testament figuratively, when eternal life is referred to, cf. Jn 4:14; Rev 21:16; 7:17.

The adjective *anudroi* 'waterless, dry' is used only in Mt 12:43 and Lk 11:24, besides here and in Jude.

The figure is regarded as a live one since the proper sense of the image is not called to mind directly. It is necessary to consider the primary senses of the words first, in order to understand the metaphor, and then the comparison must be made explicit.

What then is the point of similarity between the false teachers and "dried-up springs/wells"? Both attract people to them by appearing to be what they are not, by promising what they cannot give, by raising hopes which cannot be fulfilled. Both disappoint expectations, and neither fulfils the function for which it was intended. People expect to be able to draw water from a well. If it is dried-up, then their hopes are disappointed. Similarly, people expect to learn what is right and true from teachers, so that when these false teachers speak and behave in an immoral and wicked manner, with apparent freedom and impunity, they think that they can do the same.

The noun *homichlai* 'mists, fog', which occurs in the other figure in this verse, *homichlai hupo lailapos elaunomenai* 'mists driven/blown along by strong winds', is found only here in the New Testament. Because of this, and the occurrence of *nephelai* 'clouds' in the parallel passage, Jude 12, some MSS have *nephelai* instead of *homichlai*.

The preposition *hupo* 'by', with the present passive participle of the verb, *elaunomenai* 'being driven along', denotes agent or cause, which here is *lailapos* 'whirlwind, hurricane, fierce gust of wind'. This noun is used in the New Testament only here and in Mk 4:37 and Lk 8:23.

If the reading *homichlai* 'mists' is preferred, then the point of similarity would be that, just as mists are quickly dispersed by strong winds, so the false teachers and what they teach will soon come to nothing because of their basic instability.

If, however, the reading *nephelai* 'clouds' is preferred, then the point of similarity is the same as that in the first figure, i.e., the false teachers raise false hopes in people by their promises, just like clouds which cause people to hope for rain and then are blown away by the wind without any rain falling.

2:17d. The relative pronoun *hois* 'for them', as with *houtoi* (2:17a), refers to the false teachers.

The phrase *ho zophos tou skotous* 'the gloom of darkness' is reminisicent of *seirais zophou* 'in chains of gloom/darkness' in 2:4. Apart from these two occurrences, the only other places where the noun *zophos* 'gloom, darkness' is used in the New Testament are Heb. 12:18 and Jude 6 and 13, the last-mentioned being in conjunction with *skotous* 'darkness' as here. The phrase, which refers to a place of future punishment, emphasizes the intensity of the darkness, and in the display has been expressed by "darkest hell."

The prefect passive indicative *tetērētai* 'has been kept/reserved' echoes the use of the same verb, *tēreō*, in 2:4 and 9, and foreshadows its occurrence in 3:7. In each of these it is used in connection with *krisis* 'judgement', and here, of the place to which these false teachers will be consigned on that day of judgement.

In the display, "God" has been supplied as the agent of the (passive) action.

The Majority Text includes *eis aiōna* 'for ever', which is also included in the parallel passage in Jude 13.

2:18. The conjunction *gar* may be regarded as introducing further justification for the retribution promised in 17d, or further description, expanding upon the figures in verse 17. The latter has been presented in the display.

2:18a. The adjective, *huperogka*, which means literally, "of excessive size, puffed up, swollen," is used figuratively here, in the sense of "haughty, bombastic, boastful." Its only other occurrence in the New Testament is in Jude 16. Alford remarks that this adjective conveys the idea of "something larger than it has any right to be, something excessive," and this is very applicable here. It refers to what the false teachers have to say, describing their high-sounding speeches, which are completely lacking in truth and substance.

The noun *mataiotēs* 'emptiness, futility' is used in the genitive, following *huperogka* 'boastful things', i.e., 'boastful things of futility'. It is used only here and in Rom. 8:20 and Eph. 4:17, although the adjective *mataios* 'futile' is used elsewhere; cf. 1 Pet. 1:18 *mataias ... anastrophēs* 'futile ... ways'. What the false teachers say may sound impressive, but it does no real good; the impressiveness is merely outward.

The verb *phtheggomai* means literally "to produce a sound" or "to call out loudly" and is generally used for "speak, utter, proclaim" something. Peter used it in verse 16 of this chapter, and the only other occurrence in the New Testament is in Acts 4:18. The present participle, which is used here, can be expressed by "when they speak ... " or "by speaking ... ," to show either a time or a means relationship to the main verb *deleazousin* 'they entice'. The latter has been preferred in the display, and the whole clause can be expressed as "(by means of) boasting in a futile manner/proudly" or "(by means of) speaking in a boastful and futile manner."

2:18b. The verb *deleazousin* 'they lure, entice' is used by Peter in verse 14 also, when he speaks of enticing 'those who are spiritually unstable'. Its only other occurrence in the New Testament is in James 1:14 where it occurs with *epithumia* 'lust', as it does here.

Those who are being enticed are referred to as *tous oligos apopheugon-tas tous en planē anastrephomenous* 'those who have just escaped from those living in error'. These are probably the same people as those referred to in verse 14, i.e., *psuchas astēriktous* 'unstable souls'.

The reading *oligos* 'barely, scarcely, just' is followed in most versions, although some MSS have *ontos* 'really'. In conjunction with *apopheugontas* '(people who) are escaping', the first of these would refer to those who have only just separated themselves from a pagan way of life, while the second would refer to those who have broken away completely and are possibly more firmly grounded in the Christian faith. In the context, and in view of the reference in verse 14 to *psuchas astēriktous* 'those who are unstable spiritu-ally', the first of these seems to be the more appropriate.

The participle *apopheugontas* 'escaping' is used figuratively here, as it is also in verse 20. The use of the present tense shows that they are, as it were, still in the act of flight from their former condition and not yet firmly estab-lished in the new.

The phrase *tous en planē anastrephomenous* 'those living in error' is another figurative expression. It denotes those from whom the spiritually un-stable have just separated themselves.

The present participle *anastraphomenous* means literally 'staying, living in a place', but in its figurative use here, referring to human conduct, it has the sense of 'acting, behaving, conducting oneself' according to certain prin-ciples; and, as is usual with this usage, the kind of behaviour is more exactly described, here, *en planē* 'in error'.

The noun *planē* means literally 'wandering, roaming' but is used figura-tively here of wandering from the path of truth and, therefore, means "error, delusion, deceit." Peter uses it also in 3:17, and the related verb in 2:15 and in his first letter 2:25.

In the display, these people are represented as those who "live accord-ing to wrong principles," i.e., those still living in idolatry and paganism. There is some problem as to what is meant by "escaping" from these people, since it can scarcely mean that these new believers cease to live amongst, or associate with, their pagan neighbors. Possibly it means that they are no longer influenced by them and no longer behave like them. Instead of living according to pagan principles of behaviour, they now live according to the teachings of Christ.

2:18c.   The phrase *en epithumiais sarkos aselgeiais* 'in the lusts of the flesh debaucheries' poses some problems syntactically.

First of all, should the *en* be translated "in" or is it causal, introducing a means, and being equivalent to *dia* 'through'?

Peter uses a similar phrase in 2:10, i.e., *opiso sarkos en epithumia miasmou poreuomenous* 'walking after the flesh in the lust of uncleanness'. (See note on 2:10b.) In view of this, and of the fact that he seems to use *en* in a causal sense also in 1:1, 2, 4, 13 and 2:3, and since it also makes good sense here, this is the sense represented in the display. The false teachers use the promised satisfaction of sensual desires as a bait with which to lure these people from their new-found faith and way of life, to follow them.

The noun *epithumia* 'desire, longing' is used frequently by Peter in both his letters, cf. 1 Pet 1:14; 2:11; 4:2, 3 and 2 Pet 1:4; 2:10, 18; 3:3 (see note on 1:4).

There is a further problem as to the relationship between *epithumiais sarkos* 'desires/lusts of the flesh' and *aselgeiais* 'debauchery, licentiousness, immorality, sensuality'; cf. also 2:7 and 1 Pet. 4:3. Several possible alternatives are put forward by commentators:

1. *epithumiais sarkos* and *aselgeiais* are in apposition and are both means whereby the false teachers entice people, i.e., "by lusts of the flesh, by licentiousness." Possibly the second might be regarded as explaining the first.
2. *aselgeiais* might be used to describe or qualify *epithumiais sarkos*, i.e., "licentious desires of the flesh."
3. *epithumiais sarkos* and *aselgeiais* might be regarded as a near synonymous doublet.

There seems to be no clear reason why any one of these should be regarded as preferable, and, whichever is chosen, the meaning seems to be appreciably the same, i.e., the false teachers seek to entice these people by encouraging them to indulge their sinful desires to excess.

In the display, the noun *aselgeiais* 'debauchery, sensual indulgence' is expressed by the verb "to indulge," while *sarkos* 'flesh' is expressed by "sinful/depraved nature."

The statement (2:18c) provides a second means for 18b, which is the head of the propositional cluster 18a-c, i.e., the false teachers entice these people, by encouraging them to indulge the carnal side of their nature, by doing those evil things which they so much desire to do. The first means is stated in 18a. The verb "encourage" has been included in the statement in order to complete the sense.

2:19.   Peter now goes on to give a further means whereby these false teachers entice people to join them in their evil behaviour, i.e., *eleutherian autois epaggellomenoi* 'promising them freedom'.

2:19a.   The noun *eleutherian* 'freedom, liberty' is used especially of the freedom which stands in contrast to the constraints of the Mosaic law, looked upon as a slavery (Gal 2:4; 5:1), according to Arndt and Gingrich. But these false teachers represent freedom as exemption from the requirements of the moral law, and from obligation to serve Christ, as set out in 1:3-11. It is a false liberty of living as they please, and indulging their evil desires to the full (2:18). It is freedom from all moral restraints, which will only plunge those who trust to it back into the power of sin. They use it as an excuse to sin; cf. Gal. 5:13, and as "a cloak of maliciousness" (1 Pet. 2:16).

The subject of the present middle participle *epaggellomenoi* 'promising' is still the false teachers, and the *autois* 'to them' refers to those people they are seeking to deceive, i.e., those in 18b who have "just escaped from those living in error."

The idea that they can do whatever they want to do, which is implied in the freedom promised by the false teachers, is made explicit in the display.

2:19b.   The clause *autoi douloi huparchontes tēs phthoras* 'themselves being the slaves of corruption' provides a sharp antithesis to the preceding promise of freedom in 2:19a.

The personal pronoun *autoi* 'they themselves' refers to the false teachers, as does *douloi* 'slaves', which is used figuratively here, in the wider sense of "total subjection to" or "entirely under the control of." Its related verb *douloō* 'make someone a slave, enslave, subject someone to something' is found in this verse also; see the note on *dedoulōtai* (2:19c).

The noun *phthoras*, as used here, is generally assumed to have the sense of the moral corruption which follows in the wake of wilful self-indulgence. It also conveys the idea of spiritual death leading to final destruction, which is present also in 2:12; see the note on 1:4 and 2:12.

The present active participle *huparchontes* 'being', used here and in 3:11, is equivalent to *ontes*, the corresponding form of *einai* 'to be'.

The metaphor of "slavery to corruption" has been expressed nonfiguratively in 2:19b and c, i.e., the false teachers cannot really do as they please because they are controlled completely by their sinful nature.

The relationship between 2:19b and 2:19a could be regarded as one of concession-contraexpectation, since it would be expected that those who promise freedom to others would be free themselves, yet these false teachers are certainly not free but are controlled by their sinful nature.

Alternatively, if, as has been suggested above in the section on boundaries and coherence, the paragraph is analysed as consisting of two halves, dealing respectively, with the enticements of the false teachers (17a-19a) and the condition of the false teachers (19b-22d), then 19b, along with 20d, could be regarded as head of the propositional cluster 19b-22d, and in a descriptive relationship with the head of the paragraph, 2:17a.

2:19c. The statement *hō gar hēttētai toutō dedoulōtai* 'for by whom/what anyone has been defeated/overcome by this (person/thing) he has been enslaved' appears to have been some sort of proverb of the day. It is taken from ancient warfare, (1 Sam. 17:9), and the figure is of a person being defeated in battle and becoming the slave of the one who has defeated him. Because of this figure, it seems preferable to regard the demonstrative pronouns *hō* and *toutō* as masculine, although in the Greek they are ambiguous, being either masculine or neuter.

The verb *hēttaomai* 'be defeated/overcome by' is used in the New Testament only here and in verse 20, besides 2 Cor. 12:13, where it has the sense of "be inferior to." The perfect passive tense *hēttētai* 'he is defeated/overcome' is used here, and this, along with the perfect passive *dedoulōtai* 'he is enslaved', gives a sense of finality and completeness to the action.

The dative *toutō* with *dedoulōtai* expresses the relationship of Agent, i.e., "by whom."

The picture presented is one of complete abandonment to a sinful way of life. There is no restraint, no effort to resist their evil desires. They flagrantly indulge in those things which are contrary to God's law, and encourage others to do the same. As a result, they have become incapable of behaving in any other way, just as a person who is defeated by someone in battle can only do what the one who has defeated him allows him to do. This same thought is expressed by Paul in Rom. 6:16 and by Christ Himself in Jn 8:34.

The comparison on which 19b is based is stated explicitly here.

2:20. The initial *gar* introduces an explanation/expansion of the statement *autoi douloi huparchontes tēs phthoras* 'they themselves are the slaves of corruption' (2:19b). It is a complex verse, in that, structurally, it is a reason-result (20c and d), but the reason (20c) is itself the head of a concession-contraexpectation propositional cluster (20a and c).

2:20a. The clause *apophugontes ta miasmata tou kosmou* 'having escaped the defilements/corruptions of the world' recalls that in 1:4, *apophugontes tēs en tō kosmō en epithumia phthoras* 'having escaped the corruption in the world through lust'. Both expressions are figurative.

The aorist participle *apophugontes* 'having escaped' is expressed non-figuratively in the display as 'stopped doing/behaving'.

The noun *miasmata* 'defilements, corruptions' is found only here in the New Testament, and is used only figuratively, of moral corruption through crimes and vices; cf. also *miasmou* 'corruption, pollution' (2:10). In the Septuagint it seems to have a technical, religious sense, referring to the profanation of flesh by ordinary use, which has been set apart for sacrifice. Something of this sense may linger here, in that the body is sacred to God, and to give rein to passions is to defile it. It is regarded here then as "deeds which defile spiritually" or which "cause people to become morally depraved."

Tou kosmou 'of the world' has the sense of "everything which is at enmity with God," i.e., heathen society and its practices; cf. 1:4 and 2:18. The phrase *ta miasmata tou kosmou* 'the defilements of the world' has been expressed in the display by "those things which are pagan/heathen and which defile/corrupt a person spiritually."

There is some discussion as to whom this clause refers to. It may refer to *tous oligos apopheugontas tous en planē anastrephomenous* 'those just escaped from those living in error' (2:18b), or to the false teachers. Whoever is referred to here is also the subject of verses 21 and 22, since 20-22 clearly form a unit, with 20d as the head. In these verses Peter is saying two things about those he is describing:

1. They have gone back to their old ways after knowing the gospel, (20a-c, 21b-d, 22).
2. Their situation now, and their final condition, is worse than it was when they were ignorant of the gospel, (20d, 21a), i.e., when they were pagans. They are clearly some sort of professing Christians.

Possibly this unit is chiastic in structure:

A   They have gone back to their old ways (20a-c).
B   Their situation is now worse than before (20d).
B'   Their situation is now worse than before (21a).
A'   They have gone back to their old ways (21b-d, 22).

Those commentators who argue that those referred to are "those just escaped from those living in error" argue that:

1. *gar* 'for' looks back to 2:18 and enlarges on the awful consequences of being deceived by the false teachers and following their teaching.
2. the verb *apopheugontas* 'having escaped' (2:18) is the same as that used here in 2:20, and the *ta miasmata tou kosmou* 'the defilements of the world' (2:20) echoes *en epithumiais sarkos aselgeiais* 'through the desires of the flesh in the debaucheries' (2:18).
3. the language used in verses 20-22, and the warning which it conveys, is not harsh enough for the condemnation of the false teachers and is more appropriate as a warning to recent converts.

Those who consider that the false teachers are being referred to argue that:

1. the *gar* 'for' seems to refer back to *autoi douloi huparchontes tēs phthoras* 'they themselves are slaves of corruption', i.e., the false teachers. The *hō gar hēttētai, toutō dedoulōtai* 'for by whoever someone is defeated, by that person he is enslaved' is a parenthetical comment.
2. *hēttōntai* 'defeated/overcome', in 2:20, is exactly the same verb used of the false teachers in 2:19 explaining how they are slaves.

3. the condemnation and warning in verses 20-22 is too harsh for recent converts, who have not yet fallen away but are being tempted.
4. the whole of chapter two is a sustained polemic against these false teachers, so it seems fitting that it should continue to the end of the chapter.

In the display it has seemed preferable to regard those being referred to as the false teachers, in consideration of the arguments expressed above, and also for the following reasons:

a) It seems natural for the clause in 20a to refer to the false teachers, since they are the subject in verses 18 and 19. It would seem unnatural if those they seduce were considered to be the subject here, when they were the object in 2:18.

b) As has been said above, the whole of the chapter preceding this verse has been given over to a description of the false teachers, and it would be surprising if Peter should turn suddenly from them to describe an entirely different set of people, without in some way indicating the transition from one to the other.

c) The description in 20 and 21 of people who have known the truth and then turned aside from it accords well with that of the false teachers in 2:1, in that they also denied the truth and brought upon themselves terrible destruction.

2:20b. The preposition *en* has the force of "through, by means of," hence, *en epignōsei tou kuriou hēmōn kai sotēros Iēsou Christou* 'by means of the knowledge of our Lord and Saviour Jesus Christ'.

See note on 1:2 for *epignōsis* 'knowledge'. It is used also in 1:3 and 1:8.

In view of the final punishment which we are told befell these people (2:17), they did not know Christ truly as their Saviour. The knowledge which they had of him was not a full and saving one, but one which brought about a temporary and superficial attempt to lead a reformed life, with no real spiritual reformation.

This clause provides the means for 2:20a.

2:20c. The conjunction *de* 'nevertheless, yet' puts 20a and 20c in a concession-contraexpectation relationship.

The adverb *palin* 'again' goes with the aorist passive participle *emplakentes*, which, in its literal sense, refers to a sheep caught in a thicket by its wool. Here it is used figuratively in the sense 'be involved in'. Its only other occurrence in the New Testament is in 2 Tim. 2:4.

This use of *emplakentes*, along with *deleazousin* 'they entice' (2:18) and *deleazontes* 'enticing' (2:14), reinforces the idea of how dangerous the false teachers are. They had made a Christian profession, and, despite falling away, were, perhaps, still professing to be believers. This would make them all the more dangerous, for some would trust what they said, thinking they were true believers.

The demonstrative pronoun, *toutois* 'in/by these', refers back to *ta mias-mata tou kosmou* 'the defilements of the world', and is to be understood with both the participle *emplakentes* 'having been involved' and *hētttōntai* 'have been defeated'.

Hēttōntai 'have been defeated' recalls *hēttētai* in verse 19, when Peter made a general statement to the effect that a man becomes the slave of whoever/whatever defeats him. (See note on *hēttētai* in 2:19.) Here we have been told that it is *ta miasmata tou kosmou* 'the defilements of the world' to which the false teachers have succumbed.

2:20d.　This is the result of the reason introduced by *ei* and stated in 2:20c.

The statement *gegonen autois ta eschata cheirona tōn prōtōn* 'for them the last things have become worse than the first' appears to have been a proverb of the day; cf. Lk 9:26; Mt 12:45; 27:64.

The perfect form of the verb, *gegonen* 'has become' needs to be expressed by the present tense, "is," since "has become" conveys the idea that it was not always so and that there has been a change.

The pronoun *autois* 'for them' refers to the false teachers again.

The noun *ta eschata* 'the last things' is used of time, in the sense of coming last, or last of something that is left (Arndt and Gingrich). Here it refers to its relation with something preceding, i.e., the state of the false teachers, after they rejected the truth of the Gospel and become completely dominated by the power of sin; cf. 2:19.

The comparative adjective *cheirona* 'worse, more severe' is followed by *tōn prōtōn* 'the first', a genitive of comparison, and stands opposed to *kreitton* 'better' in verse 21.

The adjective of time, *prōtōn* 'first, earlier, earliest' refers to the state of the false teachers before they had any knowledge of Christ.

This statement can be regarded as an amplification of 2:19b, or as a second head—2:19b being the first—in a description of the false teachers extending from 2:19b-22d.

2:21a.　The conjunction *gar* introduces an amplification of 20d.

The imperfect tense *ēn* 'it was' is expressed by the subjunctive, 'it would have been'.

The perfect infinitive *epegnōkenai* 'to have known', and the aorist participle *epignousin* 'having known', which occurs later in this verse, sustain the emphasis on knowledge which runs through this letter; cf. also 1:2, 3, 5, 6, and 3:18. Each refers to knowledge of God or Christ, except for 1:5 and 6, which nevertheless refer to knowledge of a virtuous sort.

The phrase *tēn hodon tēs dikaiosunēs* 'the way of righteousness' reminds us of *hē hodos tēs alētheias* 'the way of truth' (2:2), and *eutheian hodon* 'a straight way' (2:15). All of these contrast with *tē hodō tou Balaam* 'the way of Balaam' (2:15) and all are figurative expressions which refer to a way of life, a course of conduct; in this case, one of righteousness. *Dikaiosunē* has the sense of "righteousness, uprightness" in a moral and religious sense; the characteristic required of man by God, as the compelling motive for the conduct of one's life (Arndt and Gingrich). The 'way of righteousness' then, refers to righteous behaviour, i.e., 'how to behave righteously'.

The question arises as to the sense in which they had "known" what "the way of righteousness" involved. We are told in verse 20 that they stopped behaving according to pagan principles for a time, but that they eventually returned to their former way of life. That they did so is indicative of the fact that their conversion was apparent rather than real. Outwardly, for a time, they tried to go through the motions of righteous behaviour, but they were not motivated by righteous principles. The change in their behaviour was not accompanied by a true change of heart, therefore, we can assume that their knowledge of Christ and of what is involved in living a truly righteous life was superficial. It could be said then, that they had known of or about Christ, but that they did not know him personally or experientially.

In the display, this has been expressed as "if they had never known about what it means to behave in a truly righteous manner."

2:21b. The aorist participle *epignousin* 'having known' is in the dative case instead of the accusative that would be expected, in concord with the (understood) subject of the infinitive *epegnōkenai* 'to have known' (2:21a). Instead, it shows concord with *autois* 'to them'. The (implicit) object of *epignousin* 'having known' is the same as the object of *epegnōkenai* 'to have known', i.e., *tēn hodon tēs diaiosunēs* 'the way of righteousness'. This is made explicit in the display.

2:21c-d. There are variant readings of the aorist infinitive in this clause, as follows:

1. *hupostrepsai* 'to turn back, return, turn away (once more)'.
2. *epistrepsai* 'to turn back, return to something from something'. Figuratively, it refers to a change of mind or course of action, for better or for worse.
3. *anakampsai* 'to turn back again'.

The first or second of these is usually followed, but it is generally agreed that it is difficult to decide, with certainty, which is the original reading. In favour of *epistrepsai* is the fact that Peter uses it in 2:22 and also in 2:25 of his first letter. In any case, they are semantically equivalent here, in the sense of returning to a previous activity.

The *hagias entolēs* 'the holy commandment' probably refers to the gospel; cf. also 3:2 and 1 Tim. 6:14. This would include both how a person should behave, and how a person can become a Christian. It is holy because it comes from God and also because it shows Christians how they should live in order to be holy themselves. It is expressed in the display as 'those things (which God) commanded (that they should do)'.

The rejection of this "holy commandment" amounts also to a rejection of Christ's saving power; cf. 2:2 where the false teachers "deny the Lord who bought them."

The agent behind the aorist passive participle *paradotheisēs* 'handed down, transmitted, related, taught' is made explicit in the display as "the apostles."

The latter state of these false teachers can be said to be worse than the first, in that previously they could be said to have sinned in their ignorance, (cf. 1 Pet 1:14), but now they have chosen deliberately to reject the gospel and to return to their former sinful way of life. Their consciences have become hardened so that there is less likelihood of their repenting than previously, when they had not yet received any degree of enlightenment through the gospel. The description given by Christ in Mt 12:43-45 is true of them; cf. also Lk 12:47-48.

2:22.   In this last verse of the chapter, Peter describes further the spiritual condition of the false teachers by means of two proverbs which illustrate their return to their old ways and so demonstrate that their essential nature had never been changed or renewed, despite their outward show of reformation.

Some MSS have an initial *de* 'but' to connect this verse with the previous one, but most versions omit it.

2:22a.   The noun *paroimia* 'proverb' is only used here and in the Gospel of John, cf. Jn 10:6; 16:25, 29. It indicates a figurative mode of speech and is used in the singular because the two proverbs which follow have the same meaning.

Sumbebēken autois to tēs alēthous proimias 'the thing of the true proverb has happened to them' has the sense that what has been said in these two proverbs is true of the false teachers. The statement acts as an orienter for the rest of the verse, 22b-d.

2:22b-d.   The point of comparison in these two illustrations is made explicit in 2:22d. Both point out that the false teachers have never really changed. After a temporary, superficial reformation, they returned to their old, evil ways, just as the dog returns to eat its own vomit and the swine goes back to wallow in the mud after being washed.

The first proverb (2:22b) is found in Proverbs 26:11. Dogs and swine were both regarded by the Jews as unclean animals, hence, a description of their actions is very appropriately applied to the false teachers. The two pictures also recall the *aloga zōa gegennēmena phusika eis halōsin kai phthoran* 'irrational animals born to be captured and destroyed' (2:12).

The aorist participle *epistrepsas* 'having returned, having gone back' is in the active mood, indicating that the dog returns of its own free will.

This occurrence of the noun *exerama* 'vomit' is the only one in the New Testament. The implication is that the dog returns to eat its own vomit, and this has been made explicit in the display.

The second proverb (2:22c), although not found in the Old Testament writings, was common in the Rabbinical writings, and is found in the Greek classics.

The verb *louō* 'wash' is usually used of washing the whole body. Here, *lousamenē* the reflexive middle participle is used, which is relatively rare in the New Testament.

Instead of the sense expressed in the display, i.e., after it has been washed the sow returns to wallow in the mud, some commentators consider that the sense is rather that having once bathed in filth, it never ceases to delight in it and constantly returns to it. The former sense, however, is more appropriate here.

Some versions supply *epistrepsasa* 'turns back', before *eis* 'to', from what precedes in 22b. This does seem to be the sense, although, as often in a proverb, the form is elliptical and it is not included in the Greek.

The noun *kulismon* 'rolling, wallowing' is used only here in the New Testament. Some MSS read *kulisma* which is equivalent to *kulistra* 'a place of wallowing' but these are generally regarded as inferior ones, and it is the action of wallowing which is indicated.

The genitive *borborou* 'of mud, filth' indicates location. This is the only occurrence of the noun in the New Testament.

PART CONSTITUENT 3:1-13
(Sub-part) (Role: Head₂ of 1:3–3:13)

THEME: *You ought to behave in a godly manner, since the Lord Jesus Christ will certainly come back to judge people, and at that time God will destroy this present world and there will be new heavens and a new earth where only righteous people will live.*

RELATIONAL STRUCTURE	CONTENTS
GROUNDS	(3:1-10) Although certain people will ridicule the fact that you believe that the Lord Jesus Christ will come back, he will certainly come back to judge people, and at that time God will destroy this present world.
HEAD	(3:11-13) Therefore, you ought to behave in a godly manner since God will destroy everything like this (3:10) and since only righteous people will inhabit the new heavens and the new earth which will then begin to exist.

BOUNDARIES AND COHERENCE

The boundaries of this constituent have been discussed in connection with the structure of the body of the Epistle.

This unit centres on the subject of "the Day of the Lord," which includes the return of the Lord Jesus Christ in judgement, the accompanying destruction of this present world, and how believers ought to behave in expectation of all this. The vocabulary used throughout these verses, therefore, is related to these different aspects of that day, which is referred to directly as *hēmeran kriseōs kai apōleias* 'day of judgement and destruction' (3:7); *hēmera kuriou* 'day of the Lord' (3:10); and *tēs tou theou hēmeras* 'the day of God' (3:12).

Although these verses deal with the Day of the Lord, there is a change of emphasis at 3:11. Verses 3-10 deal with the arguments of those who ridicule belief in such an event, while verses 11-13 focus on how Christians should live in expectation of that day. There are two parts to this constituent therefore, the one expository (3:1-10), and the other hortatory (3:11-13), with the former providing the grounds for the latter.

PROMINENCE AND THEME

An exhortation has greater natural prominence than the grounds on which it is based, but in this case the grounds may be regarded as being marked for prominence, because they precede the exhortation, which is the reverse of the usual order. Also, they are fully developed. The theme, therefore, is to be derived from both the grounds and the head.

SUB-PART CONSTITUENT 3:1-10
(Division) (Role: Grounds for 3:11-13)

THEME: *Although certain people will ridicule the fact that you believe that the Lord Jesus Christ will come back, he will certainly come back to judge people, and, at that time, everything will be destroyed.*

RELATIONAL STRUCTURE	CONTENTS
Situational orienter	(3:1-2) I am writing this letter to you in order to stimulate you to remember what the holy prophets said and what our(inc) Lord and Saviour commanded.
HEAD	(3:3-10) Although certain people will ridicule the fact that you believe that the Lord Jesus Christ will come back, he will certainly come back to judge people, and, at that time, God will destroy this present world

BOUNDARIES AND COHERENCE

The initial boundary of this unit has been discussed in connection with the structure of the body of the Epistle. The final boundary is marked by a change of focus in 3:11, when Peter turns from presenting the arguments of those who scoff, and refutations of those arguments, to exhorting his readers to live godly lives in expectation of the coming day of judgement. The new unit which begins at 3:11 is introduced by a Genitive Absolute construction and the adverb *houtōs* 'thus, in this manner', referring back to 3:10 and supplying a summary statement as grounds for the exhortation to follow: *toutōn houtōs pantōn luomenōn* 'since all these things will be destroyed in this manner' (3:11). A further indication of a new unit commencing at 3:11 is the use of what might be termed "behaviour" vocabulary; cf. *hagiais* 'holy', *anastropheis* 'behaviour', *eusebeiais* 'godly'.

These verses are a warning to believers about certain people who will ridicule their belief that the Lord Jesus Christ will return in judgement, and that the destruction of the world by fire will accompany his return. References to *hēmeran kriseōs kai apōleias* 'the day of judgement and destruction' (3:7), and *hēmera kuriou* 'the day of the Lord' (3:10), together with references to destruction, eg., 3:6, 7, 9, 10, all contribute to the unity of this section. The first two verses, with their first person singular verb forms, and second person pronouns, as Peter addresses his readers directly, provide a situational orienter for verses 3-10. In them he states his purpose in writing to them as he does.

PROMINENCE AND THEME

The theme statement for this constituent is based on the theme statement of 3:3-10 which is the head. The theme statement of the situational orienter, 1:1-2, is not included in the theme statement for 3:1-10, but rather serves to focus attention on this second matter which he is about to deal with.

DIVISION CONSTITUENT 3:1-2
(Paragraph) (Role: Situational Orienter for 3:3-10)

THEME: *I am writing this letter to you in order to stimulate you to remember what the holy prophets said and what our(inc) Lord and Saviour commanded.*

BOUNDARIES AND COHERENCE

The initial boundary of this paragraph is also the initial boundary of 3:1-13 and has been discussed in connection with the structure of the body.

RELATIONAL STRUCTURE			CONTENT
		Ident.of "letter"	(3:1a) This letter (which) I am now writing to you whom I love, (is) the second (letter that I have written to you).
	orienter	HEAD	(3:1b) (I have written both) these (letters to you)
contrac-tion	:HEAD		(3:1c) (in order to) stimulate you to think honestly/sincerely (about things which you know already),
	means		(3:1d) by reminding you (about those things, i.e., which you know already);
HEAD1			(3:2a) (that is, in order to stimulate you) to remember the words (which) the holy prophets spoke long ago,
HEAD2	HEAD		(3:2b) and (in order to stimulate you) to remember what our(inc) Lord and Saviour commanded,
	desc./comment of/on "what our Lord and Saviour commanded"		(3:2c) (which) the apostles, (whom you can trust, told you about).

The final boundary is marked by a change of orientation, from first person singular subject, cf. *graphō* 'I am writing' (3:1); *diegeirō* 'I arouse, stimulate' (3:1), to second person plural, cf. *ginōskontes* 'knowing' (3:3), i.e., from Peter, to those whom he is addressing.

The use of *touto prōton* 'this first/above all' in verse 3, also indicates a change of focus.

There is referential coherence in this short paragraph in the reciprocal first person agent and second person recipient references, cf. *graphō* 'I am writing' and *humin* 'to you' (3:1); *diegeirō* 'I arouse, stimulate' and *humōn . . . tēn eilikrinē dianoian* 'your pure mind' (3:1).

The use of two words with the same root, i.e., *hupomnēsei* 'remembrance' (3:1) and *mnēsthēnai* 'to remember' (3:2), strengthens this coherence.

In addition, further unity is given by the use of the following:

graphō 'I am writing' (3:1)
epistolēn 'letter' (3:1)
proeirēmenōn rhēmatōn 'words spoken before' (3:2)
entolēs 'commandment' (3:2)

These all belong to the semantic set of words relating to the communication of a message, and to the list might be added *prophētōn* 'prophets' and *apostolōn* 'apostles' (3:2), since they are the vehicles for the message.

Grammatically, the paragraph consists of one sentence in the Greek, containing two finite verbs, *graphō* 'I am writing' (3:1) and *diegeirō* 'I arouse, stimulate' (3:1), followed by an infinitive, *mnēsthēnai* 'to remember' (3:2).

The first clause in the paragraph (3:1a) serves to identify the letter which Peter is writing, as the second that he has written to them, cf. *deuteran humin graphō epistolēn* 'I am writing to you a second letter', while 3:1b provides the means by which Peter hopes to achieve his purpose of stimulating them to remember what the prophets and Christ Himself had said (3:1c-2c).

Peter states his purpose in writing the letters in general terms in 3:1c, and the means whereby he hopes to achieve it in 3:1d. Although a means proposition is usually more prominent than a purpose one, in this case the purpose proposition is regarded as being the more prominent, since the theme of the paragraph is Peter's purpose in writing the letters.

The relationship between the propositional cluster 3:2a-c and 3:1c appears to be one of contraction-amplification or generic-specific, since the content is similar. What they are to remember and consider is only implied in 3:1c and is represented in the display in only general terms, i.e., "things which you know already." It is stated in more specific terms in 3:2a-c so that a generic-specific relationship could be posited. However, 3:2a-c adds further detail to 3:1c and so a contraction-amplification relationship seems to be more appropriate.

PROMINENCE AND THEME

When two propositions are in the relation of contraction-amplification, according to general principle, it is the amplification that is prominent. The two propositions 3:2a and 3:2b are, therefore, naturally prominent and joint heads of the paragraph. The theme statement, then, is based on the two head propositions plus the means proposition 3:1b, which is necessary to complete the sense of the statement.

NOTES ON 3:1-2

3:1a.   Peter uses *agapētoi* 'dear/beloved ones' three times in this last chapter, and each time in a significant context. When he uses it in verses 14 and 17, it is followed by an imperative form of the verb, cf. *spoudasete* 'strive' (3:14) and *phulassesthe* 'beware, be on your guard' (3:17). In 1:10, where he uses the vocative *adelphoi* 'brothers', this also is followed by an imperative, *spoudasate* 'strive', which stresses the need for action.

The repeated use of the vocative in this chapter indicates the urgency and intensity of Peter's feelings, and how greatly he desires that his readers should understand his message and act upon it.

There is some discussion as to whether the adverb *ēdē* 'now, already' should be connected with *graphō* 'I am writing' or *deuteran* 'second', but this does not seem materially to affect the sense.

Tautēn ... deuteran humin graphō epistolēn 'This ... second letter I am writing to you' is taken by commentators generally as an indication that 1 Peter is the first letter, although there is no definite proof that this is so; a previous letter of Peter's to the same people, which had been destroyed, might be intended.

Even if we conclude that 1 Peter is the first of the two letters referred to here, it need not follow that those to whom it is addressed, i.e., *humin* 'to you', should live in the four Anatolian provinces named in 1 Peter, since the earlier letter, by this time, had probably reached a wider audience which Peter could be including here.

The statement is one of identification of the letter which he is writing now.

3:1b.   The relative phrase *en hais* 'in which', i.e., in both these letters, refers to the contents of them. The verb has been repeated in the display and the resulting statement provides the means for the rest of the paragraph, which states Peter's purpose in writing the letters.

3:1c.   The expression *diegeirō ... en hupomnēsei* 'I arouse ... by way of a reminder' is the same as that used in 1:13. See note on that verse.

The verb *diegeirō* 'I arouse' is followed by an accusative phrase, which here is *tēn eilikrinē dianoian* 'the pure/sincere mind'.

The adjective *eilikrinē* means literally "unmixed, unadulterated." From this it comes to mean "unsullied," and here, according to Ellicott, it probably means "untainted by sensuality, or possibly deceit." In Philippians 1:10, the only other place in the New Testament where it occurs, it is translated "sincere," and its related noun *eilikrineia*, in 1 Cor 5:8 and 2 Cor 1:12 and 2:17, is translated "sincerity." Probably the sense in Paul's letters is one of purity of motive, while here, perhaps, it is "uncontaminated by sin."

The noun *dianoia* 'mind' means "the faculty of moral reflection and moral understanding" (Ellicott). Peter uses it also in his first letter (1:13) where he tells his readers that they should keep it exercised and ready for constant use. He regards their minds as being uncontaminated by sensual passions, and their powers of thought undistorted by the destructive heresies of the false teachers. They are morally sound, with their will and affections turned to God, in contrast with the false teachers, as described in chapter 2, of whom the phrase *eskotōmenoi tē dianoia* 'darkened in understanding' (Eph 4:18) is true.

In conjunction with *diegeirō* 'I arouse, stimulate' the meaning would seem to be that he wants to stimulate them to 'honest thought', i.e., to think honestly and sincerely, and, since he hopes to do so by a reminder, the object of their thoughts must be something which they know already, so this has been stated in the display.

3:1d. The phrase *en hupomnēsei* 'by a reminder' is expressed as a means proposition, and, as in 3:1c, what they are to be reminded of is made explicit, i.e., "those things which you know already."

3:2a. The aorist infinitive *mnēsthēnai* 'remind oneself, recall to mind, remember' is one of purpose or definitiion. It expresses what Peter hoped to achieve by his reminders, i.e., that he would cause them to remember for themselves the important truths which they knew already and which are to be found in the teachings of the prophets of the Old Testament and the apostles of the New Testament.

The reference here to *tōn proeirēmenōn rhēmatōn hupo tōn hagiōn prophētōn* 'the words spoken before by the holy prophets' is reminiscent of Jude 17, except that in Jude the words are those of the "apostles of our Lord Jesus Christ."

Great weight is attached to prophecy by the apostle Peter, as we see by this and further references in his letters, cf. 2 Peter 1:19-21 and 1 Peter 1:10-12.

The noun *rhēma* 'that which is said, word, saying, expression' often takes on a special significance from the context, to mean "prophecy, prediction," as seems probable here.

The perfect passive participle *proeirēmenōn*, from *prolegō* 'foretell, tell, proclaim beforehand', which is used of prophetic utterances concerning future events and circumstances, (Arndt and Gingrich), applies to what the Old Testament prophets say, and, in particular, to the prophecies which relate to the *parousia* 'return' of Christ; cf. 3:4 and 1:19.

3:2b-c. The coordinating conjunction *kai* 'and' links 2b with 2a so that they are equal in natural prominence, and the finite verb *diegeirō* 'I stimulate', followed by the infinitive *mnēsthēnai* 'to remember', are both understood, and are made explicit in the display.

The double genitive *tēs tōn apostolōn humōn entolēs tou kuriou kai sōtēros* 'the of the apostles of you commandment of the Lord and Saviour' is an awkward construction. It seems best to take *entolēs tou kuriou kai sōtēros* 'the commandment of the Lord and Saviour' first, and *tēs tōn apostolōn humōn* 'the of the apostles of you' second, the first referring to the origin of the commandment, i.e., the Lord and Saviour, and the second to the announcement of it by the apostles. As the Old Testament prophets were the vehicle of God's message to his people, so too are the apostles vehicles of his message which we have in the New Testament.

There are a number of different opinions as to what *entolē* 'commandment, order' refers to here. It may refer to:

1. Peter's warning that they should beware of false teachers;
2. the command to be ready for Christ's second coming, and to live a godly life in expectation of it;
3. God's commandments in general.

In the context, the second of these would seem appropriate, since, throughout the letter, Peter is urging them to be ready for Christ's coming, cf. 1:5ff.; 2:21; 3:12. However, in 2:21 *tēs ... hagias entolēs* 'the holy commandment' seems to refer to the law of the Christian life, the gospel, (see note on 2:21), which would include number 2 above. It could also be argued that since *entolē* is used in parallel with *rhēmata* 'that which was said', it is probably generic and not referring to a particular command. This would also support suggestion 2. In the display, therefore, it has been expressed simply by "what our(inc) Lord and Saviour commanded."

Most authorities consider the correct reading here to be *tēs tōn apostolōn humōn* 'of your apostles'. The Textus Receptus has *hēmōn* 'of us', but both the Majority Text and the UBS agree on *humōn* here.

There is, however, some discussion in the commentaries as to who these "apostles" are. It may mean:

1. the twelve apostles;
2. Paul and his fellow-labourers;
3. those from whom the readers had received the gospel.

The word *apostolos* is used of others than the twelve apostles of Christ, e.g., Epaphroditus in Phil 2:25 and others in 2 Cor 8:23, so numbers 2 and 3 above are possible. However, as Green points out in his commentary on 2 Peter, "When the New Testament writers mean merely 'church emissary' by *apostolos* they say so, or the context makes it plain, cf. Phil 2:25," and it would seem here that Peter is referring to the twelve apostles. They alone are put on a level with the Old Testament prophets. Therefore, "your apostles" does not refer here just to those from whom his readers first heard the gospel message, rather, the phrase is stressing the reliability of the gospel, by putting the apostles to whom Christ gave it on a par with the Old Testament prophets. As Bigg says, "'Your apostles' are the men you ought to trust; do not turn to the false teachers with whom you have neither part nor lot." Instead of cleverly devised stories the apostles passed on the truth of God.

DIVISION CONSTITUENT 3:3-10
(Section) (Role: Head of 3:1-10)

THEME: *Although certain people will ridicule the fact that you believe that the Lord Jesus Christ will come back, nevertheless he will certainly come back to judge people, and, at that time, God will destroy this present world.*

BOUNDARIES AND COHERENCE

The initial boundary of this unit has been discussed in connection with 3:1-10 and also 3:1-2. The final boundary has been discussed in connection with that of 3:1-10.

The unity of this section lies in its subject matter, i.e., "the day of the Lord" (3:10); "the day of judgement and destruction" (3:7).

The chiastic structure of this section is further evidence of its unity:

A	False thesis presented (3:4), i.e.,	1 The Lord Jesus Christ has not yet returned and therefore never will.
		2 Nothing cataclysmic has happened since the creation of the world, and therefore never will.
B	Counter-argument 1 (3:5-7), i.e.,	God has destroyed the world once, by water, and will destroy it a second time, by fire. It is untrue, therefore, to say that nothing ever changes. This refutes 2 above.
B'	Counter-argument 2 (3:8-9), i.e.,	Christ has not yet come back because he wants to give people the opportunity to repent. This does not mean that he will never return. This refutes 1 above.
A'	True thesis presented (3:0), i.e.,	The Lord Jesus Christ will definitely come back at the appointed time, and the world will be destroyed.

RELATIONAL STRUCTURE	CONTENTS
CONCESSION	(3:3-7) Although certain people will ridicule the fact that you believe that the Lord Jesus Christ will come back to judge people,
HEAD	(3:8-10) nevertheless, the Lord Jesus Christ will certainly come back, and at that time, God will destroy this present world.

There is evidence for a break between verses 7 and 8, in that there is a vocative, *agapētoi* 'dear ones'; an imperative, *mē lanthanetō* 'do not overlook'; and Peter addresses his readers again by the second person pronoun *humas* 'you', in 3:8, after the exposition of arguments in verses 5-7 concerning 'the day of the Lord'. Verses 3-7, therefore, could be analysed as either two paragraphs, 3-4 and 5-7, or as a paragraph cluster. Verses 8-10 could also be analysed as either two separate paragraphs, 8-9 and 10, or as a paragraph cluster. This is discussed further in the notes on 3:3-7 and 3:8-10.

PROMINENCE AND THEME

Since the theme statements for 3:3-7 and 3:8-10 are in a concession-contraexpectation relationship with each other, the theme statement for 3:8-10 is naturally prominent, and the theme statement for this section should be based on it. However, as we see above, the structure of this section is chiastic, which means that the theme statement for 3:3-4 is also prominent, being one of the outer edges of the chiasmus. It is also the theme statement for 3:3-7, therefore, the theme statement for this section is based on the theme statements for both 3:3-7 and 3:8-10.

SECTION CONSTITUENT 3:3-7
(Paragraph cluster) (Role: Concession to 3:8-10)

THEME: *There will be certain people who will ridicule the fact that you believe that the Lord Jesus Christ will come back to judge people.*

RELATIONAL STRUCTURE	CONTENTS
HEAD	(3:3-4) There will be certain people who will ridicule the fact that you believe that the Lord Jesus Christ will come back to judge people,
concession	(3:5-7) although they know that what they say is not true.

BOUNDARIES AND COHERENCE

The initial boundary for this constituent has been discussed with reference to 3:1-2. The final boundary is marked by the following features in verse 8:

1. The vocative *agapētoi* 'dear ones', as Peter addresses the recipients of the letter directly again.
2. The imperative *mē lanthenetō* 'do not overlook'.
3. The second person pronoun *humas* 'you', after the third person forms referring to God or the scoffers, in 3:3-7.

The unity of this constituent lies in its subject matter. It presents the arguments of those who ridicule belief in the return of the Lord Jesus Christ, and refutes one of them. At the beginning, there is reference to *eschatōn tōn tēmerōn* 'the last days', i.e., before Christ comes back, and in the last verse, there is reference to *hēmeran kriseōs kai apōleias tōn asebōn anthrōpōn* 'the day of judgement and destruction of ungodly people' (3:7). In between these two references to the Day of the Lord are references to the destruction of the world by fire, on that day, and the destruction of the ancient world, by water.

Most versions do not have a paragraph break between 3:4 and 5, but regard 3:3-7 as a single paragraph. This is possible, since these verses centre round the Day of the Lord and the arguments of those who imply that this day will never come. However, it is also possible to regard 3:3-7 as a paragraph cluster, consisting of two closely related paragraphs, 3:3-4 and 3:5-7, which deal respectively with the arguments of those who scoff, and a refutation of one of those arguments. In support of this analysis is the change from direct to indirect speech in 3:5, accompanied by a new orienter, *lanthanei ... autous touto thelontas* 'when they assert this they (deliberately) overlook this fact' (3:5). The latter analysis has been followed here.

PROMINENCE AND THEME

What is the relationship between these two paragraphs? They are linked by the conjunction *gar*, which would appear to signal a result-reason relationship, i.e., they will ridicule belief in the return of Christ because they overlook the facts of the previous destruction of the ancient world. However, what Peter really seems to be saying is that these people ridicule belief in Christ's future return, and the events which will accompany it, despite knowing that the facts on which they base their arguments are not true. Those to whom Peter is writing are probably Jews and proselytes, who would know about the flood of Noah's time, and the other events referred to in 2:4-10. Since the facts about the flood were commonly known they must be choosing deliberately to ignore them.

The relationship between the heads of these two paragraphs, therefore, is one of Head-concession, and the theme statement of 3:3-7 is based on the theme statement of 3:3-4.

However, the prominence in this paragraph cluster, and also in the section 3:3-10, is far from straightforward. In the analysis presented above, the focus is on the fact that these people are deliberately ignoring known, well-attested facts, when they scoff at belief in Christ's return. An alternative approach would be to focus on the arguments on which they base their ridicule, i.e., that a long time has elapsed since Christ promised that he would come back, and he has not done so, therefore, it is obvious that he never will. Also, there have been no cataclysmic events since the world was created, therefore, there never will be a cataclysmic end to this present world. If this approach is followed, then both 3:5-7 and 3:8-9 might be regarded as comment on 3:3-4 and as separate paragraphs rather than members of paragraph clusters. The display then might be as follows:

RELATIONAL STRUCTURE		CONTENTS
CONCESS.	HEAD	(3:3-4) Certain people will deny that Christ will return, because a long time has elapsed and nothing cataclysmic has happened.
	comment	(3:5-7) This is false because there was a cataclysmic flood.
	comment	(3:8-9) This is false because God is giving men time to repent.
HEAD		(3:10) Christ will certainly come back to judge people and at that time God will destroy this present world.

PARAGRAPH CLUSTER CONSTITUENT 3:3-4
(Paragraph) (Role: Head of 3:3-7)

THEME: *There will be certain people who will ridicule the fact that you believe that the Lord Jesus Christ will come back.*

BOUNDARIES AND COHERENCE

The boundaries of this unit have been discussed already under 3:3-10 and 3:3-7.

The coherence of this short paragraph consists in the fact that it centres on the *empaiktai* 'scoffers' and their *empaigmonē* 'scoffing', what they say being quoted directly in verse 4. This has also been discussed in the notes on 3:3-7.

PROMINENCE AND THEME

These two verses consist of one sentence in the Greek, introduced by the present participle *ginōskontes* 'understanding' which acts as an orienter

RELATIONAL STRUCTURE	CONTENT
orienter	(3:3a) It is important (that you should) understand,
time	(3:3b) in the time (immediately) before Christ will come back,
contrac- tion HEAD HEAD	(3:3c) there will be people (who will) ridicule (the fact that you believe that Christ will come back).
desc. of "people" in 3c.	(3:3d) (These people (3:3c) will do whatever (evil deeds) they wish to do.
orienter	(3:4a) They will say,
concession	(3:4b) "(Although the prophets and Christ) promised (that) he (Christ) will come back,
HEAD HEAD	(3:4c) (Christ has certainly not come back, and nothing has happened which would indicate that he ever will ever come back.)
time	(3:4d) (Indeed), since the early Christian leaders died [EUPH]
grounds HEAD HEAD (evid.)	(3:4e) all things remain (as they always have been)
time	(3:4f) since (God) created (the world)."

for the whole paragraph. The future indicative *eleusontai* 'they will appear', which is naturally prominent, is followed by the participles *poreuomenoi* 'following, living' and *legontes* 'saying', which are linked by the conjunction *kai* 'and'. The second of these provides an orienter for the arguments put forward by those who scoff.

Since the focus of this whole section is on the return of Christ in judgement, it is necessary to include in the theme statement, not merely that people appeared who mocked or ridiculed, but also the object of their ridicule, i.e., Christian belief in the return of Christ in judgement.

NOTES ON 3:3-4

3:3a. The expression *touto prōton ginōskontes hoti* 'first of all you must understand that/it is important that you should understand that' is identical with that used in 1:20a (see note on 1:20a).

In most versions, *touto prōton* is translated as "first of all," but the lack of any "second" would indicate rather that "it is important" would be a more appropriate rendering.

In most versions too, the present participle *ginōskontes* 'knowing, understanding' is translated as a command, i.e., "you must know/understand." Alternatively, it is translated by "you know/knowing," when it probably agrees with the *agapētoi* 'dear ones' of 3:1. Most versions supply "you" rather than "we" as the subject.

The neuter *touto* 'this', according to Arndt and Gingrich, "is used with reference to what follows, especially before clauses that express a statement, purpose, result, or condition, which it introduces." Here, therefore, it may refer to either the information immediately following the *hoti*, (3:3-4), or to 3:3-7. In the display, the first of these alternatives is followed, since the material following the *gar* in 3:5-7 is Peter's own reasoning.

3:3b. In the phrase *ep' eschatōn tōn hēmerōn* 'in the last days', the adjective *eschatōn* is used in the sense of "last," with reference to a situation in which there is nothing else to follow it. In 2:20 it is used in the sense of "last" in relation to something which precedes.

The noun *hēmerōn* 'days' is used here to refer to an indefinite period of time and is usually translated "time."

The phrase as a whole is regarded by various commentators to signify either:

1. a time in the future, immediately preceding the second coming of Christ, a time of distress which precedes the end; cf. also Heb 1:2; Jude 18; Jas 5:3. This seems to be the sense in which Peter uses the phrase *en kairō eschatō* 'in the last time' in 1:5 of his first letter.
2. the Christian era, cf. Green "His coming to the world was the last decisive event in human history . . . With the advent of Jesus the last chapter of human history had opened, though it was not yet completed. In between the two advents stretches the last time, the time of grace, the time too, of opposition."

Meyer considers that in 1 Peter 1:20 *ep' eschatou tōn chronōn* 'at the end of the times' refers to the "whole period extending from the first appearance of Christ to His second coming," but that the reference here is only to the time immediately preceding His second coming. In the context, this would seem the more appropriate, since the focus of the whole chapter is on the day when Christ will return to judge mankind. It is this event which the scoffers seek to throw doubt upon and which is described in 3:10-12. In the display, therefore, it has been made explicit that "the last days" refers to "the time (immediately before Christ will come back)."

3:3c. *Eleusontai* is the future indicative of *erchomai*, whose primary meaning is "to come." It is also used of persons "appearing on the scene," and, in particular, of "false teachers, false Messiahs, and the Antichrist in his various forms." (Arndt and Gingrich 1.1.a.) The subject here is *empaiktai* 'scoffers, mockers', which is found only here and in Jude 18 in the New Testament. If 'appear' is used it will need to be marked with an * since this is not the primary meaning. Possibly, it might be better to say "There will be certain people."

The noun *empaigmonē* 'with/in scoffing' is not found elsewhere, although *empaigmos* 'scorn, mocking' occurs in Heb. 11:36 and the verb *empaizō* 'mock, ridicule' is used frequently throughout the New Testament. The use of *empaiktai* together with *empaigmonē* is regarded by commentators as a pleonastic Hebraism which gives prominence to the conduct of the mockers; cf. also *phthora ... phtharēsontai* 'with destruction ... they will be destroyed' (2:12). The Majority Text omits the phrase *(en)empaigmonē*.

There is some debate amongst commentators as to whether these people are the false teachers described in chapter 2, or whether they are a completely different group of people. Although there seems to be no definite evidence which would help to decide the issue, it is likely that the *empaiktai* 'scoffers' of chapter 3 are the *pseudodidaskaloi* 'false teachers' of chapter 2, for the description of the scoffers as people who live *kata tas idias epithumias autōn* 'according to their own lusts' (3:3) agrees very well with all that is said of the false teachers in the preceding chapter. People who behave as those described in chapter 2 would be very unwilling to accept the teaching which is inherent in the return of Christ, i.e., that the ungodly will be judged and condemned.

In the display, it has been necessary to make explicit what it is that the scoffers are deriding. The content of what they say (3:4) makes it clear that it is the Christian belief in the second coming of Christ. Also, Peter seems to have had this subject in mind from the start of the letter. The *epaggelmata* 'things promised' of 1:4 are the *epaggelma* 'promise' of 3:13, while other connecting links are to be found in *hē aiōnios basileia* 'the eternal kingdom' (1:11), *parousia* 'coming' (1:16), and the references to *krisis* 'judgement' and *hēmera kriseos* 'the day of judgement' (2:4 and 2:9). This doctrinal error was at the root of the moral depravity of the false teachers. In the display this might be expressed as 'ridicule (the fact that you believe that Christ will come back)'. Alternatively, it could be expressed as 'deny (that Christ will come back)' since, by their scoffing, these people are, in effect, denying the possibility of Christ's return.

3:3d. The description of those who scoff as *kata tas idias epithumias autōn poreuomenoi* 'following their own passions/living according to their own desires', is reminiscent of 2:10, where the false teachers are referred to as *en epithumia miasmou poreuomenous* 'indulging in the lust of defiling passion' (see note on 2:10). As has been said in the note on 3:3c, this gives support to the view that those who scoff are the same people as those described in chapter 2.

Peter uses *epithumia* in 1:4 and 2:18 as well as here, and in each case the sense is of "doing what is evil."

The adjective *idias* 'own' is added in order to strengthen the pronoun *autōn* 'of them'. It brings out their self-will and opposition to the law of God.

These people had rejected the Christian way of life and lived purely to gratify their own desires, considering permissible whatever pleased and suited them.

The subject of the clause has been made explicit in the display, i.e., "the people" in 3c, and the statement has been shown as a description of the people who scoff.

3:4a-f. The present participle *legontes* 'saying' is an orienter for 3:4b-f, which is the content of what the scoffers say. It has been expressed as a future tense in the display, since the event is yet to come, and the agent, i.e., "people" in 3c has been made explicit.

This direct quotation of what the scoffers say provides an amplification of 3:3c, giving details of the argument which they use in their attempt to ridicule belief in the second coming of Christ.

3:4b-c. The question, *Pou estin hē epaggelia tēs parousias autou* 'Where is the promise of his coming?' implies that the promise is unfulfilled up to this time, and will remain so.

The interrogative adverb *pou* 'where(?), which place(?)' can be used in direct questions and also in rhetorical questions which expect a negative answer, and the latter would seem to be the case here. Bruce Moore looks at this particular rhetorical question in his article in *NOT* 97 and gives the following suggested renderings:

"He promised to come, but he hasn't done it."

"Show me, if you can, this 'coming' he promised."

"Look, this promise of his to come back is turning out to be just empty words."

Commentators consider the expression to be a traditional Hebraistic formula for expressing scepticism, i.e., a denial in the form of a question; cf. Ps 42:10; Jer 17:15; Mal 2:17; Lk 8:25.

The noun *epaggelia* 'announcement' has, in later Greek, the special sense of 'promise, pledge, offer'. It can be used of men, (cf. Acts 23:21) but is often used of a divine promise, as here.

The genitive construction dependent on *epaggelia* 'promise' denotes the content of the promise; cf. also 3:9.

Peter uses *epaggelma* 'announcement, promise' in 1:3 and 3:13, rather than *epaggelia*. According to Arndt and Gingrich, *epaggelia* is only ever used to refer to God's promise; however, these are its only two occurrences in the New Testament (see note on 1:3).

In the phrase *tēs parousias autou* 'of his coming' the *autou* 'his' refers to Christ. The promise is that Christ will come again, and this has been made explicit in the display.

The noun *parousia* 'coming, advent' is used in a special, technical sense, of the coming of Christ, and, nearly always, of his Messianic Advent in glory to judge the world at the end of this age; cf. Mt 24:3; 2 Pet 1:16 and 3:12 (Arndt and Gingrich).

Meyer considers that, according to the connection of 3:2, the *epaggelia* 'promise' is that of the Old Testament referred to in 1:19ff. It would seem though, that besides the Old Testament prophecies, those of Christ himself in such passages as Matthew 24 are also referred to here. In the display, therefore, it states that 'the prophets and Christ promised that he (Christ) will come again'.

In order to express the derisive attitude of the scoffers, and their denial that Christ will return, it has been necessary to represent the rhetorical question by two propositions, 3:4b and 3:4c, the first stating the content of the promise, and the second an emphatic statement that the promise has not been fulfilled, and never will be. It is difficult, however, to express the full strength of their scorn without using the graphically brief form of the rhetorical question. The use of "certainly" and "impossible" is an attempt to do this, but this is not entirely satisfactory. The implication is that Christ has not returned and neither has there been any indication in world events that his return is imminent.

The statement of the promise (3:4b) is in a relationship of concession to the HEAD (3:4c), since the sense is, that although a promise has been made, and therefore the expectation would be that it would be fulfilled, against that expectation, it has not, for Christ has not returned.

3:4d-f. The *gar* introduces the grounds upon which those who scoff base their opposition to the teaching that Christ will come again in judgement.

3:4d. Various suggestions have been put forward by commentators as to whom the scoffers are referring to when they speak of *hoi pateres*.

According to Arndt and Gingrich, the singular *patēr* has the primary meaning of "father," i.e., immediate male ancestor. It can, however, also mean "forefather, ancestor, progenitor." Figuratively, it can mean "a Spiritual fatherhood," or it can be used as an honorary form of respectful address; cf. Mt 23:9a; Acts 7:2a. It can also be used to refer to the older male members of a church, (cf. 1 Jn 2:13,14b), while in some places the *pateres* are to be understood as the generation(s) of deceased Christians or the great religious heroes of the Old Testament, who are regarded as "fathers," even to Gentile Christians, the "true Israel." Abraham is described as "father of all those who believe" (Rom. 4:11 and Jas. 2:21).

Four main proposals have been put forward as to what *pateres* refers to here:
1. the ancestors of the human race;
2. the patriarchs and prophets;
3. the first generation of Christians;
4. each generation of men in relation to those following.

It is possible that *pateres* refers to the first generation of Christians, since the death of such "fathers" as Stephen, James and other Christian leaders (cf. Heb. 13:7) would seem to give justification to such a taunt.

However, Michael Green makes the point that every other reference to "the fathers" in the New Testament (cf. Acts 3:13; Rom. 9:5; Heb. 1:1; etc.) means the "Old Testament fathers," and this would suggest that this is the probable meaning here. Also, it is not said that things continue as they have done "since the coming of Christ," but "since the beginning of creation."

Bigg, in the ICC, also favours this sense of the word, since the church is one, as we see in 1 Peter, and "the fathers" therefore belong to all Christians.

Others, however, consider that the scoffers are referring here, not to the Old Testament fathers, but to their own and the readers' parents and other relatives. Early Christians relied on sayings of the Lord (eg., Mt 10:23; Mk 9:1; 13:30) that he would come again in their lifetime, and it was a manifest fact that many people to whom this assurance had referred had died, and neither the Lord's return nor the anticipated transformation of the created order had taken place. Paul, in 1 Thess. 4:13-18, gives explanations to quieten such anxiety .

Meyer considers that if the "fathers" is here taken to mean the ancestors, the first generations of the human race, then this makes the clause beginning with *ap' hēs* superfluous, and does not give any indication of the grounds on which the scoffers based their thesis. If, however, this is contained in the clause beginning with *ap' hēs*, then *hoi pateres* can refer only to either the fathers of the Jewish people to whom the *epaggelia* was given, (cf. Heb 1:1), or to those of the generation to which the scoffers belong. But, since the falling asleep of the fathers of Israel, before its fulfilling, could not be used as proof that the promise was of none effect, in that it referred to a time beyond that in which they lived, (cf. 1 Pet 1:10ff.), the second view is preferable.

Meyer also points out that the words quoted here are represented as to be spoken at a time then still in the future, and maintains that verse 8, which otherwise would stand totally unconnected with verse 4, also favours this view.

In the display, *hoi pateres* has been represented by "the early Christian leaders," the argument being that, since they died, no catastrophic changes had taken place, just as none had since the time of creation.

The aorist indicative *ekoimēthēsan* means literally "they slept, fell asleep." Here it is used euphemistically to mean "they died."

The preposition *apo* has the basic meaning of "separation from someone/something," and it is from this that its other meanings have developed. It is used to denote the point from which something begins, in both its literal and figurative meanings, and can be used of place and time. Here, in the expression *aph' hēs*, *hēmeras* "day" is to be understood, i.e., "from which day, from the day when"; cf. Col 1:6,9. But *aph' hēs* became a fixed formula with the sense of "since"; cf. also Acts 24:11; Lk 7:45.

3:4e. The present tense *diamenei* 'remains' indicates the continuance of an action during the past and up to the moment of speaking. Nothing significant ever changes in the world, according to these scoffers. Despite all the promises made by the prophets and by Christ himself, the world continues as it always has been and always will be. Christ has not returned and never will, so there is no judgement to fear and they can give rein to their lusts.

The adverb *houtōs* 'as' must have the sense completed by "they are now" or "as they have been." The latter makes better sense linked with *ap' archēs ktiseōs* 'since/from the beginning of creation'.

3:4f. In the display, "God" has been made explicit as the agent in the phrase *ap' archēs ktiseōs* 'since the beginning of creation'; so also has what he created, i.e., the world, referring to the sum total of everything he created.

PARAGRAPH CLUSTER CONSTITUENT 3:5-7
(Paragraph) (Role: Concession to 3:3-4)

THEME: *(3:3c) know that what they say (3:4b-f) is not true.*

BOUNDARIES AND COHERENCE

The boundaries of this unit have been discussed already under 3:3-10 and 3:3-7.

The coherence of this unit has also been discussed in connection with the above units. It consists of a refutation of the specious argument put forward by the scoffers in 3:4b-f, that there have been no previous cataclysmic events in world history, therefore there are unlikely to be any in the future, which would indicate that Christ will not return in judgement. Peter refutes this by pointing out that this argument is manifestly untrue, since God has destroyed the world once already, and intends to do so again.

PROMINENCE AND THEME

The prominence in this paragraph is far from straight-forward and has been discussed in connection with 3:3-7.

NOTES ON 3:5-7

As has been discussed under 3:3-7, most versions do not begin a new paragraph here. The NEB is one exception to this.

The *gar* introduces Peter's refutation of what the scoffers say in 3:4. The antecedent to *gar* is to be found in the assertion *panta houtōs diamenei* 'all things remain as (they have been)' (3:4e). Peter takes this, their last argument, first, and shows that what they say is completely false, having no basis in fact. Since their premise, that this is a stable, unchanging world, is false, their conclusion, that it will always be so, and that Christ will not return, is false also. God has punished sin once by the flood (Mt 24:37-39) and will do so again, but this time by fire. The scoffers are aware of this, since they know the facts concerning the creation and the flood from the Jewish Scriptures.

RELATIONAL STRUCTURE	CONTENT

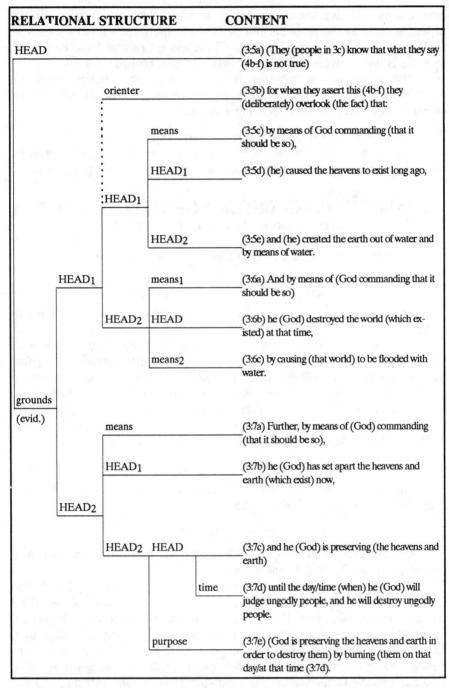

	(3:5a) (They (people in 3c) know that what they say (4b-f) is not true)
HEAD	
orienter	(3:5b) for when they assert this (4b-f) they (deliberately) overlook (the fact) that:
means	(3:5c) by means of God commanding (that it should be so),
HEAD₁	(3:5d) (he) caused the heavens to exist long ago,
HEAD₂	(3:5e) and (he) created the earth out of water and by means of water.
means₁	(3:6a) And by means of (God commanding that it should be so)
HEAD₂ HEAD	(3:6b) he (God) destroyed the world (which existed) at that time,
means₂	(3:6c) by causing (that world) to be flooded with water.
means	(3:7a) Further, by means of (God) commanding (that it should be so),
HEAD₁	(3:7b) he (God) has set apart the heavens and earth (which exist) now,
HEAD₂ HEAD	(3:7c) and he (God) is preserving (the heavens and earth)
time	(3:7d) until the day/time (when) he (God) will judge ungodly people, and he will destroy ungodly people.
purpose	(3:7e) (God is preserving the heavens and earth in order to destroy them) by burning (them on that day/at that time (3:7d).

3:5a. It seems necessary here to make explicit what is implied concerning those who scoff, i.e., that they know that what they say about the world situation and the return of Christ is untrue. The rest of the paragraph then goes on to give the evidential grounds for this statement.

3:5b. The statement *lanthanei ... autous touto thelontas* 'it escapes them when they wish this' provides one of a number of grammatical exegetical, and syntactical problems in verses 5-7.

The *touto* 'this' belongs either to *lanthanei* 'it escapes notice' or to *thelontas* 'willing'. If it belongs to *lanthanei* 'it escapes notice' then it refers to what follows, introduced by *hoti* 'that', and *thelontas* will mean "willingly, on purpose." If it belongs to *thelontas* then it refers to the contents of the preceding statement (3:4) and *thelontas* means "assert," the whole statement being "when they assert this, it is hidden from them that." This entails giving the verb *thelontas* the unusual sense of "maintaining contrary to the truth of the matter."

The second of these alternatives is preferred by some commentators, on the grounds that the position of *touto* 'this' is an obstacle to construing it as subject of *lanthanei* 'it escapes notice'. The demonstrative pronoun comes immediately before *thelontas* 'willing', and far removed from *lanthanei* 'it escapes notice'. It is preferable, therefore, to have the sense "when they assert this (3:4) it is hidden from them that."

It is difficult to be emphatic about the matter, since this use of *thelō* 'assert' is unusual, and most editors prefer the sense "they wilfully ignore that." The usage of *lanthanetō ... hoti* in 3:8 would seem to bear this out. There Peter exhorts his readers, "Do not be ignorant about this ... that," and then continues with the content in the rest of the verse. However, in 3:8 the *touto* precedes the *lanthanetō*, whereas here it does not. Also, in Col. 2:18 *thelōn* seems to have a sense of "insisting on," which would provide one parallel with the sense "assert," which is possible here.

In the display *touto* has been taken to belong to *thelontas*, and to refer to what precedes in 3:4. The statement provides an orienter for what follows in the following verse(s), introduced by *hoti* 'that'.

The content of *hoti* is regarded by some commentators as extending to the end of verse 7, but by others only to the end of verse 6, with verse 7 being an additional statement. Probably the latter is the more likely, since those who scoffed based their jibes on what had or had not happened in the past, and verse 7 deals with what will happen at a future date.

3:5c. The phrase *to tou theou logo* 'by the word of God' refers to the means by which God created the world, i.e., by commanding that it should be so; cf. Gen 1, "God said ... and it was so." It is repeated in *to auto logo* 'by the same word' (3:7), and also reference is probably made to it in *di' hon* 'through these' (3:6). This repetition gives prominence to God's overruling power in the world. He is the one who creates and who destroys.

Most versions attribute *tō tou theou logō* 'by the word of God' to the creation of both heavens and earth, but several attribute it to the creation of the earth only, because of its position immediately after the clause relating to *gē* 'earth'. However, the evidence of Gen 1:6-10 would indicate that it refers to the creation of both the heavens and the earth. Also, the deliberate antithesis between the heavens and the earth established in the beginning by God's creative word, and the present heavens and earth, which are being kept ready for destruction by the same word (cf. 3:7), requires that it should apply to both.

As some commentators point out, the phrase may also mean "Christ the Eternal Word" through whom creation was accomplished; cf. Jn. 1:3; Heb. 1:2. The same ambiguity occurs in Heb. 11:3. It is generally agreed though that this double meaning was not intended here. Only John refers to Jesus as the *logos*. Hebrews 1:2 has *huios* 'Son' and 11:3 has *rhēma* which is never used of Jesus, therefore reference to Jesus here is not acceptable.

In the display, the phrase has been represented by "by means of God commanding (that it should be so)."

3:5d.   The plural noun *ouranoi* 'heavens' is repeated in verses 7, 10, 12 and 13. In each case it refers to the destruction/dissolution of the heavens, except in verse 13, where it speaks of *kainous ... ouranous* 'new ... heavens' which will come into being after the destruction of the present ones.

According to Arndt and Gingrich, the singular form *ouranos* 'heaven' is used most frequently as referring to part of the universe, as the firmament, or sky over the earth. But Jewish mystics distinguished seven heavens, (cf. 2 Cor 12:2; Eph 4:10), and when the plural *ouranoi* is used, it is not always possible to decide when this concept is really alive and when it simply survives as a formula.

Ouranoi is used in the New Testament frequently by Matthew (as in the Lord's Prayer, 6:9), not uncommonly in Mark, rarely by Luke, and never by John (except in Rev 12:12). Paul uses the plural about as often as the singular, but only the plural in Ephesians. In other books of the New Testament, singular and plural are interchanged for no apparent reason; cf. Heb 9:23 and 24.

Peter uses the singular twice in his first letter (1:12; 3:22) and the plural once (1:4). In this letter he uses the singular once (1:18) and the plural five times, all in this passage (3:5-13), where he is dealing with cosmogony. Each time he uses the singular, it is in connection with one of the persons of the Godhead, cf. "the Holy Ghost sent down from heaven" (1 Pet 3:22); "the voice (of God) which came from heaven" (2 Pet 1:18).

According to the ICC, the plural seems to be "a mere Hebraism, the Hebrew word being plural in form, and we need not suppose an allusion to the Rabbinical theory unless the context requires it." Probably here, then, it should be translated "heaven," but some commentators prefer to keep the plural, and think that the seven heavens were in Peter's mind.

The verb *ēsan* may be regarded as relating to both *ouranoi* 'heavens' and *gē* 'earth' (cf. TEV,NEB), or as relating to only *ouranoi* 'heavens', (cf. NIV,JER). Either alternative is acceptable, and whichever is chosen, the overall sense of the passage remains basically the same.

Throughout this verse and verse 6 God is understood to be the agent in each event.

3:5e. A similar question has to be asked with reference to the participle *sunestōsa*, as was asked of *ēsan* and *tō tou theou logō* above, i.e., does it refer to both *ouranoi* 'heavens' and *gē* 'earth', or just to the latter in this case. Most translations favour the latter; cf. KJV, NIV, TEV, JER, although NEB prefers the former.

The participle *sunestōsa* is nominative feminine singular, and therefore, grammatically speaking, shows concord with *gē* 'earth', not with *ouranoi* 'heavens', which is nominative masculine plural. However, a number of commentators consider that the singular form could be the result of attraction to the number and gender of the nearer noun, *gē* 'earth', and Meyer considers that although it belongs grammatically only to *gē* 'earth', that in thought it has been applied to *ouranoi* 'heavens' also.

In the absence of any other proof, the strictly grammatical view has been followed in the display, in agreement with the majority of translations.

The verb *sunistēmi*, of which *sunestōsa* is the perfect participle active, in this context, according to Arndt and Gingrich, has the sense "be composed, compounded, consist of" combined with the sense "continue, endure, exist."

Ellicott points out that the same word is translated "consist" in Col 1:17, and he considers that "the notion is that of coherence, solidarity, and order, as distinct from chaos."

Meyer says that "*sunestōsa* expresses the idea of originating out of a combination; *sunestēmi* is often employed thus by the Greeks in the intransitive tenses."

The verb is expressed by "was formed," in a number of translations, cf. NIV, RSV, JER, TEV, and either this or "was created" would be appropriate in the context.

The noun *hudōr* 'water' is used here literally, but it is difficult to be dogmatic about the meaning of *ex hudatos kai di' hudatos sunestōsa* 'out of water and through water having been created'.

With regard to *ex hudatos ... sunestōsa* 'out of water ... was formed/created', it may mean:

1. that the earth emerged "out of/from water" in which it had lain buried (cf. Gen. 1:9). The waters that were under the firmament were gathered together into one place and the dry land appeared. Peter is referring to the watery chaos out of which the earth appeared at God's command (Gen 1:2-6) (cf. Calvin, Lillie, ICC).
2. that water is the substance from which the earth was made.

According to Meyer, the latter alternative is in harmony with the Mosaic account of creation, where the original substance is distinctly spoken of as *hudōr*. Alford, too, favours this meaning.

Although Kelly agrees that this was a commonly held belief, he thinks that to state that water was the material out of which God created the earth is reading more into the Genesis narrative than it contains. He also points out that Ps 24:2, which is a commonly cited parallel, does not fit exactly, since it affirms merely that God "established the universe on the waters."

With regard to *di' hudatos sunestōsa* 'through water was formed', it may mean:

1. "by means of water," i.e., that water was instrumental in the creation of the earth, cf. Meyer, Ellicott; Calvin states that the earth is "made firm and solid by means of water; which is true, for through moisture the earth adheres together and becomes a solid mass."

Most translations follow this alternative, cf. NIV, NAS, TEV, RSV, which can also be taken in this sense to refer to the sustaining/maintaining of the earth by water. The ICC says, "Water is at once the material and the instrumental cause of the subsistence of the earth. It is made out of the sea below, and its life depends on the rain from above."

2. "amidst, between the water," i.e., the earth is encompassed by the water above in the clouds and that below in the oceans.

The ICC maintains that *dia* never bears the sense "in the midst of" but other commentators consider that this meaning is possible, cf. Kelly. The reference for this sense would be Gen 1:6-8 where God placed the firmament which he called heaven "in the midst of the waters."

The fact that *dia* has the meaning of "through" or "by means of" in the following clause (3:6a) throws some doubt on the sense "in the midst of" here, so the majority view has been followed in the display, i.e., "(he) created the earth out of water and by means of water.

3:6a.   There has been a great deal of discussion as to what is referred to by *di' hōn* 'through which, by means of which', since *hōn* is plural, and could be masculine, feminine, or neuter in gender. It may refer to:

1. *Ouranoi* 'heavens' and *gē* 'earth' mentioned in the preceding verse. The heavens and the earth became instruments of destruction when the heavens opened to pour forth rain, and the waters from which the earth had emerged also poured forth to flood the world; cf. Gen 7:11.
2. The water mentioned twice in verse 5, which could mean:
   a. the water out of which, and the water by means of which, the world was made; or,
   b. the waters under the firmament and the waters above the firmament.
3. The water and the word mentioned in verse 5, the two agents of creation cooperating in destruction.
4. These facts/circumstances, i.e., in consequence of these things.

A number of the most used translations, (cf. RSV, NIV, TEV, JER, NEB) favour the second of these, but, as Kelly points out, it seems strange to use the plural of the relative pronoun on the basis that the singular antecedent is used twice in two different ways. Also, the repetition of "by water" with "deluged," in the same short clause, seems pointless.

It seems most likely that *di' hōn* refers to "water" and "the word of God," although the same objection as above could be made, i.e., the pointless repetition of "water." However, after the ambiguous "which," Peter may have thought it necessary to indicate that it was water which actually overwhelmed the world.

Another factor in favour of 3 above is that, in the following verse, *logos* 'word' and *pur* 'fire' appear as causes of the future catastrophe which is to destroy the world. This provides a parallel with *logos* 'word' and *hudōr* 'water' in verse 6. Further, according to Calvin, it stresses the truth that nature is not enough to support and maintain the world, but rather it contains the material for its own ruin "whenever it may please God." The very element from which this earth had its origin, and by which it was maintained, was used to destroy it at God's command.

One objection to this alternative might be that it is awkward to have the antecedent combined out of two ideas which stand in different relations and different cases in the preceding sentence.

If this sense is not followed, then option 1 might be possible, since, other things being equal, the plural relative would refer back to the plural (compound) subject of *hoi ouranoi kai hē gē* 'the heavens and the earth'.

It has been suggested that *hōn* is a scribal error and that the reading should be *hou* or *hon*, singular forms of the pronoun. It would then refer to the immediately preceding *tō tou theou logō* 'by the word of God', but there is no manuscript evidence to support this suggestion.

In the display, "by the word of God" has been made explicit in 3:6a, but "by water" has not been made explicit, since it is stated in 3:6c and it does not seem necessary for it to be stated twice.

3:6b. Peter uses the word *kosmos* 'world' in a very similar context in 2:5. There we have taken it to mean "the people who lived in the world." Does it have the same sense here? Various opinions have been put forward, as follows:

1. It refers to mankind.
2. It refers to all living creatures, i.e., humans, animals, etc.

Peter is putting forward, in this verse and the next, two cases which are parallel to a great extent, although not exactly so. He presses the analogy as far as he can.

3. It refers to the entire universe and not just mankind, or even the earth.

Alford considers that *kosmos* does not refer to just all living creatures, but neither should it be pushed to its utmost in order for it to be exactly identical with *hoi ouranoi kai hē gē* 'the heavens and the earth'. It is an indefinite common term which takes in "the heavens and the earth."

4. It refers to "order as opposed to primordial chaos, and Peter may mean no more than that the orderliness, the continuity of nature, was broken up by the flood." (Green) This would imply that it is the physical world which is spoken of, and the effects on it of the flood.

The third of these seems the most appropriate, since it would include the others.

The phrase *ho tote kosmos* 'the then world' is expressed in the display by "the world (which existed) at that time." This distinguishes it from the world which is in existence now and which will be destroyed by fire, cf. 3:7.

3:6c.   The means which God used when he destroyed the world is stated by *hudati kataklustheis* 'by water was flooded/inundated'. This is the second means, since the first has been stated in 3:6a, i.e., "by means of God commanding that it should be so."

The verb *katakluzō*, of which *kataklustheis* is the aorist participle passive, occurs only here in the New Testament. Its related noun, *kataklusmos* 'flood, deluge', occurs in 2:5 where Peter talks of the same event, i.e., the flood of Noah's time. The only other occurrences of the noun are Mt 24:38, 39 and Lk 17:27, which also refer to this event.

3:7.   The *de* at the beginning of this verse may be:
1. adversative, and translated "but," thus contrasting the destruction of the ancient world by water with the future destruction of this present world by fire; or
2. connective, and translated "and." At God's command, the world came into being (3:5). At his command also, the world was destroyed (3:6), and, at his command, it is being kept until that day when it will be destroyed by fire (3:7).

Most translations favour "but"; cf. KJV, RSV, TEV, JER. The NEB has "and," while the NIV has nothing.

Either of the two alternatives above would be appropriate and make good sense. In the display, the latter of the two has been followed, i.e., the *de* has been regarded as connective rather than adversative. Peter is refuting the arguments of the scoffers, that nothing has happened in the world in the past, which would indicate that any drastic change will occur in the future. He has pointed out that the world has been destroyed once (3:6), and now goes on to say that it will be destroyed again at God's appointed time. It does not seem to be the contrast between the two methods of destruction that is important, but the certainty of that destruction at the time which God has appointed.

3:7a. The phrase *tō autō logō* 'by the same word' points back to *tō tou theou logō* 'by the word of God' (3:5), and also to 3:6 where it is implied in *di' hōn* 'by which'.

Peter is eager to emphasize the power of God's word behind everything that happens in the universe. Whatever God commands will come to pass.

According to some readings, it should be *tō autou logō* 'by his word', but this makes little difference to the sense.

The phrase has again been expressed as a means proposition, with God as agent, as in 3:5c and 3:6a.

3:7b. The periphrastic perfect *tethēsaurismenoi eisin* 'they have been treasured, stored up' emphasizes the duration and the permanence of the act which has been accomplished. The *ouranoi kai gē* 'heavens and earth' have been set apart by God for a particular purpose. This state will only end when Christ comes to judge the world.

The RV margin gives an alternative reading "stored up with fire," but there is no record of *thēsaurizein* 'to lay up treasure' being used with the dative, in the sense required. Peter is not telling us where the fire is, but what it will do.

The *nun* 'now, the present' is used with the article as an adjective. Grammatically it belongs only to *ouranoi* 'heavens', though, in sense, it belongs also to *gē* 'earth'. The construction is similar to *ho tote kosmos* 'the then world' (3:6), and is expressed here by the phrase "the heavens and earth which exist now."

"God" is again made explicit as agent.

3:7c-d. The verb *tēreō* 'keep, hold, preserve someone/something', like *thēsaurizō* 'treasure up, store up' has the idea of being for a definite purpose or a suitable time, in this case *eis hēmeran kirseōs kai apōleias tōn asebōn anthrōpōn* 'until the day of judgement and destruction of ungodly people'. It is only God's keeping and restraining power which allows the present state of affairs to continue until the time which he has chosen to bring it to an end.

Peter uses this verb a number of times in his letters; cf. 2:4, 9 and 1 Peter 1:4.

The present participle *tēroumenoi* 'keeping, reserving' indicates the continuing nature of the action.

Eis hēmeran kriseōs kai apōleias tōn asebōn anthrōpōn 'for/until the day of judgement and of destruction of ungodly men' may denote purpose or time.

The preposition *eis* can be used of time, with indication of the time, as here, time up to which something continues, cf. 2 Tim 1:12; Phil 1:10. The heavens and earth are being preserved in their present state by God "until" the day of judgement. *Eis* may also be used to indicate a goal, to denote purpose, i.e., "in order to, for." If it is used in this sense here, it would mean that

God is keeping the heavens and earth in order that they might be part of the judgement and destruction of that day.

Peter uses *eis* 11 times in this letter and 42 times in his first letter. Of these, (according to Moulton and Geden) it is used to indicate purpose 11 times in 1 Peter and 3 times in 2 Peter, with a further 3 occasions in each letter which might possibly have this meaning. He uses it in the sense of "until" only once in each of the letters, and possibly twice more in 2 Peter. It would seem, therefore, that *eis* is more likely to be used in the sense of "for," indicating purpose. However, in the context, God's purpose in preserving the heavens and earth seems to be expressed by *puri* 'for fire', i.e., in order that they may be burned up, and *eis* introduces the phrase telling us when this will take place, i.e., God is preserving them until the day of judgement, when they will be destroyed by fire, along with all ungodly people.

The noun *hēmeran* 'day' is used here in the sense of a day appointed for a special purpose, (Arndt and Gingrich 3.b.b.), or a day of judgement fixed by the judge, referring to the day when Christ will return and the final judgement of all mankind will take place.

The noun *kriseōs* 'of judging/judgement' refers to the activity of God of the Messiah as judge, on the Last Day. It is often used to mean a judgement that goes against a person, a condemnation, and the punishment that follows. There certainly seems to be that sense included here. Peter uses the word 4 times in this letter; see 2:4, 9, 11.

Apōleias 'destruction' is also used in 2:1, 2, 3, and 3:16. Here it refers to eternal destruction, not in the sense of complete annihilation but of damnation, cf. Phil 1:28 where it is the opposite of *sōtēria* 'salvation'.

The adjective *asebōn* 'godless, impious' is found also in 2:5, 6.

3:7e.   There has been some discussion amongst the commentators as to whether *puri* 'for fire' should be construed with *tethēsaurismenoi eisin* 'they have been treasured up' or with *tēroumenoi* 'being reserved'. Alternatively, it could be considered to go with both, and they could be considered as expressing one concept.

There does not seem to be any significant difference in the meaning of the passage whichever of these alternatives is chosen. In the display, it has been linked with *tēroumenoi* since *tethēsaurismenoi eisin* does not require an adjunct, since in itself it corresponds to the *ēsan ... sunestōsa*, and it is only in the second member of the sentence that mention can be made of the future destruction by fire; otherwise, too, *tēroumenoi* would be somewhat superfluous. (See Meyer.)

Puri 'for fire' has been represented in the display by a purpose clause, i.e., in order to destroy ... by burning. God is the agent in this as He has been in the preceding verses.

The thought expressed here is further developed in verses 10 and 12.

SECTION CONSTITUENT 3:8-10
(Paragraph cluster) (Role: Head of 3:3-10)

THEME: *The Lord Jesus Christ will certainly come back to judge people, and at that time God will destroy this present world.*

RELATIONAL STRUCTURE	CONTENTS
concession	(3:8-9) Although the Lord Jesus Christ has not yet come back to judge people, because God is forbearing towards you/people,
HEAD	(3:10) nevertheless, he will certainly come back to judge people, and at that time God will destroy this present world.

BOUNDARIES AND COHERENCE

The boundaries for this constituent have been discussed in connection with the boundaries of 3:3-7 and 3:3-10.

The unity of this constituent, as with 3:3-7, lies in the fact that it centres round the Day of the Lord and the events of that day. In verses 5-7 Peter had repudiated the claim of the scoffers that nothing had changed since the world had been created. Now he answers their implication that, because Christ has not yet come back, he never will. He does this by explaining that the apparent delay in his return is because God, in his mercy, wishes to give more time for people to repent and be saved.

These verses may be regarded as a single paragraph or as two closely related paragraphs, i.e., verses 8-9 forming one paragraph and 10 the other. In the various versions there does not seem to be any general agreement as to where the paragraph breaks should be made; cf. TEV, NIV, NEB (two paragraphs); PHIL, RSV, JER (one paragraph).

In this analysis these verses are regarded as a paragraph cluster consisting of two closely related paragraphs, 8-9 and 10. The following factors support this analysis:

1. The majority of the verbs in 3:8-9 are in the present tense, while those in 3:10 are in the future tense.
2. If this constituent consists of two paragraphs, then the section 3:3-10 is chiastic; cf. notes on 3:3-10.

PROMINENCE AND THEME

The two paragraphs which make up this paragraph cluster are linked by the conjunction *de*, which, in a number of versions is translated "but". This is considered to signal that the two paragraphs are in a concession-contraexpectation relationship, with 3:10 as the Head. The theme statement for this constituent, therefore, is taken from the theme statement of 3:10.

For an alternative analysis refer to the notes on Prominence and Theme for 3:3-7.

PARAGRAPH CLUSTER CONSTITUENT 3:8-9
(Paragraph) (Role: Concession to 3:10)

THEME: *The Lord Jesus Christ has not yet come back to judge people because God is forbearing towards you.*

BOUNDARIES AND COHERENCE

The boundaries for this paragraph have been discussed in connection with the unit 3:8-10.

In these verses Peter is explaining the apparent delay in the return of the Lord Jesus Christ, and the coherence of the paragraph consists in the use of lexical items relating to time:

> *mia hēmera* 'one day' (twice in 3:8)
> *chilia etē* 'a thousand years' (twice in 3:8)
> *bradunei* 'delays, is slow' (3:9)
> *bradutēta* 'slowness' (3:9)

References to *kurios* 'Lord' and *humas* 'you', in both verses further strengthen the unity of the paragraph.

PROMINENCE AND THEME

Grammatically, this paragraph consists of two sentences, which coincide with the two verses, 3:8 and 9.

The content of 3:8 is introduced by an orienter, *mē lanthanetō* 'let not be concealed' followed by *hoti* 'that'. The content of the *hoti* clause has no verb, but *estin* 'is' is understood.

In 3:9, the two main verbs, *bradunei* 'delays, is slow' and *makrothumei* 'is forbearing, longsuffering', are connected by *alla* 'but', the latter being naturally prominent and therefore the head of the propositional cluster 3:9a-e. This proposition, 3:9c, is head of the paragraph, with the head of 3:8, 3:8b, providing a grounds for it. The theme statement, therefore, is based on 3:9c.

NOTES ON 3:8-9

In the previous paragraph, Peter dealt with the argument against the second coming of the Lord, which was based on the presumed stability of the natural order. Now he turns to the question of its apparent delay. The promise had been given in terms which caused people to think that it would

RELATIONAL STRUCTURE				CONTENT
		orienter		(3:8a) Dear ones/friends, do not overlook this fact:
	grounds	HEAD		(3:8b) the Lord (God) considers that one day (is) like a thousand years, and he considers that a thousand years (is) like one day.
contrast	HEAD	HEAD	HEAD	(3:9a) (Therefore, you should not conclude that because the Lord Jesus Christ has not yet come back to judge people) the Lord (God) delays (Christ) doing what he (Christ) promised (i.e., he would come back to judge people),
		concess.		(3:9b) (although) some (people) consider that this (9a) is so (and that Christ never will come back to judge people);
HEAD	HEAD			(3:9c) but, (you should understand that Christ has not yet come back to judge people because) God is forbearing towards you,
		contrast		(3:9d) (because) he (God) does not want anyone to perish,
	reason	HEAD		(3:9e) but he wants everyone to repent.

be speedily fulfilled, so that, when it was not, some became discouraged and doubtful.

In this paragraph, therefore, Peter is not only concerned with refuting the error put forward by the scoffers, but also with reassuring believers who may be worried by the apparent delay in Christ's return.

3:8a. Peter addresses his readers directly again as *agapētoi* 'dear ones/ friends', as he did in 3:1, and as he does so again in 3:14 and 3:17.

The conjunction *de* introduces a contrast between *lanthanei ... autous . .. thelontas* 'they wilfully ignore' (3:5), which refers to those who scoff, and the imperative *mē lanthanetō humas* 'do not you ignore/overlook', which refers to the believers to whom he is writing.

The *humas* 'you' forms an antithesis to *autous* 'they' in verse 5.

The placing of *hen ... touto* 'this one thing/fact' initially, gives prominence to what follows the *hoti* 'that', to which it refers cataphorically. Peter wants to draw their attention to an important point which they should not overlook in the midst of their doubts, i.e., God's perception of time is different from ours.

3:8b. This clause states what believers are not to overlook.

Commentators are generally agreed that *kuriō* refers here to the "Lord God," rather than to the "Lord Jesus Christ."

When the preposition *para* is followed by the noun in the dative case, it denotes nearness in space, and means, literally, "at/by the side of, near, with." Here, it is used in a figurative sense, to mean "in the sight/judgement of someone," in this case, "the Lord (God)."

There is no verb stated in the Greek, but the verb "to be" is understood, i.e., "one day (is) with the Lord (God) as a thousand years and a thousand years (is) as one day." This is reminiscent of Psalm 90:4, but "whereas the psalmist contrasts the eternity of God with the brevity of human life, Peter contrasts the eternity of God with the impatience of human speculations. God is *patiens quia aeternus* (Augustine)" (Green). Distinctions of long and short time are nothing in the sight of God. Delay is a purely human conception. God stands outside time, so human standards of calculation cannot be applied when estimating the slowness or speed with which he fulfils his promises. Because of this difference, although the judgement has been said to be "at hand" (1 Pet 4:7), the fact that it has been delayed does not mean that it will never come, which is what is implied in the remarks of those who scoff (3:4). The delay only seems long to us because we do not view it from God's eternal perspective.

This statement is a figurative one; cf. the use of *para* 'in the sight of' and the conjunction *hōs* 'as' denoting comparison. It therefore needs to be expressed in a nonfigurative way. In the display it has been represented by "The Lord (God) considers/regards one day as (being like) a thousand years and (he considers/regards) a thousand years as (being like) one day."

3:9. Peter now goes on to further explain the seeming delay in the fulfilment of Christ's promise.

In 3:7d Peter speaks of God judging and destroying ungodly people. Now, in 3:9, he speaks of God's forbearance, which is manifested in the apparent delay of Christ's return, since that will give more time for people to repent and be saved. It seems appropriate, therefore, and conveys the sense of verse 9 more completely, if the idea of judgement is made explicit in the display, in relation to Christ's return (see display). This is probably true throughout chapter 3.

3:9a. There is some disagreement among commentators as to whether *kurios* 'Lord' here refers to "God" or to "Christ." The fact that it is generally taken to refer to God in verse 8 would favour the same meaning here, but *epaggelias* 'promise' refers probably to Christ's promise that he will come back, so it is difficult to be dogmatic as to whether the "Lord God" or the "Lord Jesus Christ" is meant here. The same ambiguity occurs in 3:15.

In the display, the "Lord (God)" has been regarded as the instigator of the delay, in that, in human terms, he delays the Lord Jesus Christ from fulfilling his (Christ's) promise (see 3:9a).

The verb *bradunei* 'hesitate, delay' is found only here and in 1 Tim. 3:15, in the New Testament, and the related noun *bradutēs* 'delay, hesitation' is found only in this verse in 2 Peter. The verb is usually followed by the accusative case, but here we have the genitive *tēs epaggelias* 'about/concerning the promise'. It is suggested in the ICC that the genitive is perhaps analogous to that used commonly after verbs of "failing" or "missing," and this is applicable here. This certainly seems possible, since the implication in this paragraph and the one preceding it, seems to be that, in the eyes of some people, the delay in the fulfilment of Christ's promise holds out the prospect that it will never be fulfilled, i.e., that he will fail to accomplish what he promised to do.

Some commentators suggest that *tēs epaggelias* depends on the noun *kurios*, i.e., "the Lord of the promise does not delay," but the majority consider that it depends on the verb *bradunei*, and the latter has been followed in the display.

On the grounds that God's perspective of time is different from ours (3:8b), Peter now concludes that the delay in Christ's promised return to earth is apparent rather than real. From a human perspective, God is delaying Christ's return, but in reality he is working according to his eternal plan, and is not delaying beyond the day which he has appointed for this event, i.e., *hēmera kuriou* 'the day of the Lord'.

The proposition, which is negative, contrasts with 3:9c, which makes a positive statement as to why we have to wait such a long time for Christ to return, i.e., God is forbearing and wants to give people the opportunity to repent.

3:9b. The subordinating conjunction *hōs* 'as' introduces a clause which is in a dependent relation to the preceding one (3:9a). The relationship may be one of concession or comment. In the display, the former is expressed.

The indefinite pronoun *tines* 'anyone,some/certain people' may refer to:
1. those who scoff;
2. professing Christians who have become disheartened or impatient at the apparent delay;
3. both of the above-mentioned.

Since the term used seems to be deliberately indefinite, it has been left so in the display, cf. "some people." There would be those within and without the church who would doubt the certainty of Christ's return.

Peter uses the verb *hēgeomai* 'think, consider, regard' several times in this letter; cf. 1:13; 2:13; 3:15. When followed by a double accusative, as in 2:13 and 3:15, it has the sense "look upon, consider someone/something, (as) someone/something." Here, one accusative is stated whilst the other is supplied by the context. The noun *bradutēta* 'slowness, delay' provides one accusative, whilst we infer from the context of the preceding proposition (3:9a) that slowness or delay in the fulfilment of the promise is equated with inability or unwillingness to do what was promised, and that Christ will never come back. This inference is made explicit in the display.

3:9c.   The conjunction *alla* 'but, rather' introduces an answer to the arguments put forward by the scoffers in 3:4, which implied that Christ would never return. This is a positive statement concerning the apparent delay in the Lord's return.

The verb *makrothumeō* 'have patience, wait, be patient/forbearing' is used a number of times in the New Testament, but only here is it followed by *eis* 'toward'. More frequently it is followed by *epi* 'with'; cf. Mt 18:26, 29; Lk 18:7; Jas 5:7.

There is some discussion as to whether *eis humas* 'towards you', or *eis hēmas* 'towards us', is the correct reading here, but the former seems to be the better attested. It can be taken then as referring to the readers to whom the letter is addressed, not as a social class, but as representing all men, cf. *pantas* 'all' (3:9e).

In his first letter Peter spoke of God's longsuffering and patience in relation to mankind in Noah's time, before the flood, (1 Peter 3:20), now he speaks of it in relation to mankind and the final judgement.

3:9d-e.   These two clauses tell us why God exercises patience/forbearance. The relationship between them, linked as they are by *alla* 'but, rather', is one of contrast.

The verb *boulomai* 'wish, want, desire', which is used here, is distinguished by some commentators from *thelō* 'wish, will', in that they consider the former to express the sense 'desiring, being disposed towards something' while the latter has the sense of 'willing, purposing' to do something. One may have a sincere desire that something should come about and yet it may not do so. As Dr. Lloyd Jones puts it, "Whatever God wills inevitably comes to pass--there is a difference between God willing and wishing a thing, and what Peter says is that God does not wish that any should perish but that all should come to repentance."

The present participle *boulomenos* 'wishing, wanting, desiring' refers back to *kurios* 'Lord', i.e., "God." It is followed by two accusative and infinitive constructions linked by *alla* 'but'.

In the first of these two accusative and infinitive constructions (3:9d) the pronoun *tinas* is again indefinite, as in 3:9b, and the same verb, *apolesthai* 'to be destroyed, die', is used as it was used in 3:6 when describing the destruction of the world in Noah's time.

The negative *mē* applies to *tinas apolesthai* 'no one to be destroyed'. It might possibly be regarded as a litotes and be expressed by "everyone to be saved," cf. 2:4a and 2:5a *ouk epheisato* 'he did not spare', which becomes "he destroyed." However, the contrast between this proposition and 3:9e is seen more clearly if the negative is retained.

The verb *chōreō* means literally "go, go out/away, reach." Here the aorist infinitive *chōrēsai* is used in a figurative sense with *eis metanoian* 'to repentance'. The clause has the sense of entering into a state of repentance, with the preposition *eis* indicating the goal to be achieved. This is perhaps best expressed as "become repentant" or simply "to repent."

The participle *boulomenos* 'wanting' applies to both 9d and 9e, and the agent in each case is "God." The latter of the two (9e) has natural prominence.

The thought behind these two clauses recalls Luke 13:3 and 5 where Jesus says, "Except ye repent ye shall all likewise perish."

PARAGRAPH CLUSTER CONSTITUENT 3:10
(Paragraph) (Role: Concession to 3:3-10)

THEME: *The Lord Jesus Christ will certainly come back to judge people, and at that time God will destroy this present world.*

BOUNDARIES AND COHERENCE

The boundaries for this paragraph have been discussed under this heading for 3:8-10.

The topic of this short paragraph is *hēmera kuriou* 'the Day of the Lord'. It describes what will happen on that day, using lexical items referring to natural phenomena:

> *ouranoi* 'heavens'
> *stoicheia* 'elements'
> *gē* 'earth'

and others referring to the destruction of these:

> *pareleusontai* 'cease to exist, pass away'
> *kausoumena* 'burning'
> *luthēsetai* 'will be destroyed/dissolved'
> *heurethēsetai* 'will be burned up/disappear'.

PROMINENCE AND THEME

This paragraph consists of a single sentence of which the main verb is *hēxei* 'he/it will come'. In the Greek, the clause in which this occurs is followed by several subordinate clauses which are introduced by the relative *en hē* 'on which'. These subordinate clauses describe the circumstances of the "Day of the Lord."

The head of the paragraph, therefore, is 3:10a. However, the circumstances accompanying Christ's return are given prominence, by reason of the detail in which they are described, therefore, the theme statement for the paragraph is based upon the head, 3:10a, and also on 3:10d-f, the circumstances of Christ's return being described in more general terms.

RELATIONAL STRUCTURE			CONTENT
HEAD			(3:10a) (Although God is forbearing towards you/although God is doing this (3:9c-e)), (at) the time (which the Lord God has appointed) the Lord (Jesus Christ) will (certainly) come back (to judge people).
manner	HEAD		(3:10b) (Christ) will come back (unexpectedly),
	comp.		(3:10c) like a thief (comes unexpectedly),
	HEAD1		(3:10d) and at that time (i.e., 3:10a) the heavens will cease to exist (accompanied by) a rushing/roaring sound,
circ.	HEAD2		(3:10e) (God) will (cause) the elements/the parts (of which the universe consists) (to) be destroyed, (by) being burned,
	HEAD3		(3:10f) and (God will cause) the earth and everything in it (which God has) made, and everything (which man has) made, to be burned up/disappear.

NOTES ON 3:10

The conjunction *de* is translated "but" in most versions, cf. KJV, TEV, NIV, RSV, NEB, and this puts 3:10a, which is head of 3:10a-f, in a contraexpectation relationship with 3:9c, the head of the preceding paragraph. It might serve to clarify the relationship if 3:10 began with a summary concession; eg., "Although, God is forbearing towards you,/Although God is doing this (3:9c-e)."

3:10a. The expression *hēmera kuriou* 'Day of the Lord' is a technical term, and therefore could possibly be retained in its literal form. Alternatively, an expression such as "the day when the Lord will judge people" might be used.

There are various references in the New Testament to "the day of our Lord Jesus Christ" (1 Cor 1:8); "day of Christ Jesus" (Phil 1:6); "day of Christ" (Phil 1:10; 2:16); "the day of God" (2 Pet 3:12). It is more common, however, to speak of the Lord's return than of "the Day of the Lord," but the latter is generally regarded as referring to or including the *parousia*, or return, of the Lord. Both are spoken of as being "like a thief" (see Mt 24:36-44 and here).

In 2:9 and 3:7 of this letter reference is made to *hēmeran kriseōs* 'day of judgement', and, from the descriptions in those verses of that day, and those in 3:10 and 12 of the "Day of the Lord" and the "Day of God," it would seem that the same day is referred to. It is the day which God has appointed, and the Lord Jesus Christ is his agent on that day.

In the display, as an alternative to the literal form, "the Day of the Lord," I have chosen to represent the expression in the following way: "(at) the time (which the Lord God has appointed) the Lord (Jesus Christ) will (certainly) come back." My reason for this is that the whole thrust of the letter is to encourage believers to live holy lives, so that they may enter the heavenly kingdom (1:11), the new heavens and earth where only the righteous will live (3:13), and this depends on their being found blameless by the Lord Jesus Christ when he comes back to judge people. It is the return of Christ to judge people which is in focus therefore; cf. also "Where is the promise of his coming?" (3:4), and the reference to "his promise" in 3:9.

The term *hēmera* 'day' should not be taken as meaning a day of 12/24 hours but a period of time.

Hēxei 'will come' stands first, by way of emphasis. It helps to stress the certainty of the Lord's return, in contrast with the doubts which have been implied as to the possibility that he might never return. This emphasis may be expressed by the adverb "certainly."

3:10b-c. In the simile *Hēxei ... hēmera kuriou hōs kleptēs* 'the Day of the Lord will come like a thief' the point of similarity needs to be made explicit.

As has been mentioned above, the same figure is used by the Lord himself in the Gospels, (Mt 24:36-44; Lk 12:39). It is also used by Paul, (1 Thess 5:2), and John (Rev 16:15). The point of similarity is the unexpectedness of both events. Just as people are taken by surprise when a thief comes to steal from them, so will they be surprised when the Lord Jesus Christ returns in judgement.

The two propositions 3:10b and 10c make the comparison explicit, with "Christ" stated as the topic, and the point of similarity concerning the manner of his coming and that of the thief represented by the adverb "unexpectedly."

The Majority Text includes the words *en nukti* 'at night' after *kleptēs* 'thief', but these words are not included in the UBS 3 text.

3:10d-f. This cluster of propositions states the circumstances of Christ's return, i.e., the events which will accompany it.

The relative phrase *en hē* 'on which' refers to *hēmera kuriou* 'the Day of the Lord' and introduces the description of what will happen to the physical universe when Christ returns to judge mankind. Peter now elaborates on the brief sketch of the dissolution of the universe by fire that he gave in 3:7. He limits his view to the change that is to come to the material creation. He does not speak of other aspects, such as the resurrection of the dead. This is probably because he is concerned mainly with the arguments of the scoffers about the durability of creation, and the unchanging nature of the universe. Neither is he concerned with scientific exactness, rather, he is using popular language, which he hopes will stir the hearts and the minds of those to whom he is writing. He wants to convince them of the certainty of future judgement and the catastrophic events which will accompany it.

3:10d. Peter refers to *ouranoi* 'heavens' five times in this chapter; cf. verses 5,7,10,12, and 13 (see note on 3:5). He seems to refer to the heaves belonging immediately to the earth, the atmosphere or visible heavens; cf. also Isa 34:4 and 51:6.

Pareleusontai is the future tense of *parerchomai*, which means literally "go by, pass by" someone or something; it is used here figuratively to mean "will pass away, come to an end, disappear," speaking of "the heavens." The sense is that they will cease to be what they are now, that their present state and condition will give place to the "new heavens and earth" of 3:13; cf. also Rev. 21:1, and the words of Jesus in Mt 24:35; 5:18; Mk 13:31; Lk 16:17. The descriptions in verses 7 and 12 of this chapter are very similar.

The adverb *rhoizēdon*, which occurs only here in the New Testament, is an onomatopoeic word, used of rushing sounds, such as the hissing of a snake, the whirr of a bird's wings, the rumble of thunder, the rush of water, or the roaring of flames. It may come from *rhoizeō* 'to rush, whizz, crash', or possibly directly from *rhoizos* 'noise made by something swishing through the air'. Since the idea of fire seems to be in the forefront of Peter's mind, (cf. *puri* 'fire' (3:7); *puroumenoi* 'burning' (3:12); *kausoumena* 'being burned up' (3:10 and 12)) it seems likely that it should be translated by 'with a roaring/rushing noise', such as a powerful fire makes.

3:10e. The conjunction *de* is a coordinating one, as Peter continues with the list of events which will accompany the second coming of Christ.

The noun *stoicheia* derives from *stoichos*, which means, literally, "a row," hence the neuter plural *stoicheia* 'things arranged in a row', such as letters of an alphabet. From this it has come to refer to the following:
1. Elements (of learning), fundamental principles; cf. Heb 5:12 and possibly Gal 4:3, 9 and Col 2:8, 20
2. Elemental substances, i.e., the basic elements from which everything in the natural world is made and of which it is composed. These were usually regarded as being earth, air, water, and fire.
3. Heavenly bodies, i.e., sun, moon, and stars
4. Cosmic spirits supposed to be connected with the elements and the stars, and to dominate human destiny

Clearly here, Peter is not using *stoicheia* in the sense of "elements of learning," nor "cosmic spirits," but in a physical sense. There is however some discussion amongst commentators as to whether 2 or 3 of the above is the correct sense.

Meyer considers that it cannot refer to the four elements, because "the dissolving of fire by means of fire is unthinkable," and it would be arbitrary to limit the idea to just two or three of the elements. Also, according to him, "the position of the words shows that the expression has reference neither to the earth afterwards named, nor to the world as made up of heaven and earth." He therefore understands it to refer to "the constituent elements of the heavens," corresponding to the expression *hai dunameis tōn ouranōn* 'the powers of the heavens' (Isa 34:4; Mt 24:29), "since in the preceding *hoi ouranoi . . . pareleusontai* 'the heavens . . . will disappear' no mention has as yet been made of the destruction of heaven and earth by fire."

Kelly considers that the position of *stoicheia* between *ouranoi* 'heavens' (10d) and *gē* 'earth' (10f) signifies a third kind of cosmic entity, viz., "the celestial bodies," whose extinction or collapse was a stock feature of eschatological speculation, cf. Isa 13:10; 34:4; Ezek 32:7ff.; Joel 2:10; Mt 24:29; Mk 13:24ff.; Rev 6:13.

In opposition to both of these, Lange observes that the earth is referred to, first as an element, and afterwards as a totality. Also, in his opinion, there is nothing contradictory in the idea that the element of fire should be suspended in its action by a stronger, supernatural fire. He does not envisage a total annihilation of the elemental constituents of the world, rather, a complete change and renewal, resulting in the new heavens and earth of 3:12. Further, he regards the reference to *stoicheia* in 3:12, where the earth is not expressly mentioned, as showing plainly that it relates primarily to the earth, with the use of *de* intimating as much. Alford, however, considers that *de* followed by *kai* when reference is made to the earth, necessarily belongs with "the heavens," and that the mention of the heavenly bodies as affected by the great day is constant in Scripture; cf. Isa 13:9, 10; Mt 24:29.

As is clear from these varying opinions, it is difficult to arrive at a completely satisfying answer as to what Peter means by *stoicheia*. In the context, therefore, it seems best to follow the common meaning of *stoicheia*, i.e., the basic elements of which the universe is composed. Ellicott describes these as "the smaller parts that go to make up the whole." In the display it has been represented by "elements/parts (of which the universe consists)." This basic framework will be consumed by fire.

The verb *kausoō* 'be consumed by heat, burn up' is found only here and in 3:12 in the New Testament. In both cases it is associated with *stoicheia* 'elements', and the present passive tense is used. It denotes a violent, consuming heat, by means of which the elements will be destroyed.

The verb *luō* 'break up' something into its component parts, or 'destroy', is used by Peter in each of verses 10, 11, and 12. It is used in relation to *toutōn . . . pantōn* 'all these things' in 3:11 and *ouranoi* 'heavens' in 3:12. In different versions this has been translated as "melt," "disintegrate," "disappear," "be destroyed." In the display, the last of these has been chosen. "God" has been made explicit as the agent of destruction, here and in 3:10f.

3:10f.   *Gē* here refers to the "earth" in contrast to "heaven," but there is some debate as to what is referred to by *ta en autē erga* 'it works in it'.

Erga 'works' is passive in sense, meaning "that which is brought into being by work" (Arndt and Gingrich). But this may then refer to:

1. the works of both God and man, of nature and of art, i.e., the whole of natural creation and also all the products of human culture and civilization;
2. the works of man, in a moral sense, i.e., every action performed by man;
3. the creations of God as they are related in the history of creation; cf. Rev 10:6.

The first of these, which includes the other two, seems to be the most appropriate sense in which to understand this phrase. It has been expressed in the display, therefore, by "everything (which God has) made and everything (which man has) made on the earth."

There are a number of variant readings for the verb in this clause. They are as follows:

1. *katakaēsetai* 'will be burned up, consumed' (Majority Text);
2. *heurethēsetai* 'will be found' (UBS 3);
3. *aphanisthēsontai* 'be rendered invisible/unrecognisable', i.e., "disappear" (only found in one MS, C).

The second of these is the most difficult; cf. NIV and NEB "laid bare." Some commentators, however, suggest that the clause is, in fact, a rhetorical question, since the verb *heuriskō* frequently in Scripture approximates to "be" or "exist," and when used in the negative or cast in the form of a question, can convey the sense of nonexistence.

Arndt and Gingrich and the ICC consider that the correct reading should probably be the negative *ouch heurethēsetai* 'shall not be found'.

In the context the first of these possibilities seems appropriate and has been used in the display.

SUB-PART CONSTITUENT 3:11-13
(Paragraph) (Role: Head of 3:1-13)

THEME: *You certainly ought to behave in a godly manner, since God will destroy everything like this (3:10) and since only those people who are righteous will live in the new heavens and on the new earth.*

BOUNDARIES AND COHERENCE

The evidence for the initial boundary of this paragraph has been discussed under this heading for 3:8-10.

The final boundary is marked by the start of a new paragraph at 3:14. It is clearly introduced by the conjunction *dio* 'therefore', the vocative *agapētoi* 'dear ones/friends', and the imperative *spoudasate* 'be diligent/ zealous'.

Except for *luthēsontai* 'they will be destroyed' (3:12), which is future tense, all the verbs in 3:11-13 are present tense, and this also helps to mark it off as a unit.

Coherence is shown in the use of vocabulary relating to holy living:

hagiais anastrophais 'holy conduct' (3:11)

eusebeiais 'godliness' (3:11)

dikaiosunē 'righteousness' (3:13).

The unity of the paragraph is also seen in the use of the following words belonging to the same semantic set:

toutōn ... pantōn 'all these' (referring, by implication, to the items included in 3:10d-f) (3:11)

ouranoi 'heavens' (3:12,13)

stoicheia 'elements' (3:12)

RELATIONAL STRUCTURE				CONTENT
grounds1				(3:11a) Since (God) will certainly destroy all these things like this (3:10d-f),
HEAD	HEAD			(3:11b) you certainly ought to behave in a godly manner
	circ.			(3:12a) (while) you eagerly look forward to (the Lord Jesus Christ) returning on that day/at that time (which) God (has appointed).
		ampli./ comment on "day"	HEAD1	(3:12b) Because of (that day/time) which (God has appointed) the heavens will burn up, and (as a result) they will be destroyed,
			HEAD2	(3:12c) and the elements will be burned up, and (as a result) they will be destroyed (by God).
	concess.			(3:13a) Although (all this will happen (12b-c))
		orienter		(3:13b) we(inc) expect that
grounds2	HEAD	HEAD		(3:13c) (there will be) new heavens and a new earth,
		reason		(3:13d) because he (God) promised this (13c).
		comment/ ampli.		(3:13e) In these heavens and on this earth (only) those (people) who are righteous will live [PERS].

    gēn 'earth' (3:13)

along with the following group of words connected with their destruction:

    luomenōn 'being destroyed' (3:11)
    puroumenoi 'being burned' (3:12)
    luthēsontai 'they will be destroyed' (3:12)
    kausoumena 'being burned' (3:12)
    tēketai 'is destroyed' (3:12).

In addition, there is the repetition of *prosdokaō* 'expect, look forward to' in verses 12 and 13.

Grammatically, this paragraph consists of two sentences in the Greek: 3:11-12 and 3:13. Each consists of a main clause (3:11b and 3:13b-c respectively), with dependent participial and relative clauses.

The exact relationship between these two sentences is difficult to determine. The connecting *de* in verse 13 seems to be contrastive, and to have the sense of "but" or "nevertheless," i.e., the destruction which has been described will take place, but those who are believers and have lived godly lives can look beyond that, to the new kingdom which Christ will establish for those who are righteous. However, there seems to be a clause of concession implied here, between the description of judgement and destruction in verse 12 and the statement in 3:13 that there will be a new heavens and a new earth, i.e., although there will be devastation, renewal will follow. This prospect should motivate believers to live godly lives, so that they will inhabit this new kingdom. The propositional cluster 3:13b-e, therefore, provides a motivational grounds for the head 3:11b.

PROMINENCE AND THEME

Apart from those in the relative clauses, there are only two nonparticipial verb forms in this paragraph. They are *dei huparchein* '(you) ought to be' (3:11b), and *prosdokōmen* 'we expect' (3:13b). By virtue of the exclamatory *potapous* 'what sort of persons', which precedes it, prominence is given to *dei huparchein* '(you) ought to be', so that 3:4b is therefore considered to be the head of the paragraph. However, the grounds in 3:11a and 3:13c should also probably be included in the theme statement, i.e., since God will destroy everything like this (3:10) and since only those who are righteous will live in the new heavens and earth which will replace this present one.

NOTES ON 3:11-13

3:11. Peter begins a further exhortation to godly living. The grounds for this is the certainty that God will destroy this present world, just as he has described in the preceding verse. As in 1 Peter 4:7ff. he uses the picture of the approaching catastrophe to exhort and challenge his readers spiritually, stressing the link between conduct and belief in the Lord's return. Expectation of the Lord's return should lead to holy, godly living, since that will be a time of judgement, when each person will be consigned to either heaven or hell.

3:11a. *Toutōn ... pantōn* 'all these things' refers to all the things mentioned in verse 10 which will be destroyed, i.e., *ouranoi* 'heavens', *stoicheia* 'elements', *gē* 'earth', *ta en aute erga* 'the works in it'.

The present participle *luomenōn* is regarded by commentators as being "the prophetic present," i.e., the future prophetically regarded as present, and to express the certainty of the future event. In the display, therefore, it is expressed by either "(God) will certainly destroy all these things" or "all these things will certainly be destroyed (by God)," with "God" being supplied as the agent and "certainly" expressing the certain accomplishment of the destruction.

The clause is a genitive absolute, and one of the functions of a genitive absolute, in the Epistles, is to provide grounds. Here, it provides the grounds for the exhortation in 3:11b. In most versions, this is expressed by "since all these things will be destroyed/pass away."

The Majority Text has *oun* 'therefore' at the beginning of this sentence, but in UBS 3 the adverb *houtōs* 'thus, in this manner, so' is preferred. The latter is expressed in the display, in view of the question construction which follows, but both are implied by the general flow of thought.

Houtōs 'thus, in this manner' can refer to what precedes, as it does in 1:11, where it summarizes a thought expressed in what precedes. It can also refer to what follows. Here, it seems much more likely to refer back, i.e., "since (God) will destroy all these things in this manner/like this," referring to the description in 3:10.

3:11b. There is some debate among commentators as to whether *potapous* 'of what sort/kind' introduces a question or an exclamation.

In some translations there is a division after *humas* 'you', cf. TEV, NIV, PHIL. *Potapous* is regarded as introducing a question, "What sort of people should you be?", and the rest of the verse provides the answer, "You ought to live holy and godly lives."

Alternatively, verses 11 and 12 can be regarded as an exclamation; cf. NAS, RSV, with no break between the verses. The NEB regards it as an exclamation, but makes no break at the end of verse 11.

Potapous is used only six times in the New Testament; see Mt 8:27; Mk 13:1; Lk 1:29; 7:39; 1 Jn 3:1; and here. In the majority of cases it is expressed as an exclamation, often showing wonder or admiration. However, it makes no difference whether it is a question or an exclamation, since it can only be a rhetorical question in any case, and the rhetorical question is equivalent to an emphatic assertion; "you certainly ought to be." Strictly speaking, therefore, it is neither an ordinary question nor an exclamation. Bruce Moore in *NOT* 97, p. 27 comments that "the difficulty of assigning this to one of the rhetorical question classes is evidence that the modern Greek texts are right in not considering it a question at all."

Dei 'it is necessary, one must/has to', denotes necessity of any kind--of divine destiny or fate, of law or custom, of duty, of what is fitting, etc. Here the necessity arises from the expectation of the coming day of judgement, when the ungodly will be destroyed and the righteous will become the inhabitants of "a new heaven and earth" (3:7 and 3:13). *Dei* is followed by the usual construction of accusative and infinitive, which here is *huparchein (humas)* '(you) to be', with the *humas* 'you' referring to those to whom he is writing.

The phrase *en hagiais anastrophais kai eusebeiais* means literally 'in holy behaviours and godlinesses'. Peter uses the noun *anastrophē* 'way of life, conduct, behaviour' a number of times, in both of his letters; cf. 1 Peter 1:15,18; 2:12; 3:1,2,16; 2 Peter 2:7. He also uses the related verb *anastrephō* 'to live', in 1 Peter 1:17 and 2 Peter 2:18. This is the only place in the New Testament, however, where the plural of these two nouns is used--possibly to indicate the variety of acts involved, the different forms and directions that holy living can take. We are to strive after holiness in every part and aspect of our lives.

The noun *eusebeia* 'godliness', recalls 1:3,6 and 7, where it was also used, when Peter told them that God had given them "everything necessary for life and godliness" (1:3), and that they should add "godliness to patience" (1:6 and 7), in their efforts to live truly Christian lives. Here he exhorts them once more to make every effort in this direction. For a discussion of the semantic components of *eusebeia*, which is an important Petrine word, see note on 1:3.

Peter uses abstract nouns in the plural a number of times in both his letters. Besides here, there are the following:

> *hupokriseis kai phthonous* 'hypocrisies and envies' (1 Pet 2:1)
>
> *aretai* 'praises' (1 Pet 2:9)
>
> *aselgeiais, epithumiais, oinophlugiais, kōmois, potois, kaiathemitois eidōlolatrais* 'lasciviousnesses, lusts, drunkennesses, revelings, banquetings, abominable idolatries' (1 Pet 4:3)
>
> *aselgeiais* 'lasciviousnesses' (2 Pet 2:2)
>
> *pleonexiais* 'greedinesses, covetousnesses' (2 Pet 2:14).

It seems possible that the plural forms are used in order to express multiplicity or excess, in the case of those which refer to vices, and wholeheartedness and zeal in the case of those which refer to virtues.

Some commentators suggest that this phrase may be taken with what follows rather than with what precedes, but this is unlikely since it would mean that there is no complement to the verb *huparchein*, only a subject.

3:12a. The verb *prosdokaō* 'wait for, look for, expect' is used whether the waiting is done in hope, fear, or a neutral state of mind. It takes accusative of person or thing waited for or expected, which here is *tēn parousian tēs tou theou hēmeras* 'the coming of the day of God'.

Although believers do not know when Christ will return in judgement, they should be in a state of expectation, based on a firm belief that he will return on the day which God has appointed. Peter exhorts believers to be ready for that day, and his repetition of *prosdokaō* 'wait for, expect', in verses 13 and 14, emphasizes the importance of being prepared for Christ's coming. It adds urgency to his exhortation that they should lead godly lives in readiness for the new kingdom "where righteousness will dwell."

According to Arndt and Gingrich, *speudō*, when intransitive, may have the sense "hurry, make haste" or "be zealous, exert oneself, be industrious." When it is used transitively, it has the sense "hasten" or "strive for." In the New Testament, it is used only here and in Lk 2:16; 19:5,6; Acts 20:16; 22:18. In these other examples it is used intransitively, but here it is used transitively, with *tēn parousian tēs tou theou hēmeran* 'the coming of the day of God' providing the object.

Some commentators consider that the day of God can be "hastened," in the sense that believers can bring about those conditions which will render God's *makrothumia* 'forbearance' (3:9) unnecessary. They can do this by zealously striving to live in obedience to Christ's teaching, by evangelism, by prayer etc.; cf. Mk 13:10; Acts 3:19-21; 2 Tim 4:8. While God has his own fixed times, these are not independent of human activity. His sovereign will takes into account human zeal, unbelief etc., so that we are still responsible for playing our part in His plan. This sense is reflected in some versions; cf. TEV, NEB, PHIL.

Other commentators suggest that it is possible to regard the two participles, *prosdokōntas* 'waiting for, expecting' and *speudontas* 'hastening', as a hendiadys, with the second participle acting as a qualifying adverb to the first, e.g., "eagerly looking forward to" (Weymouth). This is linguistically possible and makes sense.

The latter of these alternatives has been represented in the display, for the following reasons:

1. The context here is godly living, and eager expectancy would be an appropriate state for those who are living godly lives, since they will be found to be blameless when the Lord returns, and so need not fear the judgement; cf. 3:14.
2. The fact that *speudō* is used transitively here and intransitively in the other examples above would seem to indicate that it is used in a different sense to "hastening away/to."
3. The fact that there is only an object phrase would seem to support a hendiadys.

The phrase *tēn parousian tēs tou theou hēmeras* 'the coming of the day of God' occurs nowhere else in the New Testament, although in Rev 16:14 we have *tēs hēmeras tēs megalēs tou theou tou pantokratoros* 'the great day of God Almighty'. It is the only place in the New Testament where *parousia* 'coming' is used with reference to the day rather than the person whose coming is anticipated.

In 3:4 we have *hē epaggelia tēs parousias autou* 'the promise of his coming', which refers to the coming of Christ; so here *parousia* is understood to refer to the event of Christ's return, with *tēs tou theou hēmeras* 'the day of God' stating when this event will happen, i.e., He will return on that day/at that time which God has appointed; cf. Acts 17:31.

3:12b. *Di' hēn*, which introduces this relative clause, has been variously translated as "wherein," "when," "because of which," while *hēn* 'which' may refer to *tēn parousian* 'the coming' or *tēs tou theou hēmeras* 'the day of God'. The sense remains substantially the same whichever is referred to.

Meyer considers that *di' hēn* should not be taken in a temporal sense, i.e., "in which," but as an occasioning cause, equal to "on account of which," i.e., "on account of the coming of the day of God." The destruction described will take place because God has appointed it for this time, just as he has ordained that Christ should return at that time also. The NIV has "That day will bring about the destruction . . . ," which is strictly causal.

In the display this is expressed as an amplification or comment on "day/time (which) God (has appointed)."

The language used here is very similar to that in 3:10. The judgement is seen in terms of fire, which destroys. It recalls, too, Old Testament passages such as Mal 4:1; Mic 1:4; Isa 34:4a; Ps 50:3.

The present participle *puroumenoi* 'being on fire' gives the means for the future verb which follows, i.e., *luthēsontai* 'will be dissolved/destroyed'. This is true also of the participle *kausoumena* 'being burned up' and *tēketai* 'melts, is dissolved'.

As with the present participle *luomenōn* 'being destroyed' (3:11), the present indicative *tēketai* 'melts, is dissolved' is the "prophetic" present, referring to a future event. The same verb occurs in the Septuagint in Mic 1:4 and Isa 34:4.

3:13a. The conjunction *de*, with which this verse begins, is translated by "but" in most versions, setting in contrast the destructive effects of the day of judgement which have just been described, and the renewal which will follow. Peter is encouraging his readers by giving them a good reason for strenuously endeavouring to live holy lives. It recalls 1:10 and 11 and 1 Pet. 1:4. However, in the display, the *de* has been represented by "although," since there seems to be a clause of concession implied here between the description of the day of judgement in the preceding verse and the statement in 3:13c, i.e., although there will be all this devastation, renewal will follow.

3:13b. Peter uses *prosdokaō* 'expect, look for' a second time in this paragraph, and again in 3:14. Ellicott comments on this tendency of Peter's to repeat a word; cf. also *apōleia* 'destruction', used three times in 2:1-3. He considers that possibly it is evidence of strong emotion on Peter's part.

There is a change here from second person plural verb forms to first person plural in *prosdokōmen* 'we expect'. Perhaps this is because Peter wishes to encourage his readers by numbering himself among them as a member of Christ's body with them.

This proposition acts as an orienter for the head of the cluster, 3:13c.

3:13c. The adjective *kainos* 'new', used here to describe *ouranoi* 'heavens' and *gē* 'earth', has the sense of "new" in contrast with something "old" which is obsolete and needs to be replaced by what is "new."

3:13d. The Christian hope of a new heaven and a new earth is *kata to epaggelma autōn* 'according to his promise', i.e., it is based upon what God Himself has promised through His prophets, e.g., Isa 65:17; 66:22. It is, therefore, expressed as a reason for the head 3:13c.

The only other use of *epaggelma* 'promise' in the New Testament is in 2 Pet 1:4.

3:13e. *En hois* 'in which' clearly refers to *kainous ... ouranous kai gēn kainēn* 'new heavens and a new earth' where everything will be at one with the Lord and obedient to His will, in contrast with the world as it is now, which is dominated by evil desires; cf. 1:4.

In the Old Testament, the Messiah is represented as the righteous one (Jer 23:5ff.) and righteousness or justice as the characteristic of the Messianic age; cf. Isa 32:16-18; 61:3. In the New Testament also, Jesus taught that the wicked will be destroyed and that the righteous will shine like the sun in the Father's kingdom; cf. Mt 13:41, 43; Rev 21; Rom 8:19-22.

Dikaiosunē 'righteousness' can be regarded as an example of personification, as it is used here in conjunction with *katoikei* 'dwells, lives'. It has been represented in the display, therefore, by "those (people who are) righteous."

Some commentators point out that the use of the verb *katoikeō* 'dwell, live' is significant in that it conveys the idea of a permanent home, in contrast to *paroikeō* which has the sense of "live as a stranger"; cf. Heb 11:9.

This statement may be regarded as either an amplification of or comment on 3:13c.

EPISTLE CONSTITUENT 3:14-18c
(Paragraph) (Role: Summary of 1:3--3:13)

THEME: *Do all you can to behave in a godly manner and guard against those who will entice you to doubt what now you firmly believe.*

BOUNDARIES AND COHERENCE

The initial boundary of this paragraph has been discussed in the notes on boundaries and coherence for the previous paragraph (3:11-13).

The final boundary is marked by the formal closing of the letter with the doxology in 3:18d.

RELATIONAL STRUCTURE

	grounds$_1$					
HEAD A	HEAD$_1$	HEAD				
		purpose				
		ORIENTER				
HEAD B	HEAD$_2$	HEAD				
		reason				
	grds$_2$	HEAD	HEAD			
			reason			
		ampli.	HEAD			
			ampli.	orienter/ transition		
				HEAD	HEAD	HEAD
						comp.
					result	
	grounds					
	ORIENTER					
		means	HEAD			
			means			
HEAD B'	HEAD$_3$	HEAD				
		orienter				
		HEAD$_1$				
HEAD A'	HEAD$_4$					
		HEAD$_2$				

CONTENT

(3:14a) Therefore dear ones/friends, (since) you are waiting for these things (to happen, i.e., all the events of the Day of the Lord),

(3:14b) do all you can (to behave in a godly (manner)

(3:14c) (in order that) he (Christ) will judge (that) you (are) completely pure/blameless [DBL], (and that you are) peacefully disposed toward each other.

(3:15a) And consider this:

(3:15b) our Lord (Jesus Christ is) forbearing/patient

(3:15c) (because he wants) to save (people).

(3:15d) Our(inc) dear brother Paul also wrote wisely to you (concerning these same matters (3:8-10)),

(3:15e) because (God) caused him (Paul) to understand (these matters, i.e., all the events of the Day of the Lord)/(God) revealed (these matters) to him (Paul).

(3:16a) In the same way he (Paul) spoke (wisely) about these matters (i.e., all the events of the Day of the Lord) in all the letters (that he wrote),

(3:16b) in which (letters) there are certain things which are difficult (for people) to understand.

(3:16c) Those people (who are spiritually) ignorant and unstable explain/interpret these things (3:16b) falsely,

(3:16d) like they also interpret the other Scriptures falsely,

(3:16e) with the result that they themselves are destroyed (by God).

(3:17a) Therefore dear ones/friends, (since) you already know (that it is dangerous to be deceived by what these false teachers say/teach),

(3:17b) guard against (this (17c-e) happening):

(3:17c) You are deceived/misled

(3:17d) by (means of) unprincipled (people) saying and doing that which is wrong,

(3:17e) so that you yourselves doubt what now you firmly believe.

(3:18a) (Instead of doing this (3:17e))

(3:18b) (behave in such a manner that you) experience increasingly (the fact that) our(inc) Lord and Saviour Jesus Christ acts graciously (towards you),

(3:18c) and get to know our(inc) Lord and Saviour Jesus Christ (in an) increasingly (personal way).

There is strong lexical coherence throughout these verses, in the two contrasting sets of words which refer to Christian virtues and blessings on the one hand:

aspiloi 'spotless, without blemish' (3:14)

amōmētoi 'blameless, unblemished' (3:14)

eirēnē 'peace' (3:14)

makrothumian 'forbearance, patience' (3:15)

sōtērian 'salvation' (3:15)

sophian 'wisdom' (3:15)

stērigmou 'steadfastness' (3:17)

chariti 'grace' (3:18)

gnōsei 'knowledge' (3:18)

and the characteristics evidenced in those who are outside of Christ, and their resulting condemnation, on the other:

amatheis 'ignorant' (3:16)

astēriktoi 'unstable' (3:16)

streblousin 'twist, distort' (3:16)

apōleian 'destruction' (3:16)

athesmōn 'lawless, unprincipled' (3:17)

planē 'error' (3:17)

sunapachthentes 'being led astray' (3:17)

ekpesēte 'fall' (3:17)

These verses contain four verbs in the imperative mood. The first two, *spoudasete* 'do all you can' (3:14b), and *hēgeisthe* 'consider' (3:15a), are connected by the conjunction *kai*, and the second two, *phulassesthe* 'guard against' (3:17b), and *auxanete* 'grow, increase' (3:18b and c), are connected by the conjunction *de*, thus forming two propositional clusters, 14a-16e and 17a-18c, with two heads to each (see display).

Possibly these two propositional clusters could be regarded as being two paragraphs, with the boundary between them marked by a combination of features in verse 17, as follows:

1. the conjunction *oun* 'therefore';
2. the vocative *agapētoi* 'dear ones/friends';
3. a return to the second person plural pronoun *humeis* 'you', and the imperative *phulassesthe* 'guard against', after the digression about Paul and his letters in 15d-16e.

However, since there is no accompanying change of topic, 1 and 3 above can be regarded as simply signaling a return to the exhortation of 14a-15c, and this would support the view that 14a-18c is a single paragraph.

There are some formal parallelisms to be noted between the two propositional clusters which form the paragraph, as follows:

1. Both *dio* 'therefore, for this reason' (3:14), and *oun* 'so, therefore, consequently' (3:17) are inferential conjunctions.

2. The vocative *agapētoi* 'dear ones/friends' occurs immediately following the conjunction in both 3:14 and 3:17.
3. The demonstrative pronoun *tauta* 'these things' is explicit following
   the vocative in 3:14, and is implicit in 3:17.
4. The present participles, *prosdokōntes* 'waiting for' (3:14), and
   proginōskontes 'knowing already' (3:17) express the grounds for the
   two heads following each.

It also seems plausible that there is a chiastic structure to the paragraph. The outer edges of the chiasmus are exhortations to action, i.e., to live
holy lives, while the inner layers are exhortations to do with doctrinal matters
which are the basis of how believers should live. Peter urges them to
"consider" the matter of the delay in Christ's return to earth, and its implications (3:15a-c), and to "guard against" having their own firmly held beliefs
shaken due to the influence of "unprincipled" people (3:17b-e).

These observations are presented in the following display:

A   Exhortation to live holy lives (3:14b-c).
B   Exhortation concerning doctrinal matters (3:15a-16e).
B' Exhortation concerning doctrinal matters (3:17b-e).
A' Exhortation to live holy lives (3:18b-c).

In this paragraph Peter provides a final exhortation and summary or
recapitulation of the body of the Epistle, as follows:

In 3:14 he exhorts them to do all they can to live godly lives in prepara-
tion for the return of Christ in judgement. This recalls the exhortation and its
grounds in 3:11-13.

In 3:15 God's forbearance and His desire for people to be saved is restated, recalling the same theme in 3:9.

In 3:16-17 there is a warning against the distortion of scriptural truths
and the ultimate destruction which will result for those responsible. This
reiterates what was said in 2:1 concerning the destructive heresies of the false
teachers, and throughout that chapter. It also recalls the "cunningly devised
fables" of 1:16, and, in contrast, the message of the Old Testament prophets
which is completely reliable (1:19-21). This warning is linked with an exhortation to guard against being swayed by such error and becoming spiritually
unstable. This also looks back to chapter 2.

In 3:18a-c there is a final exhortation to grow in grace and in the
knowledge of our Lord and Saviour Jesus Christ, and this restates briefly the
exhortation contained in 1:5-11. It also refers back to Peter's prayer for them
in 1:2.

PROMINENCE AND THEME

The four imperatives, *spoudasate* 'do all you can' (3:14b), *hēgeisthe*
'consider' (3:15a), *phulassesthe* 'guard against' (3:17b), and *auxanete* 'grow,
increase' (3:18b and c), are naturally prominent, and none of the supporting
material is marked for prominence.

The two pairs of imperatives form two complex heads for the paragraph, making it difficult to arrive at a theme statement, which may be abstracted or stated in compound form, unless there are grounds for considering that any of the main propositions is more prominent than the others.

As we have seen above, there seems to be a chiastic structure to the paragraph, and this tends to throw emphasis onto the outer edges of the chiasmus, i.e., onto 3:14b-c and 3:18b-c, both of which are exhortations to live godly lives.

The two exhortations to godly living are "Do all you can (to behave in a godly manner)" (3:14b), and, "(Behave in such a manner that you) experience increasingly (the fact that) our(inc.) Lord and Saviour Jesus Christ acts graciously (towards you) and get to know more and more about him" (3:18b-c). It seems reasonable to suppose that "in such a manner" (18b) corresponds to "in a godly manner" (14b), since they are corresponding parts of the chiasmus. The "that you experience" etc. is an anticipated result of obedience to the command, and, since this is a hortatory paragraph, the command would be more prominent. Hence, the theme of the outer layers of the chiasmus is "Behave in a godly manner."

Of the two heads, B and B', the latter has greater prominence, in that the conjunction *oun* 'therefore', the vocative *agapētoi* 'dear ones', and the imperative *phulassesthe* 'guard against' occur together. Also, since the whole Epistle, as well as being an exhortation to godly living, is a reminder to believers to be on their guard against those who will try to cast doubt on their Christian beliefs in order to lead them back to their old way of life; it seems appropriate to include 3:17b and e in the theme statement.

NOTES ON 3:14-18c

3:14a. Peter addresses his readers again as *agagpētoi* 'dear ones/friends', as in 3:1, 8, and later in 3:17. This repetition indicates the intensity of his feelings and his great concern for their spiritual welfare.

In this verse, too, Peter uses the verb *prosdokaō* 'expect, wait for' for the third time in the chapter (see verses 12 and 13). Here the present participle is used to express the grounds for the two main propositions (14b and 15b), which follow.

There seems to be general agreement among commentators that the demonstrative pronoun *tauta* 'these things' refers to what immediately precedes in 3:13, i.e., 'the new heavens and earth in which righteousness dwells'. In verse 11 he has exhorted them to live holy lives, in expectation of the dissolution of heaven and earth. Now he does so in expectation of gaining entry into the newly created kingdom which will have for its inhabitants only those who are righteous. However, it would be equally appropriate for *tauta* to refer to all the events associated with "the day of the Lord" and described in the two previous paragraphs (3:10 and 11-13), i.e., Christ's coming in judgement; the destruction of the world; the establishment of a new heavens and a new earth. The use of the same verb, *prosdokaō* 'wait for' in relation to all these matters in verses 12 and 13 would also support this.

3:14b. The verb *spoudazō* 'be zealous, eager, make every effort' has been used previously by Peter in 1:10 and 1:15; see notes on those verses.

Implied here seems to be that their striving and effort should be directed towards living in a godly manner. This has therefore been stated in the display.

3:14c. The infinitive *heurethēnai* means literally 'to be found', after someone has been searching for something, but, according to Arndt and Gingrich, it is used figuratively here, in the sense of "be considered/judged," i.e., "intellectual discovery based on reflection, observation, examination, etc." The verb is used by Peter in a similar sense in 1 Pet 1:7 and 1 Pet 2:22.

The use of the infinitive *heurethēnai* 'to be judged/considered' indicates purpose, i.e., they are to make every effort "in order to be blameless."

The adjectives *aspiloi* and *amōmētoi*, when used literally, both describe something which is without any defect or blemish, such as an animal chosen for sacrifice. Peter uses *aspiloi* in this sense in 1 Pet 1:19, when comparing Christ with a lamb "without blemish and without spot." Here, both are used figuratively, in a moral and spiritual sense, and may be translated by "pure and blameless," providing a complete contrast with the false teachers, who are described as being *spiloi kai mōmoi* 'spots and blemishes' in 2:13. As in the case of 2:13, these two adjectives may be considered to be a doublet, since there is a good deal of overlap in their meanings. If so, then "completely pure/blameless" might be a possible translation, with the adverb "completely" intensifying the force of the adjective.

This is the only occurrence in the New Testament of *amōmētoi* and *aspiloi* is only found elsewhere in Jas 1:27 and 1 Tim 6:14, where it has a similar sense.

Most commentators agree that the personal pronoun *autō* 'by him' refers to Christ when he returns in judgement. Although there is nothing in the immediate context to indicate that Christ rather than God is meant, the fact that so much attention has been focused upon Christ's return in the first half of the chapter makes it likely that Christ is referred to here; cf. 3:4, 10, 12.

Autō may be taken with *aspiloi kai amōmētoi*, i.e., "spotless and blameless in his sight," or with *heuresthēnai*, i.e., "be judged by him to be pure and blameless." The sense remains substantially the same whichever is preferred, i.e., that when Christ returns in glory, to judge mankind, believers should be able to meet him, confident in the knowledge that they have lived in obedience to his commands, and conformed to the standard which he expects; cf. 1 Jn 2:28 and 3:3. Only righteousness will survive in the new heavens and earth (3:13), so it is essential for Christians to live righteously now. It was because the false teachers were not looking to this future kingdom, but only to the present earthly one, that they lived immoral lives.

According to Arndt and Gingrich, *eirēnē* can mean "peace" as opposed to *polemos* 'war, conflict', or, figuratively, it can have the sense of "harmony" (1 Pet 3:11) or "order" (1 Cor 14:33). It can also correspond to the Hebrew for "welfare, health," cf. greetings in 1 and 2 Peter. Further, since peace will be an essential characteristic of the messianic kingdom, according to the prophets, it is also frequently regarded in Christian thought as nearly synonymous with messianic salvation, and it is under this heading that this reference is placed.

Calvin considers it to mean here "a quiet state of conscience, founded on patient waiting," while Ellicott thinks that it expresses both the condition and the consequence of being "spotless and blameless." "There is no peace, saith the Lord, unto the wicked."

Kelly thinks that it denotes the state of reconciliation with God which the restored sinner enjoys. If he is living a godly life, the expectation of Christ's return should bring him a deep sense of peace, since he has nothing to fear in the day of judgement. Lenski also considers that it is the peace which Christ has established between himself and believers which is referred to here, and this is the sense in which it is understood in the NEB, NIV, and TEV.

Since this is hortatory material, dealing with behaviour, it seems likely that the sense is of being at peace amongst themselves. It might then be expressed as "peacefully disposed towards each other." Alternatively "in a peaceful state of mind" might be used.

3:15a-c. This clause recalls 3:9, where the apparent delay in Christ's return is attributed to God's forbearance in allowing a longer time for sinners to repent and be saved.

There is some discussion amongst commentators as to whether *tou kuriou hēmōn* 'our Lord' refers to God or Christ.

According to Ellicott, *kurios* refers to God in 3:8 and to Christ in 3:18, whilst in 3:9 and 15 it is disputable as to which it refers to. However, the fact that "our" appears here before "Lord," as in 3:18, inclines him to favour "Christ" here. He also considers that if "God" was meant, it would have been sufficient to say "and account that **His** long-suffering is salvation."

The ICC also considers that it refers to "Christ," since the doxology in 3:18 is addressed to him.

On the other hand, Kelly, amongst others, thinks that *kurios* here refers to "God" since, although this sense of the expression is rare, it is practially demanded by the use of "God" in 3:8, 9 and 10, and by "day of God" in 3:12.

Meyer considers that what goes before favours "God" (cf. verses 14, 12, 10, 9, 8), but that New Testament usage favours "Christ." In either case the sense is substantially the same.

It seems appropriate that the reference here should be to "Christ," despite the inconsistency with 3:9, since in the preceding verse the last reference, in 14c, is to "Christ." Also, in the New Testament, the phrase *ho kurios hēmōn* 'our Lord' seems never to refer to "God."

The imperative *hēgeisthe* 'consider, regard', with its content *tēn tou kuriou hēmōn makrothumain sōtērian* 'the forbearance of our Lord (is) salvation', provides the second head for the paragraph.

The relationship between the two nouns, *makrothumian* 'forbearance, patience' and *sōtērian* 'salvation', has been expressed in various ways in different translations:

"longsuffering ... is salvation" (KJV);

"patience as the opportunity ... to be saved" (TEV);

"forbearance ... as salvation" (RSV);

"patience ... is our salvation" (NEB);

"patience as your opportunity ... to be saved" (JER).

Since *makrothumian* 'forbearance, patience' and *sōtērian* 'salvation' are both abstract nouns, they need to be restated in the display.

The genitive construction *tēn tou kuriou hēmōn makrothumian* 'the forbearance/patience of our Lord(Jesus Christ)' is represented by "our Lord (Jesus Christ) is patient," with "our Lord (Jesus Christ)" as agent (3:15b). This same agent is also implied in 15c where *sōtērian* 'salvation' is represented by "(he wants) to save." Here an object has to be provided in order to complete the sense. This may be either "you," i.e., those to whom Peter is writing, or the general noun "people."

The two statements (15b and c) are in a RESULT-reason relationship, and together they provide the content of the ORIENTER 15a.

3:15d-e. From 15d until the end of verse 16 consists of an amplified grounds for the two heads 14b-c and 15a-c.

Some commentators suggest that *adelphos* 'brother' in the phrase *ho agapētos hēmōn adelphos Paulos* 'our beloved brother Paul' means more than that Paul was a fellow-believer. They consider it to mean "fellow-worker" or "fellow-apostle," or some such expression which implies a closer, more restricted field of relationship. This would mean that *hēmōn* 'of us' would be exclusive, but, as there does not seem to be any conclusive evidence that this is so, it has been taken in a general sense to refer to all believers and is therefore inclusive.

The phrase *kathōs kai ... egrapsen humin* 'just as also ... he (Paul) wrote to you' may refer to:

1. What immediately precedes in 3:15a-c, i.e., the apparent delay in Christ's return gives opportunity for people to repent and be saved.
2. What precedes in verses 14 and 15, i.e., Peter's exhortation to lead a blameless life, in anticipation of Christ's return, and the opportunity of salvation.
3. *Tauta* 'these things' in verse 14, which, in turn, refers to those matters spoken of in verses 10-13, i.e., the return of Christ in judgement, the new heavens and earth, etc. and hence, the need to live in a godly manner in expectation of this.

The fact that what is being spoken of is said to be referred to in all Paul's letters (cf. 3:16) suggests that the third of these alternatives is the most likely, since Paul makes frequent reference to the second coming of Christ, whereas the content of 3:15a-c is dealt with principally in Romans.

There is considerable discussion in the commentaries as to whether one specific Pauline letter is referred to here, and various suggestions have been put forward, without, however, any conclusive evidence in favour of any particular one.

The simplest solution (cf. Green) seems to be that Peter is alluding simply to Paul's constant teaching throughout his letters about the need for holy living in the light of the coming of Christ in judgement. In verse 16, he is elaborating the point he has just made, by emphasizing Paul's teaching on these subjects. He is not necessarily making a distinction between one particular letter and the rest of Paul's correspondence.

For the identity of *humin* 'you', see Introduction to the letter.

The phrase *kata tēn dotheisan autō sophian* 'according to the wisdom given to him' refers to heavenly wisdom. Paul was able to speak about these matters only because God had given him the wisdom necessary for understanding them. Peter wants to reinforce what he himself is saying, by appealing to the fact that Paul, who had said the same things, has been enlightened by the Lord. He had been given wisdom and discernment by God, so that what he writes reflects accurately God's wisdom.

Sophian 'wisdom' has been expressed by "wisely" in 15d, qualifying *egrapsen* 'wrote'.

In 15e "God" is made explicit as agent, i.e., the one who dispenses wisdom, and "Paul" is made explicit as the one to whom wisdom is given. The clause provides the reason for 15d.

3:16.   Peter goes on to amplify what he has just said about Paul's letters.

3:16a.   The *hōs kai* 'as also' at the beginning of 3:16 has the sense of "in the same way," and refers back to what immediately precedes in 15d-e, i.e., *kata tēn dotheisan autō sophian* 'according to the wisdom given to him'.

Since it cannot be determined which and how many of Paul's Epistles Peter was acquainted with, the scope of *en pasais epistolais lalōn* 'speaking in all (the) letters' cannot be determined. It is unlikely, however, that this refers to them as a finished whole, but rather, just to those known to Peter. Each church probably made a collection of them as they became known to them.

The *peri toutōn* 'about these (matters)' defines the topic of the letters, which again is the same as in the previous verse, and *lalōn en autais* 'speaking in them' is essentially repeating *egrapsen* 'he wrote'. The clause, therefore, has been expressed as amplifying 15d.

3:16b.   In some MSS, the reading here is *en hois*, while in others it is *en hais*. The former would refer to the subjects spoken about by Paul, while the latter would refer to Paul's Epistles. The sense is not materially affected, whichever is preferred, but *en hais* has been represented in the display, because of the later reference to *hōs kai tas loipas graphas* 'the other Scriptures'.

The adjective *dusnoēta* 'hard to understand' is found only here in the New Testament. It was applied in antiquity to oracles, whose pronouncements were notoriously capable of more than one interpretation.

The clause *estin dusnoēta tina* 'there are certain things hard to understand' could mean that the actual content of Paul's Epistles was sometimes difficult to understand, because he was dealing with profound matters. Alternatively, it could mean that the expressions which Paul uses to convey his meaning were difficult to understand, being ambiguous and capable of misinterpretation.

The first of these is the more likely, since the second might imply some degree of criticism, and this does not seem to be present in the passage. Possibly Peter had in mind passages which, because of their subject matter, which was difficult to accept, perhaps, rather than difficult to understand, were misinterpreted by those who wanted to justify their own moral laxity, e.g., Rom 3:20, 28; 4:15; 5:20.

3:16c. The relative pronoun *ha* 'which things' clearly refers back to *dusnoēta tina* 'things hard to understand'.

The adjective *amatheis* 'ignorant' occurs only here in the New Testament. The sense here is of a mind which is untrained and undisciplined in habits of thought, or perhaps lacking in spiritual knowledge.

The adjective *astēriktoi* 'unstable' occurs only here and in 2:14, although in 1:12 and 1 Pet 5:10 the related verb *stērizō* 'establish, confirm' speaks of the opposite, desirable state.

Streblousin 'they twist, wrench' can mean literally to twist or screw some sort of instrument. When used of persons, it can mean "to torture, torment." Here it is used figuratively, and means "to distort/pervert" the meaning so that a false meaning results.

Some commentators think that Peter is possibly referring to Paul's doctrine of justification by faith, and the Christian liberty it brings, as opposed to the bondage of the law. Paul himself saw it as liable to abuse as immoral men perverted it to mean that, once justified, a man could do what he liked, with impunity; cf. Rom 6:1; 8:1, 2.

Peter has warned his readers already that all prophecy can be distorted (1:20), and now he tells them that the teachings of the apostles can be garbled in the same way.

This description may apply to the false teachers or to those whom they deceive. It does not seem necessary to make a distinction, since the description is appropriate to both groups of people, and so is the ensuing retribution.

3:16d. The *hōs kai* 'as also' extends the reference of *streblousin* 'they distort, pervert', which applied to the *dusnoēta tina* 'things hard to understand' in Paul's letters, to *tas loipas graphas* 'the other Scriptures', i.e., "as also they distort the meaning of the other Scriptures."

The phrase *tas loipas graphas* 'the other Scriptures' indicates that there were certain writings well known to Peter and his fellow-believers, which were referred to as "the Scriptures" and were regarded as authoritative standards of religious teaching. Paul's Epistles apparently were already regarded as belonging to these Scriptures.

Meyer considers that, although in other parts of the New Testament, *hai graphai* always means the Old Testament Scriptures, the addition of *loipas* 'other' proves that other Scriptures are here referred to. If the Old Testament Scriptures were meant, they would have been more fully designated than by being placed in the same category with the inspired writings of recent or living men. However, it is quite possible that the Old Testament and the emerging New Testament canon are intended.

Peter gives a high place to Paul's writings by placing them alongside the "other Scriptures," and this is consistent with his view of the witness of the apostles as compared to that of the Old Testament prophets, in 1:16-19.

3:16e. The phrase *pros tēn idian autōn apōleian* 'to their own destruction' recalls 2:1, 3 and 3:7 and the final destruction on the day of judgement. They bring this upon themselves by their perversion of the Scriptures, as we see from various warnings in the Scriptures themselves, e.g., Deut 4:2; 12:32; Rev 22:19. By falsely interpreting the message of Scripture so that they can indulge themselves in all manner of sin, they harden themselves and bring about their own destruction.

The *idian* 'their own' serves to intensify *autōn* 'of them'.

The sense here is expressed by a clause which is the result of 3:16c, but 16c is the head of the propositional cluster 3:16c-e since it contains the finite verb *streblousin* 'they distort, pervert'.

The agent of their destruction is made explicit, i.e., "God."

3:17. Peter returns to exhortation after speaking of Paul and his writings.

3:17a. The conjunction *oun* 'therefore' introduces a conclusion from what precedes.

Peter addresses his readers as *agapētoi* 'dear ones/friends' for the fourth time in this chapter, as he earnestly implores them to be on their guard against the influence of "unprincipled men."

The pronoun *humeis* 'you' emphasizes the contrast which there should be between *hoi amatheis kai astēriktoi* 'those who are ignorant and unstable' (3:16c), and the believers to whom this letter is addressed. The latter should not allow themselves to be shaken in their Christian beliefs, since they have been warned against false doctrine and have both the Old Testament Scriptures and the letters of Paul and Peter to teach them sound doctrine.

The verb *proginōskō* 'know beforehand/in advance' is found also in Acts 26:5; Rom 8:2; 11:12; and 1 Pet 1:20. Its related noun *prognōsis* 'foreknowledge' is found in Acts 2:23 and 1 Pet 1:2. The participle *prognōskontes* 'knowing already' recalls the *tauta prōtōn ginōskontes* 'knowing these things first' of 1:20 and 3:3. They know in advance because Peter has warned them; cf. 1:12-15 and 3:1-3. What they know would appear from the context to be the danger of being deceived by the false teachers and their followers, and following them in their heresies. This has been made explicit in the display.

This clause provides the grounds for 17e with its orienter 17b, the hortatory head of the propositional cluster 17a-e.

3:17b. The verb *phulassō* is used by Peter in 2:5 also. There it is active and has the sense "guard, protect someone," i.e., Noah and his family. Here it is middle and has the sense "(be on one's) guard against, look out for, avoid." When used in this sense, it is usually followed by the accusative of the person or thing to be avoided, or, as here, it can be followed by the conjunction *hina*, which can denote purpose, i.e., "in order that." However, according to Arndt and Gingrich, *hina* may also serve as a substitute for an infinitive that supplements a verb, or an accusative with infinitive, when it occurs after verbs with the sense "take care, be ashamed, be afraid." This seems to be the case here, since it follows *phulassesthe* 'take care, be on guard' and is itself followed by *mē ... ekpesēte* 'lest you fall', i.e., "take care ... not to fall" or "guard ... against falling." *Hina* introduces the content of "guard against," i.e., what is to be guarded against.

In the display, the command has been expressed by "guard against (this (17c-e) happening)," with the negative *mē* of the *hina* clause expressed by "against," and "(this)" representing the content of "guard against," which is stated in 3:17c-e.

3:17c-d. The verb *sunapagomai* 'be led/carried away', according to Arndt and Gingrich, is used only figuratively and passively, i.e., 'be deceived, influenced' by something. In the New Testament it is found here and in Rom 12:16 and Gal 2:13. The sense is very different in the verse in Romans but is much the same in Galatians as here.

The instrumental dative follows the verb, i.e., *tē tōn athesmōn planē* 'by the error of lawless/unprincipled (people)'. This is expressed by a means proposition (3:17d) and the participle *sunapachthentes* 'having been carried away' is expressed as a result, 'you are deceived/misled' (17c).

The adjective *athesmos* 'lawless, unprincipled' is used only here and in 2:7 in the New Testament. It probably refers to the *pseudodidaskaloi* 'false teachers' of chapter 2 and the *empaiktai* 'scoffers' of 3:3.

The noun *planē*, which means literally 'wandering, roaming', is used here figuratively, as it is in 2:18, to mean 'error, deceit, deception'. According to some commentators, it implies wandering from the path of truth, and falling into sin oneself, but not deliberately setting out to lead others astray. However, in the context, it seems more likely that there was a deliberate effort on the part of the *athesmoi* 'lawless (people)' to deceive others and cause them to sin. They themselves had turned away from Christian teaching and the principles which guided them in living godly lives, and, as a result, without these restraints, they were living disorderly, dissolute lives and wanted to cause others to do the same.

In the display *tē tōn athesmōn planē sunapachthentes* 'being led astray by the error of unprincipled (people)' has been represented by two clauses, 3:17c and d, which are in a result-means relationship.

The instrumental dative *tē ... planē* 'by ... the error' is the means by which people will be deceived, i.e., the sinful words and actions of 'unprincipled (people)'. This has been expressed by 'unprincipled (people) saying and doing that which is wrong'. They may deliberately set out to mislead others, or others may just see and hear them and imitate them.

3:17e. The noun *stērigmos* 'firmness, stability' is used only here in the New Testament, but it is used elsewhere of the fixed position of the stars and the steadfastness of a beam of light. Peter uses the related verb in 1:12 where he speaks of his readers as being 'established in the truth'. He also uses it in 5:10 of his first letter, while its antithesis occurs in 2:14 and 3:16 of this one; cf. *psuchas astēriktous* 'unstable spirits/souls' and *amatheis kai astēriktoi* 'ignorant and unstable (people)'.

The verb *ekpiptō* means literally 'fall off/from' and is used of such things as withered flowers falling to the ground. In nautical terminology it is used to mean 'drift off course, run aground'; cf. Acts 27:26, 29. Here, it is used figuratively, in conjunction with *tou idiou stērigmou* 'your own stability/ steadfastness', to mean 'you no longer firmly believe what is true' or 'you doubt what once you firmly believed'. This recalls the exhortation of 1:10, *tauta ... poiountes ou mē ptaisēte pote* 'if you do those things you will never fall'.

This clause is both the result of 17c-d, and, together with them, forms the content of 17b. Hence, together with 17b, it constitutes Head 3 of the paragraph.

3:18. The *de* which connects 3:17 and 18 is translated "but" in the majority of translations; cf. KJV, NIV, TEV, RSV, NEB. Other alternatives are 'on the contrary' (PHIL), and 'instead' (JER). One or two omit it.

The contrast marked by "but," is between the negative aspect of Peter's exhortation, in 3:17, and the positive, in 3:18. It is not between the two imperatives, *phulassesthe* 'be on your guard' (3:17b) and *auxanete* 'grow, increase' (3:18b-c), but between 3:17e, i.e., "you doubt (what you now believe)" and 3:18b-c. They are not to be deluded by false teachers so that their faith is undermined, but they are to grow in grace and knowledge of Christ.

This contrast has been expressed by 3:18a, "(instead of doing this (17e))." The *de* may be expressed by "and," or omitted.

3:18b-c. There is much debate among commentators as to whether *tou kuriou hēmōn kai sōtēros Iēsou Christou* 'our Lord and Saviour Jesus Christ' belongs to both *chariti* 'grace' and *gnōsei* 'knowledge' or just to 'knowledge'. The KJV favours the latter alternative, but the former is followed by NIV, NEB, RSV, and TEV.

Alford considers that if the phrase applied only to 'knowledge' then it would be more naturally *en chariti kai en gnōsei*, with the preposition *en* 'in' being repeated before *gnōsei* 'knowledge'. He also considers that the genitive stands in a different relationship to the two datives, *chariti* 'grace' and *gnōsei* 'knowledge' being in the first case subjective, and the second objective. Although there does not seem to be any conclusive evidence in support of either possibility, 'grace' is very commonly collocated with the Saviour, in the New Testament, and this would favour it being so here. Also, if Peter had intended the phrase to apply only to 'knowledge', he could very easily have made sure that it was not ambiguous.

The imperative *auxanete* 'grow, increase' is intransitive here, and has the sense of 'keep on growing/increasing'. It applies to both *chariti* 'grace' and *gnōsei* 'knowledge'.

Besides here, Peter uses the noun *chariti* 'grace' in 1:2 and 5:10 of his first Epistle, and in 1:2 of this one. (See note on 1:2 for further details.)

How should the clause *auxanete ... en chariti ... tou kuriou hēmōn kai sōtēros Iēsou Christou* 'grow ... in the grace ... of our Lord and Saviour Jesus Christ' be represented in the display?

"Our Lord and Saviour Jesus Christ" is clearly the agent in the action. He is the one who dispenses "unmerited favour"; who "acts graciously"; who "blesses." Those whom Peter is addressing in his letter are the recipients of the favour, the ones whom Christ blesses, but they are also the ones who are exhorted to "grow in grace." As is usually the case, *charis* is difficult to represent satisfactorily in a display, and particularly so in the context of Peter's exhortation to them to 'grow in grace', since neither the usual theological sense of "bless, do good to" seems appropriate here.

The thrust of the paragraph is that they should live holy lives in expectation of Christ's return to judge the world. Peter has just exhorted them not to be swayed by the arguments or actions of those who distort the Scriptures in order to justify their immoral life-style (17b-17e). Now, he exhorts them instead to 'grow in the grace ... of our Lord and Saviour Jesus Christ'. The sense may be that they should develop those Christian virtues which clearly show that the Lord Jesus Christ is graciously working in their lives, or, that they should live in such a godly manner that they will experience increasingly the fact that the Lord Jesus Christ acts graciously towards them. Godly behaviour and the grace of Christ go hand in hand, for without his gracious favour and influence the believer cannot sustain a godly life, and, in proportion as he grows in Christian virtue, so does he become increasingly aware of how gracious Christ is.

In the display, therefore, either of the following might be possible:

"(Become) increasingly (godly so that it is evident that) our Lord and Saviour Jesus Christ acts graciously (towards you)."

or

"(Behave in such a (godly) manner that) you experience increasingly (the fact that) our Lord and Saviour Jesus Christ acts graciously (towards you)."

The latter of these has been expressed in the display.

It might be necessary for "our Lord and Saviour Jesus Christ" to be expressed by a verbal phrase, i.e., "Jesus Christ (who) saved us and rules over us."

3:18c. Peter draws his letter to a close very much as he began it, on the subject of growth; cf. 1:5ff. The Christian life should be one of continuing development, as the believer grows in knowledge of Christ and his Word, and in the Christian virtues enumerated in 1:5-7.

Both *gnōsis* and *epignōsis* are used by Peter to mean 'knowledge'. He uses the former in 1:5, 6 and here in 3:18, and the latter in 1:2, 3, 8, and 2:20.

Greenlee, in *NOT* 63-82, suggests that when *epignōsis* is used there is emphasis placed on the truth of the knowledge referred to, while *gnōsis* can be used of either true or false knowledge. (See note on 1:2.) Another possibility is that the distinction is between knowing Christ as a person (*epignōsis*) and knowing about Christ (*gnōsis*). It is difficult to be certain since there does not appear to be conclusive evidence in favour of either. Whichever sense is intended, the important fact is that the knowledge spoken of guards against heresy and apostasy, and encourages growth in the Christian life.

EPISTLE CONSTITUENT 3:18d
(Proposition) (Role: closing of the Epistle)

THEME: *I pray that Jesus Christ may be glorified now and forever.*

RELATIONAL STRUCTURE	CONTENTS
	(3:18d) (I pray that) he (Jesus Christ may) be glorified now and forever.

BOUNDARIES AND COHERENCE

The body of the Epistle was brought to a close in 3:18a-c, with Peter's final exhortation to his readers to grow in the grace and knowledge of our Lord and Saviour Jesus Christ, thus returning to his prayer of 1:2, that they should experience increasingly God's grace and peace as they grow in their knowledge of him.

The Epistle now comes to an abrupt conclusion, without any personal remarks or greetings, unlike Peter's first Epistle. The introduction had been comparatively brief also, as Peter quickly got into his subject without much preamble. He is conscious of the importance of his message, and wishes to unburden himself of it, no doubt urged on by the knowledge that his death, when it comes, will be sudden; cf. 1:14.

PROMINENCE AND THEME

This doxology consists of only one proposition, which is therefore the head and the theme statement.

NOTES ON 3:18d

According to Arndt and Gingrich, *doxa* means "brightness, splendour, radiance." Everything in heaven has this radiance, especially God himself; cf. 1:17. The concept has been widened to denote the "glory, majesty, sublimity" of God, and the concept of "might" and "power" is also present.

Peter uses *doxa* four times in this letter, (1:3; 1:17; 2:10; and here). He uses it no less than ten times in his first letter, where he describes the state of being in the next life as participation in the radiance or glory; cf. 1 Pet 1:11 and 5:1 and 4. He also uses it to refer to human "magnificence/splendour" of any sort; cf. 1 Pet 1:24.

Here, the glory is addressed to *autō* 'him', which refers back to *tou kuriou hēmōn kai sōtēros Iēsou Christou* 'our Lord and Saviour Jesus Christ'. As is usual, no verb is expressed in the Greek, but the verb "to be" is usually understood, i.e., "to whom be glory." This may be expressed in the display as, "may our Lord and Saviour Jesus Christ be glorified," or "(I pray that) our Lord and Saviour Jesus Christ may be glorified."

The expression *eis hēmeran aiōnos* 'until the day of the age', is found only here in the New Testament. Later liturgical expressions became stereotyped and *eis tous aiōnas* became the accepted form very quickly; cf. Rom 16:27. Most commentators regard it as equivalent to this or *eis ton aiōna*; cf. 1 Pet 1:25, but Meyer considers this to be too inexact. He thinks that *hēmera aiōnos* is the day on which eternity begins—as contrasted with time—which, however, at the same time, is eternity itself.

According to Arndt and Gingrich, *hēmera* is a day appointed for a special purpose, especially the day of judgement, while *aiōnos* 'time, age' can mean "very long time, eternity," and be used of time gone by and also time to come, which, if it has no end, is also known as eternity. In doxologies it is usually expressed as "forevermore."

Peter uses a number of expressions throughout chapter three which are in keeping with this:

> *eis hēmeran kriseōs kai apōleias tōn asebōn anthrōpōn* 'until the day of judgement and destruction of ungodly men' (3:7)
> *hēmera kuriou* 'the day of the Lord' (3:10)
> *tēs tou theou hēmeras* 'the day of God' (3:12)

The preposition *eis* 'to, for' with accusative of time, indicates duration of time, i.e., "until." Since the implication of the phrase *eis hēmeran aiōnos* 'until the day of eternity' is surely "forever," that is how it is represented in the display.

The *amēn* is generally regarded as being of doubtful authority, and may have been added later by a copyist, since it is usual in doxologies.

REFERENCES

GENERAL REFERENCES

Alford, Henry. 1875. *The Greek Testamenmt* (Vol.4). London et al.: Rivingtons, Deighton, Bell and Company.

Arndt, William F. and F. Wilbur Gingrich. 1957. *A Greek-English Lexicon of the New Testament*. Chicago: The University of Chicago Press.

Beekman, John and John C. Callow. 1974. *Translating the Word of God*. Grand Rapids, MI: Zondervan.

Bigg, Charles. 1901. *A Critical and Exegetical Commentary on the Epistles of St. Peter and St. Jude*. Edinburgh: T. & T. Clark.

Bratcher, Robert G. 1984. *A Translator's Guide to the Letters from James, Peter, and Jude*. United Bible Societies.

Callow, John C. 1982. *A Semantic Structure Analysis of Second Thessalonians*. Dallas, TX: Summer Institute of Linguistics.

————. 1983. *A Semantic Structure Analysis of Colossians*. Dallas, TX: Summer Institute of Linguistics.

Callow, Kathleen. 1974. *Discourse Considerations in Translating the Word of God*. Grand Rapids: Zondervan

Calvin, John. *Calvin's Commentaries* (Vol. 22). Grand Rapids, MI: Baker Book House.

Ellicott, Charles J. 1860. *A Critical and Grammatical Commentary on 2 Peter*. London: John W. Parker & Son.

Gill, John. 1853. *An Exposition of the New Testament (Romans - Revelation)*. London: william Hill Collingridge.

Green, E.M.B. 1961. *2 Peter Reconsidered*. London: The Tyndale Press.

Green, Michael. 1968. *The Second Epistle of Peter and the Epistle of Jude*. Grand Rapids, MI: Wm. B. Eerdmans Company.

Greenlee, Harold. 1982. "A Note on 'Knowledge'." *Selected Technical Articles Related to Translation*, No. 6, pp. 30-31. Dallas, TX: Summer Institute of Linguistics.

Henry, Matthew. 1685. *An Exposition of the New Testament: Vol. 10. 2 Peter-Revelation*. London: Thomas C. Jack.

Kelly, J.N.D. 1969. *A Commentary on the Epistles of Peter and of Jude*. London: Adam & Charles Black.

Kittel, Gerhard, ed. 1964. *The Theological Dictionary of the New Testament*. Tr. by Geoffrey W. Bromiley. Grand Rapids, MI; Wm. B. Eerdmans Company.

Lange, John D. 1971. *Commentary on the Holy Scriptures* (Vol. 9). Grand Rapids, MI: Zondervan.

Lillie, John. 1978 Reprint. *Lectures on the first and Second Epistles of Peter*. Minneapolis, MN: Klock and Klock.

Lloyd-Jones, D.M. 1983. *Expository Sermons on 2 Peter*. Edinburgh: The Banner of Truth Trust.

Meyer, H.A.W. 1881. *Critical and Exegetical Commentary on the Epistles of Peter and Jude*. Edinburgh: T. & T. Clark.

Moore, Bruce R. 1972. "Doublets," *Notes on Translation*, No. 43 Dallas, TX: Summer Institute of Linguistics.

Moulton, W.F. and A.S. Geden. 1926. *Concordance to the Greek Testament*. Fifth Edition. Edinburgh: T. & T. Clark.

Poole, Matthew. 1685. *A Commentary on the Holy Bible: Vol. 3: Matthew - Revelation*. Edinburgh: The Banner of Truth Trust.

Smith, Robert E. and John Beekman. 1981. *A Literary-Semantic Analysis of Second Timothy*. Dallas, TX: Summer Institute of Linguistics.

Travis, Edna J. 1981 *Exegetical Helps on Second Peter*. Dallas, TX: Summer Institute of Linguistics.

VERSIONS

The Analytical Greek New Testament. 1981. Ed. by B. Friberg and T. Friberg. Grand Rapids, MI: Baker Book House.

The Eight Translation New Testament. 1974. Wheaton. IL: Tyndale House Publishers.

The Good News Bible. 1976. The Bible Societies. England: Collins.

The Holy Bible: Authorized (or King James) Version. 1611.

The Holy Bible: New International Version. 1979. London: Hodder and Stoughton.

The Living Bible. 1974. Tr. by Kenneth N. Taylor. England: Coverdale House Publications.

The New American Standard Bible. 1973. New York: A.J. Holman.

The New English Bible New Testament. 1961. Oxford and Cambridge.

The New Testament in Modern English. 1960. Tr. by J.B. Phillips. London: Geoffrey Bles.